D1881166

INDIAN FAMILIES AT THE CROSSROADS

INDIAN FAMILIES AT THE CROSSROADS

Preparing Families for the New Millennium

Editors

David K. Carson, Ph. D.,
Cecyle K. Carson, Ph. D.,
Aparajita Chowdhury, Ph. D.(Eds.)

GYAN PUBLISHING HOUSE

NEW DELHI-110002

Indian Families at the Crossroads:Preparing Families for the New Millennium

Rs. 690/-

© David K. Carson, Cecyle K. Carson, Aparajita Chowdhury

ISBN: 81-212-0929-3

All rights Reserved. No Part of this book may be reproduced in any manner without written permission

Published in 2007 in India by
Gyan Publishing House
5, Ansari Road, Darya Ganj,
New Delhi-110002
Phones : 23282060, 23261060
Fax : 011-23285914
E-mail: books@gyanbooks.com
Website: www.gyanbooks.com

Lassertype Setting by: Rudra Computer Graphics, Delhi
Printed at: Salasar Imaging System, Delhi

Dedications

To my incredible sisters: Debi Blue, my hero and confidant, and Gloria Houser, who I admire beyond measure; and to my step-mother, Peni Carson, who embodies unconditional love. ***(DKC)****.*

To my three children, Farah, Brock, and Shena, who have taught me much about being a parent, just as I hopefully have demonstrated my unconditional love for them. They have allowed me to share in their lives — the adventures, experiences, and joys of childhood, adolescence, and early adulthood. My life has been richer than I ever imagined because of them. ***(CKC)****.*

To my immediate and extended family, who are responsible for what I am today. ***(AC)***

Contents

Preface

Contemporary families in India are indeed at a crossroads. On the one hand, millions of Indian families have found a way to stay cohesive and resilient during these times of turmoil and rapid change. In reality, family has always been at the foundation of this diverse and expanding society, and Indian people today continue to place marriage and family life as their highest value and priority. Children and adolescents are given a special place in the family and community, and interdependency, support, and nurturing across the generations are uniquely valued in the Indian family system. Parents and extended family members remain the primary socializing agents of children, a practice no longer evident in many regions of the world. Parents and adult children tend to maintain close ties even when great geographical distances separate them.

On the other hand, modern Indian families are encountering complex and disturbing problems that are heightening the risk for parents, children, and extended family members. The majority of the approximately 80% of Indians who live in villages and rural areas are still poor, lacking in social resources and supports, and generally isolated from the mainstream society. Urban dwellers also are experiencing a multitude of difficulties, which are challenging for traditional family structures and relationships, and putting marriages and families at risk. These problems, both urban and rural, include: a prevalence of poverty and disease;

overcrowding; water and air pollution; migration of individuals and families from rural to urban areas due to a lack of viable employment and vocational opportunities; a gradual weakening of age-old traditions including transformations in religion, caste, and other social institutions; natural disasters that make transportation, communication, and modernization difficult; ethnic conflicts and ongoing political instability; increased crime, social violence, and terrorism; inadequate housing and sanitation; poor nutrition and health care; illiteracy and low quality (and sometimes non-existent) education for children; minimal enforcement of child abuse and child labor laws; and especially in rural areas, the continual promotion of early marriages and large families which facilitates more than impedes the cycle of poverty.

Other changes are having far-reaching implications in Indian family, social, cultural, economic, and political life. These include the widespread growth of education (especially women's education), the impact of the mass media and modern communications, westernization (i.e., gradual adaptation of values and life-styles of western nations), industrialization and modernization, and economic liberalization. In the age of electronic media, including televisions and computers even in remote areas, the Indian family is being exposed to ideas, ideals, and values swept across from distant societies. More recent crises in families encompass many of the same kinds of problems that have plagued countries in the West at least since the 1960's. These include, for example, marital strain and dissolution, parent-child conflicts, various forms of family violence, substance abuse, juvenile delinquency, school dropout or low school attainment among the lower class, and excessive pressures in many middle and upper class families for adolescents and young adults to achieve academically. Given these conditions and difficulties, the future and well being of the Indian family is uncertain. Indian families face a wide variety of everyday problems, including the stresses and strains of rearing children, conflicts with in-laws, difficulties associated with various chronic illnesses, and developmental delays and disabilities of children or other family members.

The majorities of urban dwellers today, and even many rural citizens, prefer to live in small nuclear family units. At the same time they want to maintain close relations with their extended family and have them available during times of crisis. This practice has created role strain, ambiguity, and conflict between family members (such as authority over children between mothers and their mother-in-laws), as well as confusing expectations for children. Moreover, unlike the scenario in the traditional joint family system, elderly members today not only have few roles to play in child socialization, but also in educated families are less likely to live with their adult children and grand children due to increased mobility. In many families the result is an absence of clear and consistent role models for the child beyond his or her own parents. In addition, partly due to safety reasons, parents are becoming more restrictive of their children in having free time to interact with peers, either at school or in the neighborhood. This not only reduces children's social network but also tends to instill feelings of fear and distrust. The mass media (especially the electronic media) also aggravates the situation by creating unrealistic aspirations in children and parents, including a "you can or should have it all" mind set.

Exposure to "western thinking" (European and American) has brought about changes in attitudes towards traditional methods of disciplining, toilet training, feeding, and other child-rearing practices. However, because traditional attitudes have not been completely abandoned, many parents alternate between permissive and strict (authoritarian) child-rearing, thus creating anxiety and confusion in children and making them more vulnerable to behavioral or emotional disorders. Marital difficulties, coupled with inadequate or conflict oriented co-parenting practices, are also becoming more prevalent as women are breaking out of traditional roles, becoming educated in greater numbers, and advocating for equal rights both at home and in the work place. With so many women employed outside the home today, some Indian researchers contend that children's needs are not being met, and that there is little time for parents to listen to and converse with their children. Studies of female-headed households have shown that these women face numerous problems. Some researchers assert that this increase in single-parent families has contributed to a greater percentage of children and adolescents experiencing serious difficulties. This may be more common in middle and lower class families, where alternative childcare provisions are often not available. In sum, increased role strain, marital difficulties, parent-child conflicts, feelings of guilt, and status confusion are commonly observed among working women, even though there are some economic and self-esteem related advantages. Since more women in India are joining the labor force without proper support and assistance, often in the face of extended family and community opposition, an increase in family difficulties is to be expected.

Also contributing to family problems is a school curriculum and environment that often does not meet children's needs, be they academic or personal. It is not uncommon for teachers to use strict and sometimes physical punishment to maintain order, with which today's Indian youth are not always in agreement. Perhaps most notable in educated families are the extreme pressures for children to achieve academically so they can gain entrance into the prestigious colleges and universities (often with little free time with peers or family play time). This pressure tends to increase the vulnerability of older children and adolescents to various personal and relational difficulties.

Although Family Life Education (FLE) as an academic discipline and professional field is new to Indian society, it has tremendous potential to educate and assist people in leading a rewarding and growth-promoting life, as well as in preventing a host of social ills and mental health problems. This edited book in part examines the need for Family Life Education in contemporary Indian family life, while also addressing many of the contemporary issues and problems confronted by Indian couples and families. Each chapter, to a greater or lesser degree, emphasizes the practical application and practices in the multiple areas of Family Life Education. Its purpose is to help professionals and concerned citizens in their understanding of contemporary Indian families. The potential benefits of Family Life Education to Indian society are discussed throughout. The concluding chapter includes a discussion of target groups and settings for Family Life Education training programs. Also presented is a justification for and outline of a "training-the-trainer" approach to Family Life Education (including a lay-training component) so that families in this country of over one billion people will have a greater opportunity to cultivate a happier and more fulfilling life.

In sum, this book explores the range of marital and family difficulties in light of the undercurrent of social and economic changes in India today, and examines how a Family Life Education "movement" might take root in the context of the current mental health system and social service practice. As part of a comprehensive mental health effort in India, Family Life Education on the community level holds great promise as a keeper and restorer of the family unit. However, as has been mentioned, the idea of Family Life Education is relatively new in India, and with few exceptions it has not been integrated with current mental health and social welfare programs. Yet, the notion that couples and families need on-going support and useful information about family life appears to be in the early stages of acceptance in professional circles. This country is ready for a preventive approach to marital and family difficulties. The authors discuss the content, scope and potential benefits of family life education training and services in meeting the tremendous needs of married couples and families in India today. It is the sincere hope of the Editors that this book will fill an important gap in the Indian family science literature and serve as a catalyst for needed changes in social policy and community development programs.

D.K.C,
C. K.C, &
A.C

List of Contributors

T. Banoomathi – Reader, Department of Home Science, Queen Mary's College, Chennai, Tamil Nadu, India.

Cecyle K. Carson – Associate Professor, Department of Communicative Disorders, University of Central Florida, USA.

David K. Carson – is a Professor of Psychology at Palm Beach Atlantic University Orlando, Florida USA.

Aparajita Chowdhury – Professor of Home Science, and Director of Women's Studies Research Center, Berhampur University, Orissa, India.

Rita Choudhury - Reader, Department of Home Science, Dhenkanal Women's College, Dhenkanal, Orissa, India

Bijayalaxmi Das – Rtd. Home Scientist, Orissa Education Services, Orissa, India.

Ms. Sanjukta Das – Senior Lecturer, Department of Home Science, Niranjan Women's College, Aska, Orissa, India.

Tapati Das – Reader and Head, Department of Home Science, R.D. Autonomus Women's College, Bhubaneswar, Orissa, India.

Ms. Visala Patnam, Professor and Head, Department of Child Development and Family Relations, College of Home Science, Marthawada Agricultural University, Parbani, Maharastra, India.

Ms. Fauzia Khan, Executive Member of Marthawada Agricultural University and Member of Legislative Assembly, Maharastra, India.

Urmimala Das - Research Associate, Women's Studies Research Centre, Berhampur University, Orissa, India.

Arundhati Rath, Reader, Post Graduate Department of Home Science, Berhampur University, Orissa, India.

N. Jayapoorai - Professor, Department of Human Development and Family Studies, Avinashilingam Deemed University, Coimbatore, Tamil Nadu, India.

Indumati Pattnaik – Early Childhood Educator, FUNSKOOL, Bhubaneswar, Orissa, India.

Manoj Manjari Pattanaik – Senior Lecturer, Department of Law, Berhampur University, Orissa, India.

Sucheta Priyabadini – Assistant Registrar, Kalinga Industrial Training and Technology, Bhubaneswar, Orissa, India.

K. Vaijayanthimala – Rtd. Home Scientist, Department of Home Science, S.B.R. Government Women's College, Berhampur, Orissa, India.

1

Gender Issues in Family Life

Reeta Choudhury

Gender is one of the most powerful variables influencing development from conception to death. Gender based differences have penetrated the social fabric of Indian families to the extent that the outcome has been manifested in various forms of discrimination and inequality. These biases can be observed in the process of socialization of children, gender role-relationships, development of adult roles, and identity and status of the female in Indian families. The author discusses key gender issues prevalent in contemporary Indian families and the challenges put forward by them. Specific recommendations for change include gender sensitization, inculcating androgyny in children, and providing family enrichment programs and family life education on a widespread basis to help bring about gender equilibrium in Indian families.

Gender is considered an important construct existing between men and women in almost all societies of the globe. Apart from class, age, race, religion and ethnicity, gender is an integral dimension of social stratification, putting the female at the level of disadvantage, and varying in degree, across time and space within and across societies.

Today, at the turn of the Century, we hear slogans and mandates to consider the whole world as one, to remove all barriers of caste, class and religion, and to build a prosperous, peaceful and harmonious community, free from violence, disease, poverty and injustice. However, what we observe in everyday life are indifferences, discrimination, inequality and bias within our own families. Gender is perhaps one of the most powerful variables that impacts development from the moment of conception to death. The horrendous stories of selective foeticide, female infanticide, low female literacy, unfavorable sex ratios, dowry deaths, and the unenviable status of the widow all speak of gender bias in a patriarchal society such as India. Thus, the life events of an individual born into an Indian family are totally gendered. The birth itself receives a differential welcome depending on sex. The expectation for conformity to social norms (socialization patterns), access to education, role and status in marriage, and family are also gendered. Hence, gender based inequalities permeate the very fabric of family and cultural life in India.

Women are a large segment of the population in India and contribute immensely to the well-being of the family and society. Yet, their contribution has remained unaccounted for and invisible for centuries, only because of their gender. A review on the status of Indian women reports that women's suppression is deeply rooted in the social structure of Indian society – in traditions, religious doctrines and practices, within the educational and legal system, and within the families. Women are oppressed, suppressed and segregated, and are considered inferior, secondary individuals. The manifestations of acquiring a lower status and position in the family are revealed in the development indicators based on decreasing sex-ratios, increasing infanticide and foeticide, higher maternal mortality rates, inadequate health services, low literacy rates of females, higher drop-out rates of girls in schools, and less opportunities to develop female talents (Sen, 1996). Indeed, gender bias and discrimination are experienced in all aspects of family life in India.

Women in modern society constitute half the population of the country. In spite of the constitutional guarantees on equal rights and opportunities for both men and women, an inequality based on gender still persists. In modern India, in spite of greater enrollment in education, more legal provisions, political opportunities, and better health care facilities, the status of women in families and society continues to be extremely low. There are crimes committed against women in their families as a fetus, as an infant, as a bride who does not bring enough dowry, as a wife who does not produce a male child, and as a widow whose life without her husband is considered worthless. Above all, if she is a working woman she is allowed to slave from dawn to midnight, working fourteen to eighteen hours per day between two jobs. This is how human survival, development, and responsibilities have been gendered in Indian families. Furthermore, industrialization, liberalization and migration have brought about some obvious changes in the stereo-typed concepts of masculinity and femininity in the family, affecting such factors as household composition, residence patterns, specific kinship relationships, and male and female attitude and behaviors. These changes have posed a challenge to the family organization, as well to the role and status of both men and women within the family.

The present discussions are based on certain theoretical assumptions and sociological insights that will provide a more thorough scientific understanding into the issues of gender in a more purposeful manner. Key questions must be addressed, such as:

How and why men and women are similar and different?

How are they groomed in the families to perform certain gender roles in a given society?

Why are there so many gender inequalities and biases persisting in Indian families?

What is the present status of females in society?

Theoretical Perspectives: Understanding Gender

Sex and gender constitute perhaps the single most important dimension for discrimination between individuals. Sex is constitutional, whereas gender is acquired. Gender refers to socially influenced characteristics, or the role and relationship that exist between men and women in a given social context. It is generally used when judgments are made about either biological or environmental causes (Berk, 1996; Deux, 1993). Virtually, all societies expect the two sexes to adopt different gender roles. A gender role is the pattern of behavior and traits that define how a female or male should act in a particular society. Women are typically viewed as nurturing, soft, shy and submissive, and the roles assigned to them are confined to the domestic sphere of child care and home related activities. The tasks and responsibilities of women are focused on relationships and interpersonal spheres. Males are recognized as tough, independent, and aggressive. The role assigned to them in households is as the bread-earner, administrator, and protector of the family. These activities reflect male dominance within the family system. These characteristics and behaviors viewed as desirable for males and females are considered the gender-role norms that form the foundation for society's expectations and standards concerning what men and women should be like (Pleck, 1977). Further, these norms generate gender-role stereotypes, and through the process of gender typing, children develop gender-linked beliefs, roles, and identities (Huston, 1983). Hence, the differences between the two sexes are determined by several factors — biological, cognitive, social and cultural.

Socialization of Male and Female Children in Indian Families

In India, gender influences the socialization process from birth onward. Children experience gender-based differences in their relationships with others (boys are generally more preferred and loved than girls), in distribution of family resources, and in the entitlement to family membership, food, nutrition, health care, education and recreation. In this patriarchal setup, male children enjoy a special status and are highly valued in the family through parental responses and behaviors, family rituals and practices, and social customs and traditions. Sons are considered an "*asset*" and daughters a "*liability*" to the family. The preference for a male child is an age-old practice in Indian families. The birth of a male child is greeted with joy and the status of the mother is elevated when she gives birth to a male.

However, a female child is frequently unwanted in families in India, irrespective of caste, class and religion. Females are exposed to severe indifferences in the behavior and attitude of family members starting from birth. This gender difference in the family continues throughout the life span. The most important and visible attitude of the family towards the growing female child is of her "*guest status*" in her home. She eventually realizes that her stay in the family is '*temporary*,' and that she does not have any right to membership, property and affiliation. A young female in an Indian family is considered a '*Parayadhan*' or someone's (would-be-husband) property. This idea is conveyed to her through various family practices, songs and rituals (Dube, 1988; Mazumdar, 1981). Moreover, the discriminatory attitude of family members toward the young girl starts from a very early age. With long feeding hours for the boy, delayed toilet training, better health care attention, and greater play opportunities, these facilities and care for the female baby are limited if not nonexistent in many families.

During adolescence, marriage is viewed as the ultimate goal of a girl's life in India. A young girl is trained to be a good wife and mother, the practice which is still continuing in the present-day family in spite of the career options given to middle and upper class girls. In Indian culture, chastity is cherished as a more precious gift than life itself. So, girls are over-socialized from childhood onward toward family roles and responsibilities and informed of their subservient roles in a patriarchal society, which is to learn modesty and self denial and to develop proficiency in household tasks and child care through intensive participation in the home. M. N. Srinivas (1960) coined the phrase "*girls learn to be mothers even before they are wives*", which refers to the sibling care assigned to girls in their home. In contrast, a boy of the same age is given higher status, involved more in decision making, assigned newer responsibilities, and has the opportunity to develop a greater sense of autonomy and self-worth.

A series of studies conducted by Saraswati and her associates (Saraswati & Dutta, 1988, 1990) suggests that boys are socialized for occupational competence and girls are socialized for competence in household activities in Indian families. As Dube (1988) observed, there is a natural-ness to gender in India which is based on the division of work and labeling of tasks as feminine and masculine, beginning in childhood.

Female children are also taught to cultivate qualities of '*sewa*' or service, tolerance, and self-restraint within the feminine role and to acquire qualities of adjustment and docility as part of her grooming for marital roles (Dube, 1988). Thus, girls in India often suffer from feelings of low self-worth, an inferiority complex, self-depreciation and low self-esteem throughout life (Cormack, 1961; Kakar, 1978). Such sex-biased attitudes are widely prevalent in Indian families, where boys and girls continue to be socialized for their gender-appropriate adult roles. This is evident in the findings of some studies on working women (see e.g., Bharat, 1992; Ramu, 1987, 1989; Shukla, 1988). The findings in general indicate a sex-based division of domestic responsibilities. Despite women's heightened employment status and career positions today, it is unlikely that family systems are allowing for a great deal of change in gener roles. However, the joint family system is characterized by more rigid gender-based socialization than what is observed in the nuclear family structure in contemporary India.

Status of the Female Child and Women in Contemporary Indian Society. Today, rapid socio-economic development in India has created some changes in the lives of female children and women today. This is especially the case in the position and status of educated urban women who seem to reap the benefits of constitutional, political and economic rights provided in a democratic society. On the other hand, increased incidences of female foeticide, infanticides, dowry deaths, sexual harassment and gendered-based violence have degraded the status of females in families and the society. The idea that "women are the companion of men, gifted with equal mental capacities and have the right to dignity, to participate in every minute of details of the same activities of men, and the right of freedom and liberty" has still remained a myth in millions of Indian families.

2001 Census of India and National Family & Health Survey-2 (NFHS), 1998-1999, Report on the Status of Women in India. The 2001 Census of India survey report reveals the following: gender ratio of 933 females per 1000 males and the female literacy rate has increased to 51% from 35% in 1991. Also, there have been some positive changes in the conditions of women over the past decade, as the overall gender ratio has stayed at about 970 females to 1000 males from 1991 to 2001. Child gender ratio is 927 females per 1000 males. The National Family and Health Report highlights the status of the female child and women in present Indian society. It revealed that 85% of married women need permission to visit friends and relatives, 52% of married women are involved in decision making about their own health, 60% of married women have access to money, and that 33% and 32% of girls are married by the age of 15 and 18, respectively.

Fifty-three percent of males and 34% of the child population (6+) complete primary school. These indicators of the male and female population in India give a slightly improved position of females in Indian society; however, on the social parameters the improvement rate is exceedingly limited.

National Report on the World Summit for Children Held in 1990. This report states that the life expectancy at birth for females has been steadily rising and has overtaken the male life expectancy of 59 years. Although the sex ratio has remained constant, the maternal mortality rate is 407 per 100,000 live births in 1998, which is a matter of concern (office of the Registrar General of India, 2000). Females in India did not have equal access to nutrition, health, and medical care in spite of the major gains and only 50% of women are literate. However, no significant improvement has been observed in the social attitude and behavioral practices inferred to females.

The Report of the National Committee on the Status of Women in India Towards Equality. This report highlighted the process of the declining status of women and pointed out that this deterioration has accelerated in the last three or four decades. The committee has mentioned several disturbing trends, such as disparity in access to health care and medical service, the increasing gap between men and women in literacy, and the inequality with regard to education and training for employment. The most conspicuous issues of families related to the lower status of females are: decreasing sex ratio, increasing female infanticide and foeticide, malnourishment and undernourishment among girls and women, and higher maternal mortality rate due to inadequate health care and medical services. All these reports on the status of women in Indian society indicate that gender is the single most factor posing constraints in the development of females in this rapidly developing nation.

Gender Disparity in Childhood. Gender based inequalities exist in almost every aspect of the growing female's social and cultural environment. The important familial factors responsible for creating disparity and discrimination are a patriarchal mind set, rigid sex-role stereotypes, and socio-economic powerlessness. Every sixth female death in Indian families is specifically due to gender discrimination. A female child is neglected and discriminated against at home in the following area.

Health, Education, and Development. Gender bias persists in the allocation of both quality and quantity of food, and health care. The male health environment differs from that of the female by the former being more out doors, the latter being mostly around "the dark smoke-filled kitchen", which suggests that exposure to infection may be gender-specific in households. Among the poor, discrimination against female children, coupled with inadequate purchasing power, means that young girls have lower calorie intakes, consume less complementary food and less solid food compared to boys. This resulted in a considerably high mortality level among low-caste female infants at 196/1000 in 1990, as compared with 125 males per 1000 live births.

The gap between the participation rate of boys and girls in elementary education is the largest. The incidence of drop-out and stagnation among girls is nearly twice that of boys, especially in rural areas. Even in non-formal education, girls form only 1/3 of the total enrollment. Schedule Tribe (ST) and Schedule Caste (SC) girls have the highest drop out rate at the primary level, with 68%-73% and 53.39%, respectively. For the average female child in India, the prevalence of poverty, coupled with low female status and living mostly in a rural family set-up, aggravates her disadvantaged status significantly. A girl's childhood years are crowded with domestic chores, and the self-image created for her at home is one of worthlessness servitude and dependence. She is socialized to be submissive and acquiescent – as a daughter, sister, wife and mother. Early marriage and childbearing poses constraints in a female's self-development. Large numbers of females are involved in hazardous labor activities. These include serving as bonded slaves and being forced into prostitution by family members, especially in poor rural and urban slum families. Girls from poor families become victims of sexual exploitation and substance abuse, and they are sometimes sold off for a meager amount of money at a tender age. Certain noxious practices such as sexual abuse of minor daughters and daughters-in-laws occur within the family, which to date the public at-large generally does not acknowledge.

Child Labor (Working Girls)

Gender discrimination and abuse can be seen in various areas of child labor. For example:

- The labor of young females and that of women remains totally invisible and unaccounted for within the family, as it is carried out in the domestic spheres and as a social norm, household tasks defy qualification and monetary value.
- Large numbers of girls are involved in full time economic activity outside the home, and boys who are often part-time workers are privileged to go to school for some hours of the day, which is completely restricted for girls.
- The bulk of the rural female working child population is engaged in caring for younger siblings, cooking, cleaning, fetching fodder and fuel for the household, and further assisting their parents in the fields.
- In the cities, girls usually work eight to ten hours a day. In most cases, they do not get separate wages, as they generally work with their mothers.

Identity of Indian Women

The identity of Indian women, until today, has been associated with the social roles she performs. These are acquired through the values, behavioral expectations and socialization patterns learned in the families, such as '*Beti*', '*Suhagin*', '*Mata*', and '*Vidhva*'. These secondary constructs are derived from the cultural construct of gender identity in Indian families, which exemplifies and supports gender inequality. Indian females are labeled as weak, fragile, dependant and submissive. The identity of women is submerged in prescribed roles, clear-cut and limited aspirations, and selflessness within the family.

The effect of urbanization, liberalization, industrialization, migration, and other socio-economic upheavals have affected Indian families in numerous ways. There are increasing numbers of single parent families, female headed households, and dual career families where there is the emergence of a new identity for Indian women. The striking feature of the contemporary family system is the changing gender roles from strict gender-based sex roles in traditional families, to alternative family patterns based on liberal, egalitarian sex roles. Indian females are trying to give themselves a new identity, which is most conspicuous among urban educated rural families where females are taking active participation in the decision-making process, family savings, and legal matters. Gradually a transformation is taking place in the identity of Indian women as a human being to stand and live for herself and not simply sacrifice for others throughout her life.

Women as Agents Perpetuating Gender Biases in the Family

As one proverb said, "*Women are women's worst enemies*". It is generally observed in traditional Indian families that senior women constitute the prime agents in the socialization process of the family. Female children are trained from a very early age by their grandmothers or elderly aunts to submit and surrender to their male counterparts, or to simply adjust and accept future inequalities. These senior women themselves have led a life of oppression and subjugation from their childhood, thus perpetuating the vicious cycle of gender bias and discrimination in their own family.

In the affined family, the cycle of discrimination and injustice continues by the transfer of reign (power) to the mother-in-law and assisted by the sister-in-law. New wives from outside the family can become victims of domestic violence in the form of wife battering, dowry, and incest-related violence. Further, Thangamuthu and Rasi (2002) reported that discrimination against the female child was found to be more pronounced in the female-headed household than in male-headed ones. Thus, gender bias does not seem to be a solely male-inspired phenomenon, and it goes against the notion of a patriarchal attitude of men who are usually held responsible for the gender-biases in the family.

Gender and Family Violence

Gender-based violence is commonly observed in Indian families, where women are sometimes victimized at all stages of life, from conception to death. They are threatened by infanticide, incest, child prostitution, rape, wife battering, psychological abuse, sexual abuse, and harassment. Harmful traditional practices include early marriage, repeated pregnancy stresses, widow burning (sati), dowry torture and death, and sometimes selling of young female children to be raised as commercial sex workers.

Domestic violence includes physical, sexual or psychological aggression or coercion and a pattern of behavior that is employed to control the other, usually by men over women, to maintain power and supremacy. In Indian families, normally the abuse is directed at girls and women. The violence includes female battering (mostly wives), burning, emotional blackmail, mockery or ridicule, threats of abandonment, confinement to the home, and withholding of money or other family support. Domestic violence against females is a routine affair in many families. The most common form of domestic violence is battery (beating of women and girls by men). The wife is normally the victim of such violence with serious physical injuries and emotional scars from the traumatic experience of beating. It is presumed that in India, women tolerate this violence because they witness the same treatment being done to their elders and therefore consider it a normal behavior. The high level of acceptance of wife beating suggests that women may feel powerless against such violence and will tend to accept it without question.

Another form of gender-based violence is sexual abuse toward women even young girls. Sexual abuse includes rape, sexual assault, sexual molestation, sexual harassment, and incest. In families, the perpetrator is usually a family member, relative, neighbor or close associate of the family.

Consequence of Violence on Women's Health

Gender-based violence has a serious impact on the health and overall well-being of females both directly and indirectly. Violence suffered by women can have fatal consequences, inducing suicide and homicide. It can sometimes affect sexual and reproductive health. The consequences can include psychological breakdowns, depression, and other forms of mental and emotional illness. In terms of reproductive health, the impact of violence may lead to unwanted pregnancies, transmission of STD/HIV, low birth-weight babies, forced abortions, and sex selective abortions.

Challenges for Indian Families Today

The primary gender challenges faced by both males and females and the family unit as a whole in contemporary life are as follows:

- Change in men's traditional control over women, which poses a challenge to patriarchal relations.
- Increase participation of women in the decision-making process and occupants of high status roles.
- Increase participation of men in household tasks and child rearing.
- As per the constitutional and legal provisions of equal rights to both men and women, sharing authority, responsibility, property and family identity are paramount.

- Providing reproductive rights to women solely.
- A socialization process that is similar for both boys and girls.
- Observing family rituals and ceremonies in favor of females, along with males.
- Provisions for working women who can succeed at home, in marriage, and in parental roles, as well as in a worker's role to be independent and compete in the job.
- Acceptance of the development of a more androgynous personality in Indian children.
- A change in attitudes/commitments of males and females towards marriage and family life.

Suggestions and Future Directions

The cultural make-up of Indian society is distinctive in its deep-rooted support of gender differences. Although the present socio-cultural scenario surrounding the family system has changed dramatically, gender roles and identities have changed little in traditional Indian families, which constitute the majority of the population. Despite an increase in women's education, employment, and occupational status, the policies and programs for women's development have brought about only slight improvements in the status of females within families. Regardless of constitutional guarantees and amendments, there is still a difference between what is preached and what is practiced in attaining gender equality. The following suggestions and recommendations are proposed in an effort to help bring about gender equilibrium within and beyond the family.

Positive gender sensitization. The emphasis on positive gender socialization is on creating greater self-awareness and self-awakening with regard to the worth of all people to a family and to society. The recognition of the contribution of both males and females through gender sensitization programs has been identified as the key formula in bringing '*gender equality*' within the family. Each individual should be sensitized of her/his respective roles and responsibilities within the family and should be taught to respect others. The valuable contribution of females both '*visible*' (Monetary) and '*invisible*' (household tasks and other activities at home) should be given due accountability. Males should be taught that no development is possible without the partnership of both male and female. Furthermore, a woman herself should build a positive self-image, develop confidence to think critically, and foster decision-making factors. Also, she should develop competence and efficiency in all the activities she performs to gain control and autonomy in the family.

Inculcating androgynous traits in children. In recent years there have been many life events occurring that have transformed the conventional standards regarding men's role and women's role in families. These changes have put tremendous pressure on family security and well-being in India. In this transitional state of a changing environment, both males and females are experiencing a psychological change in them which is a challenge to the traditional gender-role stereotypes and gender-typing of both men and women in the family. Hence, the contemporary family requires more flexibility and open attitudes of its members, for there to be a change in the gender-roles for better adjustment and coping, even in the most adverse situations.

Researchers have espoused the view that gender-typing prevents both males and females from developing into a full and complete being. Therefore, individuals (both men and women) need to be more androgynous. Androgyny prepares one to be independent and tender, assertive and understanding, yielding masculine and feminine traits. Further, androgyny proposes that one's psychological well being will be maximized when one has androgynous gender-role orientation that enable one to engage in situational effective behavior without regard for its stereotype as being masculine and feminine.

Such a behavioral concept (androgyny) has also been relevant in the Indian cultural-context, where the proper amalgamation of the so-called "*masculine*" and "*feminine*" personality traits is evident in the concept of "*ardhanariswar*" (half male-half female). There should be a distinctive shift in the socialization pattern of male and female children in India, right from infancy to adulthood; emphasizing the development of both masculine and feminine traits within the personality (obvious of the gender to which one belongs).

Greater degree of control and autonomy has been regarded as an essential element of contemporary family life. Hence, through various control-enhancing programs, such as women to be placed in more responsible jobs, women will develop decision making abilities. Additional responsibilities beyond the home boundaries may equip women to develop a more positive self-concept that can incorporate both masculine and feminine characteristics, thus contributing to autonomy and control.

Family life enrichment and education programs. These programs empower individuals and the family to face crisis situations confidently. The scope and objectives of these programs may include the following aspects of family life.

- Attitude development about goals for family wellbeing
- Education for enrichment of family interactions and relationship
- Education for preparation for different stages of family life span
- Strengthening the family's interaction with other systems

Family life education programming can help each family member learn how to work toward the betterment of the family as a whole. It can also prepare couples for a healthy marriage and a happy parenthood. Family life education helps to reduce to family stresses and strengthens family life. At the local and community level, it can help parents learn how to raise emotionally healthy children who will be well prepared to be ideal partners and parents in the twenty-first century in a way that gender becomes an enhancing rather than debilitating agent.

References

Berk, L.; E (1996). *Child development.* New Delhi Prentice-Hall of India Pvt. Ltd.

Bharat, S. (1992). *The Two Pay Cheque Couple: An analysis of their housework, decision making, sex role perceptions and attitudes.* Bombay: TISS

Census of India Report 2001- *Office of the Registrar General of India 2000*, New Delhi.

Cormack, M. (1961). *The Hindu women.* Bombay: Asia Publishing House.

Deux, K. (1993). Commentary. Sorry wrong number – a reply to Gentile's call. *Psychological Science, 4*, 125-126

Dube, L. (1988). On the construction of gender Hindu girls in patrileneal India. *Economic and Political Weekly, 23*(18), WS 11 – WS19.

Govt. of India (1974). *Towards equality.* Report of the National Committee on the status of women in India, New Delhi.

Huston, A.C. (1983). Sex typing. In P. Mussen (Ed.) *Handbook of child psychology:* Vol. 4 Socialization, personality, and social development (4th ed.) (pp 387-467), New York: Wiley

Kakar, S. (1978). *The inner world: A psycho-analytic study of childhood and society in India,* Delhi: Oxford University Press.

Mazumdar, S. (1981). *Socialization of Hindu Middle Class Bengali women.* South Asia Bulletin.

National Family Health Survey-2, (1998-99). *A Report: International Institute for Population studies,* Mumbai, 2000.

National Report on the World Summit for Children, (1990). *Dept. of Women and Child Development, Ministry of Human Resource Development.* Govt. of India.

Pleck, J. H. (1977). The Psychology of sex roles: Traditional and new views In L. A. Cater and A. F. Scott (Eds). *Women and men: Changing roles, relationships and perceptions* (pp. 181-200) New York. Praeger.

Ramu, G. H. (1988). Marital roles and power perception and reality in the urban settling. *Journal of Comparative Family Studies, 19,* 207-227.

Ramu, G. H. (1987). Indian husbands: Their role perceptions and performance in single and dual earner families. *Journal of Marriage and the Family, 49,* 913-915.

Saraswati, T. S.; Dutta, R. (1990). Poverty and human development: Socialization of girls among the urban and rural poor. In G. Mishra (Ed.), *Applied social psychology in India* (PP. 141-169), New Delhi: Sage.

Saraswati, J.S.; Dutta, R. (1988). Current Trends in developmental psychology: A life span perspective. *In J. Pandey (Ed.), Psychology in India: A state-of-the art* (pp. 93-152), New Delhi: Sage.

Shukla, A. (1988). Marital role behavior and marital relationship among single and dual career families. *Indian Journal of Clinical Psychology, 15*, 84-88.

Srinivas, M.N. (1960). *India's villages*. Bombay Media.

2

Family Violence: Impact on Family Life

Manoj Manjari Patnaik

Deeply rooted in the wider societal milieu, family violence is manifested in marital, parent-child, grandparent-youth, sibling, and adult-child/elderly relationships. Operating in the closest human unit characterized by dependency relationships, family violence often results in grave injury to the victim and has an undeniable impact on family members. This chapter examines various types of family violence, causes and consequences, and efforts to prevent and contain the problem in modern day India.

Violence is an everyday occurrence in Indian family life irrespective of class, culture, status, society and religious affiliation. Wife beating and physical maltreatment of children are the two most common forms of family violence, and this is not a recent phenomenon. Family violence is a problem not only confined to our society, but also is common in most areas of the world. The growing nature of the problem has captured the attention of professionals from all walks of life, including therapists, researchers, politicians, judges, and the social intelligentsia. It is one of the greatest threats to any society, with India as no exception. Studies on family violence suggest that most people in the world have, at some time or another, witnessed or been the victim of some form of violence, and that family members are most at-risk (Levinson, 1989). The various types of family violence as observed across the lifespan include:

- Infancy: Abuse and Neglect, including Foeticide and Infanticide
- Childhood and Adolescence: Physical Punishment or Chastisement (beating, kicking, slapping, burning, etc.), Sale of Child, Child Marriage, Child Prostitution, Child Labor, Sibling Abuse, Child Rape and Molestation.
- Adulthood: Wife Battering, Killing of Young Brides (bride burning), Forced Suicide of Wives, Sister Beating.
- Old age: Neglect or Abandonment of the Aged, Battering, Exploitation (physical, material, or financial), Forcing the Aged to Commit Suicide.

Historical Roots of Family Violence

Socially sanctioned domestic violence has occurred since ancient times. Hinduism and other patriarchal religions have affirmed the male dominated family structure. The husband was held responsible for his wife and children's behavior and was admonished to beat them when they committed a serious wrong or mortal sin. Philosophically, this practice was not to be done with rage but out of charity and concern for them. The beatings were viewed as 'protection' for their soul. Assaults on wives and children have long been considered a family issue rather than a legal matter. Traditionally, the courts have been reluctant to invade the privacy of the home or to intervene and usurp a man's authority over the members of his household.

The available literature on the history of family violence in India is scarce. Documentation of the problem is deliberately denied as both society and law have been condoning violence to wives and children for centuries. Despite the lack of concrete evidence, however, family violence in India has a long history. To some extent it has been verified through oral tradition, as well as reflected in mythologies and legends. Although the magnitude, intensity, and control of violence have varied with time and place, it has existed in all segments of Indian society for centuries.

Traditionally in India womanhood has been respected and held in high esteem, yet violence has persisted. The problem of marital violence is as old as Sita who was deserted by Lord Rama (*The Ramayana*). On a baseless and unfounded allegation of infidelity Lord Jagannath deserted the Goddess Laxmi and Draupadi was publicly tortured, assaulted and humiliated by her in-laws, the Kauravas (*The Mahabharata*). Her husband Rishi Goutam turned Ahalya to stone, Parsuram killed his mother at the urging of his father Rishi Jamadagni, and King Karna the great giver sacrificed his little son Brushaketu to keep his promise. The same violence continues, being positively reinforced with age and time, following the dictum of Manu 'the perpetual tutelage of women' and the reaffirmation by Santh Tulshi Das that Donkeys, drums and women deserve to be beaten, "Dhol, Ganwar, Sudra, Pasu, Nari: Yeah sab he Tadan ke adhikari".

Legally sanctioned family violence existed in India since the time of recorded history. The equality of right and status conferred on women during the Vedic period. (4000 to 1000 B.C.) suffered a setback in the post Vedic period. Manu, the first law giver and codifier of Hindu Law, stressed the dependent status of women Manu in Chapter IX verse 3 of Manu Smriti, saying:

> *"While young she remains under the control of her father, after marriage under the control of her husband, on his death and in old age under the control of her sons; she does not deserve complete dependence at any time".*

The same viewpoint finds expression in the works of other *Smritikars* and legal commentators like Yajnavalkya and Vigyaneswara. Yajnavalkya, in his Smriti Chapter 1 and Verse 85 states:

> *"After father, women are kept under the control of husband and then under the control of the son. In their absence, under the control of Kinsmen, but are never to be left free"(Sen, 1984).*

Regarding the nature and extent of the husband's control over his wife and children and power of chastisement, Manu (in Chapter VIII, Verse 299-300), declares:

> *"A husband has no right to do anything more than inflict moderate chastisement upon his wife, son and servant only as a punishment for an offence or a mistake using a string or a light rattan and taking care to strike on the back and never on the head".*

Kautilya, in his famous treatise Arthasastram, emphatically approves of these kinds of practices (Sharma, 1963). Thus, the legally sanctioned power of physical correction over one's wife and children if they are guilty of a mistake or an offence received philosophically and religious support throughout the ages and was practiced in everyday life until in 1924 when the right of the husband to inflict corporal punishment on wife was first denied by law courts (Kondal Vs. Ranganayaki AIR 1924, Mad. 49, P.55).

Although there have been a variety of improvements in recent years in the law and justice system's response to the problem of domestic violence in India, these policies are only now being put into effect. Still, policies and their implementation are highly inconsistent. The old laws are a reflection of our social altitudes, and such deeply entrenched attitudes take a very long time to change.

Family Violence in Contemporary India

Violence at home is a private affair with a few or no bystanders and no real time or opportunity to help the victim. The accused is often times the only witness to the violence (Chawla, 2004). The family, once considered a fortress for women and children's safety and security and a place of peace and solace, has turned out to be the breeding ground of violence (Ahmed-Ghosh, 2004). It is an irony, as Martin (1978) observes, that ".....family, the most intimate association to which the majority of people belong, is an unrivalled source of strength and comfort. But its very closeness can also intensify the worst of human relations. Love may be corrupted to envious possession and discipline to cruelty. And above all the private focus of hopes and fears may foster dual standards of private and public behavior".

The pervasiveness of the problem in India has not been fully documented. It is one of the least reported of all crimes relative to actual frequency of occurrence (Chawla, 2004). Except for police records that are loosely maintained and a few privately conducted investigations, no nationally represented study provides data concerning the incidence of family violence in India (Ahmed-Ghosh, 2004; Chawla, 2004). Despite the absence of any uniform national investigation into the problem, there is enough evidence to show that family violence does occur in India, and that marital violence in particular is widespread though largely hidden (Chawla, 2004; Fernandez, 1997). However, due to the private, personal and sensitive nature of the problem in India, scholars have not yet been able to overcome the theoretical and methodological issues involving family violence. Increased privacy, inequality between the sexes, and legitimization of violence through cultural and social norms, are some of the factors responsible for family violence (Williams, 1992). Since the family is a source of comfort and nurture for its members and regarded as sacred, family members who are victims of violent behavior rarely seek outside help when it occurs. Outside intervention for personal or family problems is generally looked down upon in India (with few exceptions); thus, violence within the family tends to be trivialized or ignored. Yet, the collection of empirical data on family violence in India began in the 1980's. According to statistics reported in India 2000 of the National Crime Record Bureau (NCRB), crime against women has increased 4.1% from previous years and Dowry death cases has increased 4.4 percent. This is a clear indication that violence in families is increasing and needs to be seriously addressed on both community and national level.

There are several key expressions of violence in families. These are discussed as follows.

Marital Violence. We are living in a violent society where millions of women are victims of marital violence (Chawla, 2004). Wife battering is a global phenomenon and not simply an aberration in the behavior of a class of emotionally disturbed men. It is a manifestation of male dominion over women, and of the patriarchal attitude that views women, especially wives, as the property of men. The problem of marital violence is not a recent experience. Women in our society have been subjected to humiliation, torture, exploitation and neglect for as long as we have had written records of social organization and family life. However, it is only recently that the problem has come to the widespread attention of activists, academicians, professionals, and the public at large, with growing awareness of the undesirability of physical and mental violence and the need for efforts to contain and prevent it.

Marital violence is just beginning to be recognized as an important social problem. Today's social and political climate that emphasizes civil rights and sensitivity to possible infringements of these rights has led to a broader understanding of the historical subjugation of women. In India marital violence takes several forms, including: (i) conjugal violence (ii) sexual violence (iii) alcohol related violence (iv) protective reaction violence (iv) stress-associated violence, and (v) violence associated with dowry (Chawla, 2004; Fernandez, 1997). The psychological, emotional, and relational consequences of all the manifestations of violent behavior can be devastating, and it is not unusual that death results (Pagelow, 1981). Violent behavior toward women is often viewed as normative and sometimes even mandatory in family relationships (Fernandez, 1997). However, much of contemporary society disapproves of these acts of violence or assaults on women. Indeed, "No husband has the right, irrespective of the community to which he belongs, to do physical violence to his wife. And if he does so, she has every right to resist" (Tulsa V. Pannalal, 1963). Given that marital violence is a significant social problem, incidence data need to be gathered with regard to family violence for the purposes of policy formulation, intervention and prevention. Yet, the vast majority of cases in India go unreported because of the private and secretive nature of the family. The belief that wife battering and cruelty is solely linked with dowry harassment is mostly a myth. Wife abuse is a much more pervasive and complex phenomenon and cannot be attributed primarily to the dowry system (Chawla, 2004). This shift in public attitude has made it possible for marital violence to emerge as a socio-legal problem of compelling intensity, demanding recognition from professionals and society at large.

Violence Against Children. Another form of family violence is physical abuse of children. It has become widespread in Indian society and occurs among both the economically disadvantaged as well as advantaged (Chawla, 2004; Segal, 1995). Parents often consider such behavior as an effective way of teaching and controlling children (Hunter, Jain, Sadowski, & Sanhueza, 2000). However, violence against children is not a recent phenomenon. Historically, parents have wielded absolute authority over their children's life, as can be seen in certain Epics and mythology (Sen, 1984). Violence against children today manifests itself in a variety of ways, including physical battering, physical or emotional neglect, sexual abuse (including child rape, molestation, and prostitution), emotional or psychological abuse, abandonment of children, and the selling of children for profit (Chowdhury, Pattnaik, & Patro, 1994).

The child abuse literature in India indicates that child maltreatment has its own set of negative consequences or harmful developmental outcomes for children and youth (see e.g., Chawla, 2004; Chowdhury et al., 1994; Deb, 2005). For instance, abuse tends to lead to more abuse, contributes to delinquency and aggressive behavior in children, and increases the likelihood of adult criminality. Hence, violence tends to beget violence. "The children inherit a legacy of violence, a gift of tyranny, which they in turn will pass into their children — one generation of violence begetting another – and so on" (Maria Roy, 1977, p. 139). There is considerable evidence for the intergenerational transmission of family violence (Freeman, 1977). The continuance of this syndrome erodes the basic structure of the family and society. Maltreated children also express more anger toward, and have more conflict with, their family members than non-maltreated children. They exhibit more internalizing disorders (e.g., depression and various anxiety disorders) than non-abused children and are less pro-social In addition, abused children tend to manifest a variety of other cognitive, emotional and social difficulties, including troubled relationships with peers, impaired social cognition, lack of empathy, and poor performance. Sexually abused children often suffer from a variety of behavioral and emotional problems. These include like depression, guilt and shame, learning difficulties and higher rates of school dropout, sexual promiscuity, runaway behavior, somatic complaints, and sudden changes in mood, to name a few (Gelles & Conte, 1990). Child abuse and neglect is a social ill with which India as a nation has yet come to understand or be able to provide solutions.

Violence Against the Elderly. Elder abuse is described as the newest and most hidden form of violence in the home (Jamuna, 2003). Older parents are being assaulted and injured by their children and other relatives, often those who are their primary care providers. Elderly abuse is frequently a more subtle form of violence against the elder members of the family. Accurate estimates of this form of intra-family violence are difficult to come by because family loyalty and dependency in a country like India prevent elder persons from reporting abuse. Maltreatment of the elderly includes both passive and active neglect, physical abuse and mental anguish, marital abuse, medical abuse, and self-abuse (e.g., self-mutilation) (Jamuna, 2003). Elder abuse also includes violation or denial of rights that occur when elderly couple are financially exploited or forced out of their dwelling and into another setting against their will (Fernandez, 1997; Jamuna, 2003).

Major demographic changes have occurred over the last half-century which help explain why problems of the elderly and the silent problems of elder abuse are capturing the attention of professionals and the general public. Improved health and technological conditions have created a demographic shift in favor of the aged in India. The average life expectancy has increased from 32 in 1947 to 62 in 2000 and is likely to be 75 by 2010 and 80 by 2020. Census-based data produced by the Centre of Development indicates that India has the highest population of elderly people in the world. Seven percent of the people in India are above 65 years of age, a number approaching 100 million. Sixty percent of these individuals are women. The rapid aging of the population has resulted in an increased need for long-term care of the elderly. This is especially so as socio-economic structures change rapidly, and as the security and support provided by both extended and joint family members are waning. Today the responsibility of caring for aging parents fall almost entirely on the shoulders of one or more of the adult children. This phenomenon leads to caregiver burden and burn-out, which are major contributors to elder abuse and neglect. The increasing burden of home care also has an impact on the financial resources of families. Furthermore, the increased entry of women into the employment sector reduces time and energy for care of their elderly relatives. In Indian society, household caregivers are usually women. They are responsible for the care of the aged parents more than other members of the family, and it is they who may be most likely to abuse the aged. Overburdened with other family responsibilities, workplace problems, and other stresses of parenting one's own children as well as caring for one more aging parents or relatives, the caretaker is at greater risk for resorting to violence as an emotional outlet. There is some empirical support for the notion that the stress associated with caring for an older adult in the home is mainly responsible for violence against elders (Legal Research and Service for Elderly, 1979)

The possibility of financial gain is also cited as one of the common reasons for physical and emotional abuse of the elderly. Recently an elderly couple from east Delhi, through a letter sent to the Delhi High Court, alleged that their son and daughter-in-law tortured them and forcibly took possession of their property. The court directed the police to provide protection to the couple and institute criminal proceedings against the abuser. This would perhaps be the first case of its kind that has engaged the attention of the judiciary (Times of India, 2003)

Another manifestation of elder abuse is that the abuser has harmed herself or himself. This view, based on the theory that "violence begets violence", states that the victim parents may at an earlier time have been the abuser; but that now the abuse has been targeted against oneself – often in the form of self-mutilation. Needless to say, these forms of self-abuse can often lead to disability or death.

One additional explanation for the occurrence of elder abuse is that society today places little value on the aged (Jamuna, 2003). This has not the case historically in India. Age was synonymous with wisdom, and respect and honor were given to elders. Unfortunately, older people "are but paltry thing, a tattered coat upon a stick" who are no longer seen as making much of a positive contribution to family and society. This is especially true for elderly women, who, in a patriarchal society are less valued, less educated, and seen as more of a burden on family life. Reports on elder abuse consistently identify females of advanced age as the most likely victims (Anantharaman, 1980, Lan & Kosberg, 1979). The abuser is often a middle-aged female and typically the daughter-in-law of the victim. Ramchandran et al. (1999) found that family living conditions are significant factors affecting the mental health of the elderly, with higher reported incidences occurring in low income families. However, elder abuse in India occurs throughout all segments of society and is one of the most serious problems that needs to be addressed by both local and state governments, professionals, and concerned citizens.

The Impact of Family Violence on Individuals and Families

Research in recent years has documented extensively the effects of family violence. Since the consequences of physical violence have been the most obvious and immediate, they have received the most empirical attention. Deaths associated with the dowry system in India are among the most common expressions of family violence. According to Crime Bureau of Indian statistics, during the year 1997-1998 Dowry Deaths were 6006 and 6917, respectively, accounting for a 15.2% rise in this offence. Violence in any form has both short- and long-term effects on individuals and families. Family violence suffered by women in particular often has consequences that include suicide and homicide (Nagda, 2003). In other cases women suffer serious physical injury during attempts at bride burning and other forms of murder. As the common targets of family violence, women and children also suffer injuries that include major and minor cuts, fractures, damage to internal organs, burns, and injuries associated with sexual abuse (Nair, 2000).

Jaswal (2002) explored the relationship between domestic violence and the state of women's health by examining records of medical college hospital and community based health facilities. Of the total 12,987 cases studied, women in the age group of 18-30 years reported the most incidents of violence. More cases of domestic violence were reported by women with chronic illnesses such as tuberculosis and gynecological morbidity (Jaswal, 2002). The majority of the wives who experienced domestic violence also suffered from multiple health hazards, including sexually transmitted infections and disease (STI/STD), depression, anemia, and high/low blood pressure. These abuse-related outcomes were especially high in families that were poor and uneducated.

Martin et al. (1999) studied wife abuse in India in relation to its effects on reproductive health. These investigators found that abusive men were more likely to engage in extramarital sex and contract sexually transmitted infections and diseases, thereby placing their wives at risk for acquiring these diseases. Such abusive sexual behavior may also result in an increased rate of unplanned pregnancies (Martin et al, 1999). Indeed, violence against women has a major impact on their physical, sexual and reproductive health. Common outcomes are unwanted, unplanned, and frequent pregnancies that often result in both forced and sex selective abortions. Sexual abuse, including forced intercourse within marriage and refusal to use male contraceptives, puts women at risk of HIV/AIDS and other sexually transmitted diseases. The threat of violence by the male partner makes it difficult for women to choose and practice contraceptives of their choice (Nagda, 2003).

According to the International Centre for Research on women (ICRW), family violence is a major contributor to depression, anxiety disorders, somatic disorders, and broken families (ICRW Study). This United States based organization conducted a study in seven states of India. This study, which included a sample of 10,000 women, found that incidences of severe physical violence were high, and that 95% of the victims did not leave their marital partner but continued to endure the abusive relationship. The majority of wives who had experienced domestic violence also suffered from multiple health hazards (e.g., STI/STD) or a host of psychological and emotional disorders. However, despite this survey, the impact of family violence on the mental health of women has not been systematically studied in India. Verbal and emotional abuse can also contribute to the deterioration of the mental health of the individual and her/his ability to parent effectively and function as a full-fledged member of society (Nair, 2000).

Another manifestation of domestic abuse, and one that is often overlooked, is that of the economic suppression and exploitation of women. Oppression of women in the workplace, or exclusion of them from high status and well-paying jobs, is another form of control. This type of abuse forces women into low paying or non-paying jobs. Financial exploitation is sometimes linked with physical violence against women, as well as physical and emotional neglect (Nair, 2000).

Witch killing, another form of violence practiced in *adivasi* (tribal) families and communities, also keeps women away from obtaining access to land. In fact, fear of violence or retaliation prevents millions of women (widows, divorcees, deserted, and other kinds of single women) from claiming their legal rights to property inheritance. On the other hand, the basic economic dependence of women and their resourcefulness render them fearfully weak and dependent, thus making it difficult for them to stand up and challenge the violence and power used against them in the family.

Efforts to Address the Problem of Family Violence

Attempts to address the problem of family violence include: (i) intervention and treatment in the post violence situation, i.e., after the incident of violence has occurred; and (ii) prevention of violence before it takes place. A number of programs have aimed at treating known cases of family violence and preventing abusive behavior through, for example, psychological and family counseling, family enrichment programs, self-help groups in shelter homes short stay homes, comprehensive emergency social services, crisis intervention programs, police intervention programs (i.e., crime women cells, anti-dowry cells), and day care centers. These programs are geared toward assisting known victims of violence. However, the greatest need in India today is the prevention of violence in families. Violence in the home can be reduced if we have full employment opportunities, the elimination of poverty, and guaranteed health care for all citizens. Changes in the law and public policies that influence family life are also needed to help prevent violence in families.

To uphold the constitutional mandate and enact the promise of an egalitarian, non-exploitative, secular, and democratic social order (Articles 12 to 35 of the Indian Constitution), the government has enacted various legislative measures to ensure equal rights, counter social discrimination and violence, and provide support services to vulnerable groups. However, none of these laws directly addresses the problem of *domestic violence*. Thus, unaffected by an ineffective justice delivery system, family violence over the years has escalated. Inefficiency of the police, loopholes in judicial system, non-cooperation of victims and their family members to report incidences of abuse and neglect, outdated methods of investigation and hostile witnesses, have all contributed to this social malady. To bring about a fundamental change, citizens must accelerate changes in legal codes and the court system and move the country away from the traditional notion that family violence is just a conflicting situation at home, and that courts should not interfere. All citizens are entitled to equal protection under the law. Legal procedures for dealing with domestic violence need be streamlined, and police need to be trained to cope with and manage domestic violence efficiently. However, family violence is best prevented by family members themselves. But how can families prevent something about which they are not fully knowledgeable, nor have the resources and supports in their communities to prevent? It is in this regard that Family Life Education (FLE) holds its greatest promise. Information about all forms of abuse and family violence need to be a central part of any widespread FLE "movement" in India, as well as creative and time-proven strategies for strengthening both the nuclear and joint family system.

References

Ahmed-Ghosh, H. (2004). Chattels of society: Domestic violence in India. *Violence Against Women, 10*(1), 94-118.

Anantharaman, R.H. (1980). Self concept and adjustment in old age. *Journal of Psychological Research, 23* (2), 55-58.

Chawla, S. (2004). India. In K. Malley-Morrison (Ed.), *International perspectives on family violence and abuse: A cognitive ecological approach* (pp. 265-281). Mahwah, NJ: Lawrence Erlbaum.

Chowdhury, A., Pattniak, S., & Patro, A. (1994). Psycho-social profile of abused children in India. *Early Child Development and Care, 104,* 85-93.

Deb, S. (2005). Child abuse and neglect: The Indian scenario. *Social Science International, 21*(1), 3-19.

Fernandez, M. (1997). Domestic violence by extended family members in India. (Interplay of gender and generation). *Journal of Interpersonal Violence, 12*(3), 433-455.

Gelles, R. (1987). *Family violence.* Newbury Park, CA: Sage Pub.

Gelles, R.J., & Coute, J. R. (1990). Domestic violence and sexual abuse of children: A review of research in the eighties. *Journal of Marriage and the Family 52,* 1045-1058.

Hunter, W.M. (2000). Risk factors for severe child discipline practices in rural India. *Journal of Pediatric Psychology, 25(*6), 435-447.

Jamuna, D. (2003). Issues of elder care and elder abuse in the Indian context. In P.S. Liebig & S.I. Rajan (Eds.), *An aging India: Perspectives, prospects, and policies* (pp. 125-142). New York: Haworth Press.

Jaswal, S. (2002). *Methodological issues in assessing domestic violence from health records.* Tata Institute of Social Science, Mumbai.

Kautilya (Translated by Pandit Anantram Kar Sharma), Kautilya Artha (1963). Sastram, Bhubaneswar : Orissa Sahitya Academy, p. 425.

Legal Research and Services for the Elderly. (1979). *Elderly Abuse in the USA.*

Levinson, D. (1989). *Family violence in cross-cultural perspective.* Newbury Park, CA: Sage Pub.

Manu (Translated by Ram Shankar Ray), Manu Samhita or Manu Smriti, (1927). Cuttack: Dharma Grantha Store, p. 240.

Martin, J.P. (1978). *Violence and the family.* Chichester, England: John Wiley & Sons.

Martin, S.L., et al, (1999). Sexual behaviours and reproductive health outcomes. Association for Wife Abuse in India, *JAMA, 282* (20).

Nagda, B.L. (2003). Violence and health of women. *Social Welfare, 50*(9).

Nair, U. (2000). *Domestic violence and its impact on the health of women: Experience from Rural Vadodara, Gujrat.* SORT, Vadodara a Monograph.

Omvedt, G. (1990). *Violence against women: New movements and new theories in India.* New Delhi: Kali for Women.

Pagelow, M.D. (1981). *Woman battering: Victims and their experiences.* Beverly Hills, CA: Sage Pub.

Rane, A,J. (Ed.) (1991). *Research on Child Abuse in families: Review and implications. Research on families with problems in India: Vol. II.* Murali Desai, Tata Institute of Social Sciences, Mumbai.

Segal, U. A. (1995). Child abuse by the middle class? A study of professionals in India. *Child Abuse and Neglect, 19*(2), 217-231.

Times of India (2003), 31.12.

Tulsa V. Pannalal, (1963). All India Reporter. MP 5.

Veeraraghavan, V. (1995). Violence in families: A bio-psychological and natural perspective. *Trends in Social Science Research,* 2 (1), 83-93.

Williams, K.R. (1992). Social sources of marital violence and deterrence: Testing and integrated theory of assaults between partners. *Journal of Marriage and the Family, 54* (3) PP. 620-629.

Yajnavalkya Smriti, quoted by P.N. Sen. (1984). *An introduction to Hindu jurisprudence.* Allahabad: Allahabad Law Agency.

3

Women's Work and Family Interface

Urmimala Das

Socio-economic and demographic issues have forced women into the labor force in India. Economic participation of women outside the home has influenced the roles and relationships between men and women, and gender-based social attitudes and behaviors in general. This chapter discusses the status of working women in modern India and related issues and difficulties that affect the family. The author offers proposals for alleviating pressures and problems and foresees a future which includes an improved quality of family life through a more balanced interface between work and family.

Indian women are born workers. They work throughout all stages of life. In addition to their domestic responsibilities they earn money for their families and capital for the nation. Historically, Indian women accepted their gender role of child bearing, child rearing, and master over all other household chores. In this traditional division of labor, men were the chief breadwinners. For centuries Indian society has been patriarchal. Masculine values have regulated sexuality and reproduction, and were expressed through specific cultural metaphors. Overt rules prohibiting women from specific activities and denying certain rights were commonplace. More subtle expressions of patriarchy occurred through a type of symbolism communicating messages about the inferiority of women. This can be seen through legends highlighting female self-sacrifice and self-effacement, and through ritual practices which day in and day out emphasized the role of women as a faithful wife and devout mother (Desai & Krishnaraj, 1987). Another factor, caste, also contributed to keeping women in their place in family and society. Caste not only determines the social division of labor but also the sexual division of labor. In higher castes women were exempt from working outside the home. Physical mobility was also restricted through caste norms.

Prior to Irfan Habib and Bipin Chandra, it is difficult to construct a complete picture of the economic structure of India. However, historians and many feminist scholars (Khare, 2003) have noted that colonialism and the rise of capitalism in the Indian economy has changed the way of life. Socio-economic demands and demographic compulsions have forced women into the labor force. The number of women with family responsibilities who also work at a paid job has increased significantly in the last 20 years and is expected to keep growing; however, one of the common problems of a working woman in India is over work. She plays the multiple roles of housewife, mother and wage earner. Her relentless attempts to bridge the gulf inevitably fail, often contributing to anxiety, confusion, and conflict. The required changes, including a redefinition of roles, reallocation of responsibilities, and radical change in familial and societal support for resolution of conflict, does not seem to occur (Das, 1999). According to Engel (1891) over a century ago ..... "The emancipation of women may only be possible when women can take part in production on a large social scale and domestic work no longer claims anything but an insignificant amount of her time".

Demographics of Work Force Participation of Women in India

The discussion in this chapter is based on the data of Census, Government of India Census and International Labor Organization (ILO) and the body of basic research currently available to us. A statistical analysis of the work participation of women during the three Censuses of the past century reveals a declining trend for both women and men. However, the data show a marginal increase for females in comparison to males. Table 1 reveals that the workforce participation rate of women (WFPRW) was increasing in the early decades of last century, and that mid century it went down. In 1971 it declined to as low as 14.2 percent. From 1971 onwards it has steadily increased and reached 25.6 percent in 2001. These percentage, however, are deceptive if one looks at absolute numbers involved. The main rise in the three Census years (1981 to 2001) comes from the rural sector, i.e., 23.06 percent, 26.76 percent and 30.97 percent, respectively (see Table 2). In rural areas women belonging to socially weaker sections were forced to work because of their economic needs. This increase though was greater for males in urban areas (Khare, 2002). The urban sector, to which large numbers of people are migrating, shows a very slight increase in three decades, i.e., 8.3, 9.19 and11.55 percent, respectively. This means that the secondary and tertiary sectors are not showing the expected increase.

Table 3 includes data about the division between main and marginal workers. Even though the number of female main workers has increased by 44.24%, as contrasted to male workers who have increased 21.51%, the percentage increase hides the fact that initially the number itself was less. There is, however, an increase in marginal workers by 33.74%, i.e., 10% more than that of the growth in population. The gender differential here is quite obvious. While male marginal workers have increased only 0.98% of the population, female workers have registered an increase of 6.26%. Population percentage-wise the growth rate is 15.48% for males and 37.31% for females — a 22.0% point growth rate in comparison to males. This indicates a trend of deepening marginalization of female workers, which means less and less entitlement to any means of survival.

The number of informal sector women workers, such as hawkers and vegetable sellers, is reported to be quite substantial. Employment of women in the public sector unit in urban areas has gone down. Thus, women are generally working in low-income jobs. As an agricultural country, India needs the contribution of female cultivators and agricultural labourers. Male cultivators have declined in the decade 1981-1991 from 43.7% to 39.62%, while female cultivators have risen from 33.2% to 34.18% (See Table 3). Male migration to urban areas and the number of female-headed households subsisting on meager landholdings can be the only reason for this rise. Census data hardly give any indication in landholdings among cultivators to determine their real worth.

The percentage of female agricultural workers has gone down in recent years from 46.18% to 44.83%. At the same time we should consider that there are nearly 42 million more male cultivators than women cultivators. There are 6 million more female laborers than cultivators. However, the calculation and assessment of percentages is quite deceptive in analyzing the basic realities of women's access to land and to employment opportunities. Percentages for working women in the areas of livestock, forestry, mining and quarry have also declined. In the household industry, women's participation has gone up from 4.59% to 4.63%, a slight increase. The exploitation of women in the export oriented garment industry is a well-documented fact.

Conspicuously, all age groups share in the decline of female work participation roles. This trend becomes clear by the figures in Table 4 (ILO data). In this period, there was a 9.5% decline in male participation rates while the corresponding figure for females was 31.1%. The difference in the participation rates between the two sexes show that it is on an increasing function of age (except for the age group of 60 and above). The smaller difference in the younger age group is mainly due to the decline in the female participation rate.

Data in Table 5 reflect the female employment status more clearly. The information shows that between 1971 and 1988 the share of women in casual employment increased in rural and urban areas. In other words, female employment in India is getting increasingly more casual. This is mainly because employers wish to avoid the provision of maternity leave and other social and economic benefits for workers. Hence, they recruit women as casual workers. Secondly, with the increase of subcontracting in the production process, employment in general, and women's employment in particular, is being gradually transferred from the organized to the unorganized sector.

It has been argued that women in India show reluctance to enter into the labor force, and perhaps that is why their participation rates are low. This argument holds if unemployment among women is negligible, or at least is lower as compared to men. However, the available estimates of female employment do not support this idea. In Table 6 data speak about unemployment among women, which is consistently higher than that of men during all periods of the survey (1961-88) both in rural and urban areas.

Sector-based distribution of employment indicates that nearly 80% of women workers in India are concentrated in agricultural activities. The major shift in women's employment in this sector is from the agricultural laborer category to cultivators. "Cultivators" in this Indian census signify that either an employer or family workers are engaged in cultivation. Women in the Indian context belong mainly to the latter category. It is therefore obvious that the status of women between three census periods has marginally shifted from agriculture to unpaid family worker, but that the share of men in this sector has declined. This may be partly due to migration of females from rural areas to urban areas. The percentage of men declined in the household industries, while that of women increased between 1971 and 1981 and declined between 1981 and 1991 (see Table 6). In non-household industries, the share of men showed improvement between 1981 and 1991 and declined between 1981 and 1991. The share of women in non-household industries improved during the three census periods.

In sum, all of the evidence suggests that women have moved down to lower paying or unpaid work even in higher paying sectors, and that the advancement of women is measurably slow compared to that of men. Moreover, several studies (Subramaniam, 1997; Banerjee, 1985; BAUD, 1992) analyzing the pattern of women's employment in the manufacturing industry have shown that women are being excluded from most skilled jobs and are concentrated in lower paid jobs and industries. Development in India has generally excluded women from high-level jobs and pushed them into marginal occupations.

Social Position of Women in India

The above analysis gives the impression that, after Independence, complex variables have influenced women in different ways. Census data analysis on the status of working women creates contradictory images. In rural areas, small towns and slums, women still suffer economic and social oppression. While the vast majority of upper-caste women today are still confined to household activities and involved with the interests of kith and kin, at the bottom level of the rural hierarchy, women do both intramural and extramural work. One positive trend is that middle class educated women, particularly those who are working, are moving about more freely and generating an impression at least that the status of women in India has substantially improved. The entrance of more women into the political arena reinforces this impression.

Despite some improvements, the condition of women continues to remain much the same, even though there have been some improvements in their overall quality of life. Rising violence against women has been a negative indicator of her status. The female mortality rate has shown a declining trend for the last century. Up to the age of 34, the female death rate is much higher than that of men. One study (Feinstein, 1979) on differential access to healthcare showed that females received significantly less medical attention than males. Education, urbanization and industrialization have yet changed the outlook for a more gender-neutral health culture. In India nearly 100,000 women die every year due to abortion and childbirth, a figure 100 times higher than in developed countries. Two-thirds of pregnant women are anaemic. Pregnant women loose immunity to malaria and are more susceptible to viral infections.

Indian Census data reveal a lower level of female literacy (i.e 54%), although there has been some increase in the literacy rate (39.29% in 1991 to 54.16% in 2001). Gross enrolment of girls in Class I to V is 82.9% and for boys it is 100.9% (1991-99); whereas, in Class VI-VIII these figures are 49.1% and 65.3%, respectively. The dropout rate for girls in primary classes as compared to boys is high, i.e., 41.2% in primary and 61% in upper primary classes. On the whole, it is clear that although enrollment in school is steadily increasing with each census recording, there remain substantial differences in male-female rates of participation. Obstructing factors include the high cost of education, young age of marriage for girls, female seclusion, increasing violence against women, and the fear of high costs of dowry. The rise in education has not been proportionately reflected in employment figures for women, i.e., only 15.9% of women are engaged in the organized sector. There is a tendency of overcrowding in the agricultural sector without any structural change. With few exceptions industrialization has not been able to give a space to women in planned economic development.

In terms of political decision-making and administrative activities of women, the figures are not encouraging. Only 10.4%

of women are in the Indian Administrative Service (IAS), and the figure for women in the Indian Police Service (IPS) is only 3.3%. In the central legislature 8.4% members are women (1999); whereas, this percentage is even smaller in state assemblies (i.e., 5.6%). In the Central Council of Ministers, 10.9% of ministers are women. Reservations for women in PRIS (Panchayat Raj Institutions) gives an encouraging figure, i.e., 31.3% (1997) seats are occupied by them. It may also be that many educated women in India today prefer the freedom of nuclear families to joint family systems. Traditionally in India the joint family has controlled women's labor, sexuality and reproduction. Women are now becoming aware of such patriarchal controls and are aspiring for equality, which is threatening to the men (Desai, 2000).

In India the work participation of scheduled tribe women is the highest, i.e., 43.74% as contrasted with 25.98% for scheduled caste and 22.23% of the total population (1991, Census). Most people who belong to the scheduled tribe population live in rural areas and are engaged in the primary sector. A crucial problem associated with such women who are engaged in primary, agricultural and other unorganized sectors is care of their children. Non-availability of food, shelter and affordable care remains a chronic problem, causing immense hardships to working parents. Although we have not yet learned the full effects of such pressures on the family, we know that they are most severe on women belonging to marginalized socio-economic groups. It is vital that feminists and other pro-family advocates recognize the complex interrelationships among gender, class, race, ethnicity and age in structuring the fates and fortunes of women in employment (Anne Witz, 1993). In India it is the upper caste women who are mostly in the white-collar jobs, whereas tribal women experience the turmoil of casual low level work within a gender biased labor market. The latter work for long hours and receive subsistence pay without any job security. This is a type of repression that Indian society can no longer afford, nor should tolerate any longer (Phizacklea & Wolkwitz, 1995).

Patriarchy and Working Women

Women work not only for income but also for achievement and satisfaction that comes from using their skills and being recognized for them. Meaningful and recognized employment also helps buttress the status of women in society. Years ago, Halter (1971), Goode (1963), Myrdal (1956), and Ginsberg (1962) observed that industrialization and equal employment contributes to egalitarian relations between men and women both within and outside the family. However, industrialization in India has largely failed to bring about an elevation in the relative position of women. Even most highly educated and well-paid women remain subservient to patriarchal norms. These norms are evident in the allocation of roles, responsibilities and control in the distribution of resources. As a wife and mother she has to observe all rituals that establish her role and goodness in the family and society. Further, working wives do not necessarily maintain full control over their earnings. The great majority of working women studied by Kapur (1974) reported that they were not allowed to spend even their earned money in the way they would like to spend it, and that they had to give their pay to their husbands and in-laws. In addition, many working women are allowed to go only to the workplace and few if other places unless they are with their husbands. These restrictions have caused a great deal of conflict in modern households.

Dual Responsibility and Role Conflict

Advancements have been made in the education of women and their economic opportunities while there has been a decline in conservatism. However, many women according to Mohanty (1999), "..... are still struggling with the dilemma: employment will bring economic security, but it may create problems in the family. Problems may include: children of an employed mother may miss her at meal times, she will have less time to entertain relatives and guests, and the pressures of work may be reflected in her dealing with family members, which may in turn disturb the family peace and happiness". It may not be easy for a woman to resolve the conflicts resulting from her double responsibilities- at home and in the work place (Bhoite, 1987). The wife's employment according to Srivastava (1978) may create a problem in adjustment at work as well as in her family. Any illusion about her being a super woman is bound to be frustrating for her and painful for her family (Davis, 1975).

These concerns and risks are real. Still, educated women in India are greatly in favor of having jobs primarily because it is economically beneficial for them, making them financially independent. Working gives dignity and a higher status to the women in India. Further, employed women feel satisfied that they are contributing something to the welfare of their family and society.

The middle and lower class working women carry greater responsibilities at home and outside, than those who only work inside the home and they suffer from feelings of guilt about neglecting children and other family members. There are many problems existing in the lives of working women, some are overt and others are hidden. Working women do not necessarily maintain full control over their incomes. Dhingra indicates that a large number of women reported that their husbands were inconsiderate and often demanded a traditional wife. Husbands crave for the wives earning, but they cannot change their authoritarian attitudes with regard to their wives and family (Reddy, 1986). They want continued performance of house hold chores by wives in addition to job demands but they still treat them the same as a non-working wife.

Poverty and mental depression are problems of women who work at lower-level. Stress and a sense that they lack the power to improve their circumstances seem to be the chief causes of low confidence and self-esteem. There is an immense physical and emotional burden as well as a dual responsibility on these working women's families. Because of their busy lives there is little time left for leisure and recreation or even for simple relaxation.

Women say that their husbands demand work from them because it is a women's exclusive duty even though they are earning wages., but then they are abused for alleged negligence of the husband and family for having been employed (Reddy, 1986). A working woman is made to feel that her employment is an equally important role without any changes in her familial role. However, if a working wife takes it easy and neglects her home and children, then she is not only accused of being vain, inefficient, and useless as a wife, housewife, and mother, but is made to feel guilty for her being so. Thus, she feels torn between the duties of her home and work because she wants to be very efficient and successful both as a worker and as a housewife. Role conflicts leave working women feeling guilty. Being a wage earning member of society, a wife has privilege to move freely, to demand her equal treatment by her husband, and to have a relationship of co-partnership with her husband. If a wife did not feel like listening to her husband or refused to share a bed she was accused of having sex with others. This was the particular mindset of husbands and proves to be humiliating for wives. Recently, husbands have started sharing in household work and childcare, but it has still not become common because of the persistence on the part of both men and women of traditional ideas about sex roles.

Impact of Work on Women's' Health

Stress in the lives of working women with children, caused by dividing their loyalties between family and career, may be a cause of physical and emotional problems resulting in strains to family life. Carrying out almost single-handedly all the duties and responsibilities of home life strains a working women and makes her tired and irritable. This in turn is liable for making her an unpleasant and unenjoyable company to her husband and children. Also, the unavailability of childcare during working hours of parents remains a major problem. All these factors serve to severely limit a woman's chances of upward mobility.

Stress is created from high demands coupled with high constraints and low support on working women. Stress can lead to insomnia, headaches, indigestion, muscle cramps and aches, fatigue, not being able to concentrate, depression, tension, impulsive and hostile behavior, and irregular periods (Magezis, 1996). Chowdhury's (1995) findings confirm that multiple roles are more of a disadvantage for a working mother than for a non-working mother. This can be linked to recent various family crises in India, which include mental strain and dissolution, parent-child conflicts, and family violence. It is important to recognize the extent to which women in this mechanized world have become alienated from their work at home and socially isolated because of increasingly urban lifestyles. For men and children, home serves as a leisure space, for women it is a workplace, so then work and leisure become inextricably mixed. Thus, the real labor involved and considerable energy invested in work in the home is demanded from women. The idea of a woman's role as a mother and wife as the true purpose of a woman's life further complicates the problems of working women. Marriage has been considered as an unwritten contract which confines wives to child and home keeping responsibilities. Many women are demanding new options for careers and rejecting household responsibilities as their sole job.

A number of studies have come to the following conclusions. As more choices exist for women in terms of daily employment and long term work commitments, including options for work inside or outside the home (or a combination of both), the divisions between work and leisure are likely to breakdown. Women find work and leisure more satisfying when neither is enforced nor precluded by societal conventions. The employed mother manages her double load but as a result she has less leisure and less time with her children. The amazing thing is that she can manage work and home life efficiently and effectively. Employed women watch less TV and are more engaged in organizational and societal activities. Employed women, in spite of the fact that they undergo higher strain than housewives, are willing to embrace both important aspects of their lives—family and work.

Gender problem in the workplace

Apart from mental health, women's general health may be affected due to typical adverse work experiences and pregnancies. Sexual harassment in the workplace may lead to psychological trauma. Moreover, working women may suffer from a number of psychological problems created by male co-workers and male bosses. Sometimes, the male boss with the advantage of his position and official status tries to exploit her sexually (Reddy, 1986). Sometimes the egos of male colleagues or a male boss may be injured by the competence of a woman resulting in sexual harassment. Males may also gossip and fabricate derogatory stories about women co- workers. One such story is that she is having intimacies with her male boss and/or colleagues. The woman is forced to either go along with the story or reject it. By rejecting the story she has to accept her dim promotional avenues, humiliation and marginalization in the workplace. If a woman is the boss, male and female subordinates do not obey her. If she becomes reserved and strict and demands discipline, she is considered as too masculine, dictatorial, and harsh. When the lady boss is polite, courteous, and kind she is not taken seriously and her orders are neglected. She is sometimes mistaken as a woman interested in men and an inefficient boss. Indian society does not want a woman to be an efficient, confidant, assertive, and dominating personality. Families of such women do not want her to make independent decisions for her personal life. Still, in most of the cases the dehumanization of gender-based social division of labor is established in Indian lifestyle. Resource theory, role overload theory, and exchange theory (American and/or European theories) can all be used to explain the misery of working women but not to a very great extent in the Indian context.

Tentative Suggestions

As society's expectations become more flexible, marriages should be made comfortable and couples should realize how many years they have to experiment with various ways of working, being at home, and being with their children. Double household planning and geographic distances are part of the new flexibility. It is important to recognize that different life stages can invite different role and interactional patterns without threatening the integrity of the family life space. New roles and new lifestyles can continue to develop in a healthy functioning family up to the end of the life span. Most working women do not have choices. However, when there is a fusion of work and leisure by choice, life satisfaction increases. At the moment, if rigid attitudes towards gender-based division of labor are modified, men will be fully liberated to enjoy homemaking, thus family life will be richer and household responsibilities can be shared with husbands and children to benefit all of family members. Children's sharing and involvement in household labor is valuable for all family workers. Care of the children can be accomplished inside or outside the home by qualified caregivers. Working women have raised a number of issues and demands to improve their lives. Some specific issues are as follows:

(a) Childcare must be available during all hours and should be seen as a woman's right rather than a privilege.
(b) Equal treatment to part-timer workers.
(c) Equal wages for men and women.
(d) Expanded training and education for women.
(e) Maternity rights, benefits and protection.
(f) Support and help networks in the workplace.
(g) Assertiveness.
(h) Knowing one's rights.
(i) Women's unionization is a woman's power to combat sexual harassment.
(j) Affirmative action programs.

Perspectives

How to interface of family and work is a crucial question of both ideology and practice. Women are so closely identified with family in thought that reconceptualizing the gender boundaries requires rethinking kinship and the role in the labor market, while also taking into account the organization of household labor and the primary responsibility of caring for domestic maintenance. As of yet, social thinking about family roles reflects a male oriented approach, which distorts women's experiences, while maintaining the gendered nature of family experience. (Hessuferree, 1987).

The aforementioned analysis of women's experiences in the work place and in family life has given enough reasons to consider traditional family practices as problematic. It is neither a search for ways for women to balance family and work, nor is it a woman's role, attitude or personality, which can bring a better future for family life. Women are not treated as individuals but (both in and out of family) as a family in herself conceptually. Gender issues need attention among researchers of family life education. "Structural Functionalism", "Exchange theory", and "interactionism" are three most important schools of thought aimed at perpetuating the monolithic model of the family. They emphasize consensus and continuity of traditional family organization and ignore the significance of variations of family forces, conflict, and inequality in family life. Heterosexual family interface with working women's lives creates problems such as: pathogenic families, role conflict, mental and physical health hazards, and varied work place problems. It also poses far deeper serious problematic propositions like erosion of the heterosexual family, a reverse (or gender neutral) socialization, the rise of individualism, family violence, equality, and the issue of production and reproduction.

Under the ongoing transitional phase in the evolution of the concept of the Indian family, any prescription or suggestion will treat the outer symptoms and not the underlying problem. For example, social support networks at home and in the work place may reduce tension and relax the mental stress of working women but they do not address the disease of the society. It treats the individual and does not focus on social construction of gender as its underlying analysis. Likewise, "role sharing" is meaningless because the notion of role focuses attention more on individuals than social structure and implies that "the female role" and "the male role" are complementary (i.e., separate or different but equal). These terms strip power and create conflict; and it is significant that sociologists don't speak of "class roles" or "race roles" (Stay & Thorne, 1985). The most difficult task of women is maintaining

Table 1
Female Labour Participation
(1901-2001)

Year	*Female Workers as % to Female Population*	*Male Workers as % to Male Population*	*Population Sex Ratio*	*Female Workers per 1000 male workers*
1901	31.70	61.11	972	504
1911	33.73	61.90	964	525
1921	32.67	60.52	955	516
1931	27.31	54.04	946	408
1951	23.31	54.04	946	408
1961	27.93	57.12	941	460
1971	14.22	52.75	930	215
1981	20.85	53.19	936	367
1991	22.23	51.56	927	-

Source: Processed from Census of Government of India (1901 to 1991).

their position as wives and mothers, while meeting the demands of their job at the work place. First of all, women need to be considered as individuals by elevating their status both at home and at work. The next important process is to change the direction of family socialization principles so as not to perpetuate the practices of gender domination and subordination. Family socialization should aim at establishing democratic relationships, which are devoid of patriarchal hierarchies.

Table 2

Work Force Particiation by Sex and Place of Residence (values in percentages)

	RURAL		URBAN	
Year	*Males*	*Females*	*Males*	*Females*
1961	58.27	31.39	52.40	11.09
1971	53.46 (-4.71)	13.09 (-18.13)	48.82 (-3.58)	6.61 (-4.48)
1981	53.77 (0.31)	23.06 (9.97)	49.06 (0.24)	8.31 (1.7)
1991	52.28 (-1.49)	26.76 (3.70)	48.92 (-0.14)	9.19 (0.88)
2001	52.36 (0.08)	30.97 (4.21)	50.85 (1.93)	11.55 (2.36)

Note: Figures in parentheses indicate decadal shifts

Sources:

1. 1961,GOI,Vol.VIII,M.P. Part II A—General Populations
2. 1971,GOI,M.P.series-10,Part II B—1,Economic tables.
3. 1981,Primary Census abstract,Part II B-1.
4. 1991,GOI,Series 13,M.P, Part II A, General Populations tables.
5. 2001GOI,Provisional tables,Paper—2,M.P.

Table 3

Distribution of Main Workers by Sectors

Sl. No.	*Sector*	*1971*		*1981*		*1991*	
		Male	*Female*	*Male*	*Female*	*Male*	*Female*
1.	Cultivators	45.9	29.84	43.7	33.2	39.62	34.18
2.	Agricultural laborers	21.54	50.86	19.56	46.18	21.01	44.83
3.	Livestock, Forestry and Fishing	2.24	1.91	2.34	1.85	1.94	1.58
4.	Mining and Quarry	0.54	0.40	0.62	0.35	0.69	0.31
5.	Manufacturing						
	a) Household Industry	3.42	4.24	418	4.59	2.08	3.49
	b) Non-household Industry	6.70	2.77	8.92	3.55	8.88	3.81
6.	Construction	1.36	0.65	1.8	0.80	2.31	0.63
7.	Trade and Commerce	6.37	1.78	7.33	2.04	8.93	2.22
8.	Transport, storage and communication	2.84	0.47	3.32	0.38	3.51	0.31
9.	Other services	9.07	7.08	9.22	7.05	10.78	8.26
	Total:	100	100	100	100	100	100

Table 4

Age Specific Work Participation Rates

Age years	*1950*		*1960*		*1970*		*1980*		*1985*	
	Male	*Female*	*Male*	*Female*	*Male*	*Female*	*Male*	*Female*	*Male*	*Female*
10 – 14	41.4	28.1	33.6	25.3	25.8	20.8	18.0	16.2	15.8	13.8
15 – 19	77.0	38.3	69.4	35.4	62.4	31.0	55.0	26.5	53.8	25.4
20 – 24	93.6	45.4	90.4	42.4	89.2	36.4	88.0	30.4	87.8	29.3
25 – 39	97.7	52.3	97.6	49.5	97.6	43.9	96.9	38.1	96.8	36.5
40 – 59	97.0	48.3	96.3	46.1	96.1	41.3	95.7	36.6	95.4	34.7
60 and above	7.5	24.6	75.2	21.3	70.2	18.6	65.1	15.7	62.7	14.6
Total	61.3	30.5	57.5	28.5	54.9	24.8	54.2	21.7	55.1	21.6

Source: ILO.

Table 5

Female Employment Status

Year	*Self Employed*	*Rural Regular Employees*	*Casual Workers*	*Self Employed*	*Urban Regular Employees*	*Casual Workers*
1972-73	64.5	4.1	31.4	48.5	27.8	23.7
1977-78	62.1	2.8	35.1	49.5	24.9	25.6
1983	61.9	2.8	35.3	45.8	25.8	28.4
1987-88	60.9	3.6	35.5	47.1	27.5	25.4

Source: Visaria, P and Minhas, B.S. (1991), "Women Work", *The Indian Journal of Labour Economics*, Vol. 34, No. 3, 1991

Table 6

Unemployment Rates in India

Concept/Year	*Rural Areas*		*Urban Areas*	
	Male	*Female*	*Male*	*Female*
Weekly Status				
1961-62	3.7	6.5	3.0	3.3
1972-73	3.0	5.5	6.0	9.2
1977-78	3.6	4.0	7.1	10.9
1983	3.7	4.3	6.7	7.5
1987-88	4.2	4.3	6.6	9.2

Source: Visaria, P and Minhas, B.S. (1991), "Women Work", *The Indian Journal of Labour Economics*, Vol. 34, No. 3, 1991.

References

Annewitz, (1993). Women and work. In Victoria Robinson & Diane Richardson (Eds.), *Introducing women's studies* (p. 243). London: Macmillian.

Banerjee, N., (1985). *Women and Industrialisation in Developing Countries: Occasional Paper No.71.* Calcutta, Centre for Studies in Social Sciences.

Baud, Isa, (1992). Gender and forms of production: Labour intensive industries in India and Mexico. *Economic and Political Weekly, 24*(34), 6.

Bhoite, A. (1987). *Women employees and rural development: Problems of employed women in rural areas.* Delhi:Gian Publishing House, Pp.23-49.

Chowdhury, A. (1995). Employed mothers and their families in India. *Early Child Development and Care, 113,* 65-75.

Das, T. (1999). Employed women and problems of child care. In J.K. Baral & A. Chowdhury (Eds) *Family in transition: Power and development. New Delhi: Northern Book Centre,* Pp.139-147.

Davis, R. (1975). *Women and work.* London:Hutchinson.

Desai, N, & Krishnaraj, M. (1987). *Women and society in India.* Delhi: Ajanta Publications, P.28.

Desai, M. (2000). Public policy and the family in India. Paper presented and the Nineth National Conference on Women's' Studies, Hyderabad, January 8-11.

Feinstein, K. (1979). *Working women and families.* London: Sage Publications, P. 16.

Goode, W.J. (1963). *World revolution and family patterns.* London: The Free Press of Glencoe.

Ginsberg, E., and Associates, (1967). *Lifestyles of educated women.* New York: Columbia University Press.

Halter, H., (1971). Sex roles and social change. *Acta Sociological Special Issue on Sex Roles, 14:* 1-2.

Hess, B.B., & Ferree, M.M. (1987). *Analysing gender: A handbook of social science research.* New Delhi: Sage Publications.

Kapur, Promillia.(1974). The changing status of working women in India. Delhi: Vikas Publishing House.

Khare. (2003). Changing contours of female workforce participation rates in India. *Women's Link*, April – June.

Magezis, J. (1996). *Women's studies teach yourself books.* New Delhi: Sage Publications.

Myrdal, A. (1956). Women's Double Life. *Social* Welfare, 3:9.

Reddy, C., & Raghunadha, R. (1986). *Changing status of educated working women.* Delhi: B.R. Publishing Corporation

Srinivas, V. (1977). *Employment of educated married women in India: Its causes and consequences.* Delhi: National Pub., P-99.

Stacey, J., & Thorne, B. (1985). The missing feminist revolution in sociology. *Social Problems. 32*(4), 301-316.

Subramanian, K.M. (1977). *Wages in India.* New Delhi: Tata McGraw Hill.

4

Impact of Technology on Family Life

Bijayalaxmi Das

During the last few decades, technology has affected Indian families in numerous ways. The impact of technology on family life is extremely important, and it requires a proper understanding to provide maximum benefits for the general welfare of the family. Quality of life has changed due to developments in technology. This chapter discusses the beneficial and harmful effects of technology on family life and proposes suggestions for making use of technology in ways that will enhance quality of life.

Technology is all-pervasive in industrial societies in the 21st Century and is increasingly impacting developing societies. Technology now affects us before we are born and even after we die. How and if we are conceived now frequently depends on technology. Once a child is conceived, technology allows for fetal monitoring and even in utero surgery if necessary. At the other end of the life cycle, parts of our bodies may continue to exist after our deaths as transplanted organs or as frozen sperm or embryos. It is now entirely possible to produce offspring many years after one's death. Consequently, the notion of what it is to be a mother, a father, and to have a family is being redefined everyday.

The impact of modern technology on a family can be recognized by a review of the changes in the roles and contributions of each family member to the family's well-being. Some changes are the result of interaction with and exposure to other cultures and these should be differentiated from those directly resulting from technological advances. In trying to assess the significance of the changes in family life brought about by technology, we must recognize the fact that these changes are gradual and that there are significant variations between countries. These variations may be due to cultural differences and occur between those who are economically comfortable and those who are economically deprived. The topic of technology and family is significant for a variety of reasons. Modern technology is directly related to family issues and social problems. It brings new opportunities and challenges to individuals, families, and the society at large. The technological revolution has also impacted the structure and function of families in many societies. Technology offers opportunities for both developing countries and those that are already developed, but the dispersion of technology will contribute to the modification of family relationships, attitudes, and values.

Tasks which traditionally took hours to accomplish can now be done in a matter of minutes. With this reality, wives are able to seek employment outside the home or to take on outside work which can be done at home. Advances in modern technology take basic economic pressures off an increasing number of people, raise standards of living, and bring the prospect of a more secure and satisfying family life. This reflects the rise in the status of young wives and children, which is one of the great transformations of our time. There is now a new approach to equality between males and females. Each has its own particular role, but the boundaries are no longer so rigidly defined or performed without consultation—husbands and wives are partners to some extent (especially in high income families).

Since human beings first fashioned primitive hand tools, technology has continuously transformed the way we live through the nature of our relationships with each other and the manner in which we interact with our environment. The technological advancements that have marked the past two decades have come into our homes and our workplaces and have begun to change how we think about ourselves and the world around us. From modern air travel to mass communications to computers, our professional and personal lives have not just been affected by technology—they have been deeply altered by it. Changing in how we think and analyze information is at the core of the challenges we face as we seek to shape technology to benefit humans. Otherwise, we will merely be shaped to fit the agenda and pace set by technology's machines.

For women, this technological way of looking at issues and finding answers is very troubling for at least two reasons. First, by ignoring the human element and human dimension of all decision-making, technological decision-making reduces and even excludes personal feelings and desires. Secondly, technological decision-making ignores the historic reality of women's alienation and exclusion from the decision-making process. It makes no room for their views or the views of other vulnerable groups including children, the poor, or the less powerful person in the family. They become no more than statistics, whose presence is problematic for technical planners and embarrassing for the government. In the past, women have been excluded and absent from the decision-making center. Their priorities and needs have rarely been taken into account by the powerful institutions that make these formal decisions. What they do as wives, mothers, workers, and professionals is an integral part of who they are. They are not just one or the other, they are both. For instance, talking about work and talking about childcare often go hand-in-hand.

Technology has been deemed a prime causal factor in the overall transformation that has affected the life of millions of people, as well as their perceptions of social values. Technology essentially is a main characteristic of contemporary civilization, pervading the entire society for better or worse. This is not a new revelation, however. The story has been told repeatedly for almost two centuries since the industrial revolution erupted in England and expanded to the rest of the world. The past industrial revolution and new technology are not comparable though. Both were born of technical progress, but they are distinct systems, one industrial and the other technological. They are different and to some extent antagonistic, bringing forth different outcomes. During the past two centuries, the progressive development of capitalism has relied heavily on workers, transforming peasants into producers of manufactured goods. The recent technological advances in the industrial countries have made people practically nonessential, except as consumers.

Technology: Its Impact on and Challenges for Family Life

In many parts of the world, technology is creating huge problems to go along with its benefits. Invariably, we are invited to believe that the way to solve these problems is to create yet more technology. In some cases, technology may be part of the problem rather than the solution.

It is important to realize that the cultural, economic, and even political impact of technology may be quite unforeseen. Throughout most of human history, performing arts were live. The artist (actor, singer, or dancer) was in the same place as the audience at the same time. One limitation was the distance of the artist from the audience in order to ensure the largest audience but still allowing them to see and hear the whole performance. Quite elaborate technological solutions existed at that time. For example, the astonishing acoustics of the Greek amphitheaters alleviated that problem.

Viewed historically, the rate of technological change is increasing exponentially. Primitive wheeled transport existed for hundreds of years. Watt steam engines were in use for 90 years or more. Advances developed in the 1930's were written off in some 30 years; in the 1970's and 80's advancements might be around five years. Equipment, in particular software, being introduced today will be superceded and rendered obsolete in as little as six months. In carefully selected cases it is possible to leap into present technologies. This is an option well worth considering in the context of technologies that support families.

One obvious example is in the field of communication technologies. There is no plausible reason why remote and disadvantaged regions or even marginalized groups should not conceptualize themselves as low tech areas with high tech communication systems. As suggested elsewhere, high tech communications make distance learning and working and the creation of virtual multinational family businesses possible. In this case one could envision young people who have left their families and regions and re-located elsewhere. They are in a position to distance work and support the families and communities they have left behind, which is viewed as being to everyone's advantage. A practical example would be in the field of medicine where alternative treatments based on local plants and herbs or perhaps acupuncture techniques could be linked with Western technology to create virtual organizations capable of offering alternative treatment options to young people and the families they let behind. In the process, cross-generational interaction and solidarity could be created.

Many technologists pursue the introduction of technology with a sort of missionary focus. Some do it because it is profitable for them or their employers. For others, it is a deep conviction that it constitutes progress and it is their *raison d'être*. In some cases, it actually seems to be a matter of having a solution and looking for a problem. More sensitive design methodologists often point out that the correct definition of a problem will constitute as much as 75% of its solution. We would be well advised to re-examine how we define family problems and how we identify the origins of those problems to find the most elegant and humane way of solving them.

The twentieth century represented a period of transition to this new model of the family, which developed right after World War I. By and large, during the process of industrialization, rural to urban migration led to insecure settlements, poverty, and family instability. A major consequence for the evolution of the family was that survival was sought through protective self-reliance (including procreating numerous children), regardless of the detriment to economic and social conditions, the environment, and community life.

This situation, although real and terrifying in most instances, resulted chiefly from external factors that were due to improve as the century progressed, particularly as material growth proved sustainable. Improved material conditions, the expansion of educational opportunities, the decline of infant mortality, and more effective medical care resulted in a smaller family size. Many more people born in this century could hope to live long enough to know their grandchildren and live a married life of 35 to 40 years. In addition, the early development of commerce and industry induced a sense of familial ownership, where two generations could own a family farm. What was not anticipated was how a longer life expectancy would later lessen familial bonds of such enterprises in favor of production-oriented public organizations. Within the family the authority of the father still prevailed due to the security brought about by assertive labor movements in Europe, as well as the rapid gains in productivity within the United States.

The situation did not remain static. With the rise of the technological revolution, the social institution of the family seemed to disintegrate and become one of the weakest social organizations. Technology-related changes brought forth new patterns of power relations within the family. The emancipation of women, with their newly gained independence and ensuing empowerment, has encouraged new changes in family structures, roles, and functions. Furthermore, technology has been fundamentally involved in the realm of life and death via advances in contraceptive methods and the decrease in infant mortality, enhancing and augmenting food security, hygiene, and health care. The dramatic reduction of population growth in industrialized countries and the alarmingly rapid population growth in developing countries contrast aspects of technical exertion, having deeply modified the age structure of the populations. This has brought forth unprecedented problems in the evolution of the concept of family. Finally, technology has introduced different perceptions of time and power into the social environment, altering the composition of the nuclear family.

Although the traditional family in developed countries appears only as a remembrance of the past, the concern about family has not faded. The old model gave way to new forms that are more permissive. The concept of family today does not refer to a specific model, nor is it characterized by the disappearance of the nuclear type. The concept of family is characterized by the coexistence of various forms. Most of these forms are not made legitimate by marriage; however, all are acknowledged as either a private contract between two persons (implicit or not), or by one parent's decision to rear the offspring of a casual relationship alone. The best formula depends on the desired outcome. The question about the uncertainty of family life involves the future of society and what is meant by well-being. In summary, it seems that the liberalism usually limited to the global economy, has managed to impact social structures as well.

Traditional social structure is being altered, particularly the concept of social class. New workers are emerging that possess a more technical background. They are being entrusted with wider responsibilities and they feel that they are not blue-collar workers anymore. Mobility and readiness to change jobs and locations has become an important aspect of the employment market, since interchangeability of job-related activities is increasingly difficult. This was further facilitated by the development of communications systems, including faster transportation systems and instantaneous ways of inter-connecting persons via the telephone, fax, or internet. Interestingly, a side effect of technology is the preference given to the recruitment of temporary specialized consultants over permanent staff assigned to one location. Short-term professional mobility and a feeling of insecurity have both increased. This has destabilized families as the rising number of divorces has shown. Technology replaces the job and not the worker. The worker is no longer qualified for the job and becomes expendable, as exemplified by the disappearance of couriers, due to the extended use of the fax machines.

While the population of the world has more than tripled during this century, fertility levels in Western countries have declined below the level necessary for long-term population replacement. This resulted broadly in smaller-sized families with one or two children. This decline can be attributed to the ability to plan conception, acknowledgment of the individuality of each child, and economic choice. More people are living longer, family size is shrinking; and individual family members have become more independent. Even the most traditional families have undergone transformation. Increasing longevity requires that a balanced existence take place within the family between the older generations and the children. The number of single parents has increased, and many grandparents have succeeded in keeping up with their independent existence. In most cases solutions have been found outside of the family. On one hand, the grandmother who was conveniently available as a baby-sitter for the working mother has now found activities which conflict with that task. On the other hand, children are less ready to take responsibility for the elderly, even just to keep them company. Children's own interests and activities are too numerous and diverse.

The commodity market has become more age-specific, stressing the generational gap. Adolescents are consumption oriented and commodities now target their age group. Teenagers have part-time jobs and between schooling and paid work, they are affected by the general increase in work hours. The cost of a college education in the United States has increased considerably, and in many instances students have to take out loans in order to pay for their schooling. In Europe, state-controlled, free education increases in the private sector, as seen in England. This adversely affects family income. The choice of a professional career becomes oriented toward earning potential and is less guided by personal propensity, possibly contributing to the rise in job instability.

The elderly play a role in the commodity market as well, whether it be travel, cruises, or medications being marketed to them. Moreover, the extension of a health service market allows older people to be placed in improved nursing homes, reducing the family back to its nuclear arrangement. With medical care and technological devices, the elderly have been able to lead a life separate from their married children and so remain independent for a longer period.

In European countries where medical insurance is part of the social security system, pharmaceutical industry advances are highly advertised and have increased public belief in their efficacy. Demand for specific new products has risen accordingly, and the whole system of social security is in jeopardy because of this excess demand. With medical insurance being at risk of collapsing, the family unit becomes more vulnerable since each of its members might be left, as in the United States, to pursue contracts with private insurance companies.

Medical expenses have also grown due to more sophisticated modes of treatment, by means of new devices or medications. The cost of treatment has led insurance companies to become overcautious and eligibility for medical insurance can be denied. Once probability-based, these organizations have now narrowed their risk to zero to keep from losing profits.

A wider dissemination of information has permitted self-care to expand. People in the field of health have succeeded in creating a market for inexpensive and relatively safe products. These help individuals avoid going to the doctor for minor health problems and help people to be more physically independent, especially senior citizens.

Research in the medical field has become very sophisticated, and the cost has escalated. Most of the effort has been directed toward finding a cure for cancer and heart disease, as they are the leading causes of premature death in Western countries. What is chiefly needed is an educated public. It is not the abundance of information that gives real access to health care and hygiene, but a well organized selection of information. Advice from competent social workers and technicians is still the most important requirement to help people trying to understand contradictory announcements, reports, or literature about healthcare.

Beneficial and Harmful Effects of Technology – Ranging from Domestic to Medical Intervention

Due to tremendous technological growth, the scientific world has flooded the market with consumer goods that make life much less complicated for the woman at home. Refrigerators, grinders, mixers, cookers, ovens, and washing machines help get the job done quickly, leaving women with more spare time. Besides an explosion of consumer goods, things were changing within the industry as well. With the arrival of sophisticated machines, manual labor became less and less necessary. Businesses grew so much that people had to organize, plan, and come up with strategies to cope with the situation.

Oppressed women saw the opportunity to show their capabilities with technological developments. Coupled with incentives and reservations offered to them by governments, women increasingly began to leave their homes in search of an identity. They wanted to prove their worth by earning the very pay packets with which men had condemned them to a life of servitude. While some men encouraged women to use there spare time for intellectual growth and earn extra money in the process, others ridiculed this phenomenon. Men who scoffed at women's efforts to share the work force with them were sure that the women would fail miserably. These men forgot that the focus had shifted from manual labor to mental work. Women, who had well planned their homes, began to manage factories and organizations with ease. They could do almost every job that men could do, sometimes even better.

With these drastic changes, women at times forgot or neglected their role at home. Some women were very content with the new role that enabled them to earn money in their spare time. The more ambitious ones however began to change their careers. They felt a need to prove themselves, but it could come as a price paid by their families. Young children could grow up to be insensitive if their mothers did not show them the love and care they needed. As a result, female children may not learn the values of motherhood. However, a career contributes tremendously to one's identity and self esteem. To manage their dual commitments to home and work, women depend on modern technology.

The new millennium is approaching rapidly. Advanced countries are rapidly inventing new space-aged gadgets and appliances. Where is the Indian culture in the scheme of things? Much progress has been made in the past 50 years since India's independence. There are e-mail and internet centers in big cities. Most children are aware of computers and many are computer literate. Those who are not are being persuaded to take up computer courses by parents. Parents are also thirsting for knowledge about computers, so they are not left behind in understanding this new medium of communication.

Many two-income families (husband and wife both work) are happy to spend money on appliances that will add to their comfort. However, many homes in India do not have refrigerators because they are still considered a luxury item. A kitchen counter that has a built-in cutting block to chop things, a sink to wash in, water for cooking, and a dishwasher that will clean up the dirty dishes—

these would be considered a dream come true for Indian families when 1/3 of our population is still cooking outdoors. A woman is able to save time and energy by using modern gadgets, but money cannot always be saved because these gadgets and modern equipment cost money to acquire in the first place.

Refrigerators, ovens, grinders, washing machines, and all types of modern gadgets make the life of a woman at home much easier and help her do her job more quickly. To some extent she saves time on cooking, washing clothes, or any other household work. By storing vegetables, fruits, meats, and fish in the refrigerator she saves time and energy from going to the market daily to buy all those things. A negative drawback to all this is that health can be affected by reduced physical labor. For instance, grinding *masala* (spices) with a grinding stone and washing clothes in a traditional method, contribute to physical exercise. Modern technology provides machines for these types of work. Cooking by wood fire adds a better taste to food while cooking by aluminum and stainless steel pots do not. Preserving fruits or vegetables by adding preservatives or keeping them in a refrigerator causes vitamins and minerals to be lost.

Air conditioners have greatly increased the comfort levels in homes, workplaces, departmenl stores, cars, and trains. The work output increases in offices with air conditioning, making the demand for air conditioners greater. Therefore, more companies started manufacturing air conditioners and their prices are steadily decreasing. However, the coolants used by air conditioners are harmful to the ozone layer of the earth's atmosphere; as a result more ultraviolet light from the sun reaches the surface of the earth, increasing the risk of skin cancer.

To look more attractive and beautiful, women use cosmetics, soaps, shampoos, facial creams, and lipsticks. In previous years women relied on natural substances like turmeric powder, sandal wood powder, cream, milk, fruits, tulsi leaves, and cucumbers as their cosmetics to keep their skin and body healthy. The use of modern cosmetics sometimes causes skin allergies, rashes, and other complications. If complications do arise, women have to go to the doctor and spend money on medications to alleviate their symptoms.

Families now have cars and scooters. Some are necessary and some are status symbols. These vehicles are used even for short distances and money is spent on gasoline. By using vehicles, the atmosphere is polluted, and drivers suffer from tension and stress.

Exposure to Western thinking has brought about changes in attitudes towards traditional methods of disciplining, toilet training, feeding, and other child rearing practices. Traditional attitudes have not been completely abandoned though. Many parents alternate between permissive and strict child rearing, thus creating anxiety and confusion in children and making them more vulnerable to behavioral and emotional disorders. Marital difficulties, coupled with inadequate or conflicting co-parenting practices, are also becoming more prevalent as women are breaking out of traditional roles, becoming educated in greater numbers, and advocating for equal rights at home and in the work place. With so many women employed outside the home today, some Indian researchers contend that children's needs are not being met and that there is little time for parents to listen to and converse with their children. Studies show that the female-headed households face numerous problems. Some researchers assert that this increase in single parent families has contributed to a greater percentage of children and adolescents experiencing serious difficulties. This may be more common in middle and lower class families, where alternative childcare provisions are often not available.

The impact of modern technology has raised the strain, marital difficulties, parent-child conflicts, feelings of guilt and insecurity, and status confusion that are commonly observed among the working women and high and middle class families even though there are some economic and self-esteem related advantages. However, the potential of such technologies to support family health programs, job creation schemes, and education could be significant even for the disadvantaged groups and those in more remote areas. In this context some see the internet as some sort of technological panacea. However, as pointed out earlier, this technology is double-edged. It potentially holds the ability to access the world's cultural and educational resources; however, there is material on the internet which is deeply offensive, sacrilegious, and thoroughly obscene to many cultures. These concerns can however be addressed by having a local NET Node Point and a Local Area Network based on the local languages and reflecting indigenous cultural and other values. Another concern, already highlighted in America and Europe, is internet addiction. Manifestations include reluctance to join family events, spending more and more time connected to the internet, becoming isolated, increasingly irritable, and preferring electronic relationships to those with family and friends. Ironically, one of the counseling services for the addiction is available on the internet itself, costing $30.00 for a session with an addiction therapist.

In contrast, positive developments must be stated which are already being facilitated by internet technology. Tele-pathology is one example; a breast cancer specialist in London has already diagnosed a patient in Edinburgh via the internet. Specialists would like to see five times as many breast cancer cases referred for a second expert opinion, and Tele-pathology will make this possible. These polarized examples have been cited so that it will be clear that there are a number of different application options for a given technology and that the technology should not be accepted at face value.

It is frequently suggested that the only way in which underdeveloped regions or countries can develop their economies and enhance the wellbeing of their people is to catch up with the technologically advanced nations. This can be a long and painful process and can leave countries in a position of continuously attempting to catch up with what is essentially a moving target.

One way of partly overcoming this problem is by planning to leapfrog in particular areas. The sheer rate of technological change can actually facilitate this. Traditional and new family models are both reflected in the media and advertisements. This has mirrored the instability of contemporary society as well as the conflict among transitional values. Western commercials, for instance, generally address the ideal nuclear family that remains the model alongside preserved values. At the same time the news media, movies, and some television industries portray the emergence of manifold families (e.g. cohabitation, deliberate single parent, or same gender unit) which are acknowledged in a few European countries, Sweden and France for instance, as a binding contract between two consenting adults, mostly for property devolution. Thus, such a society has perpetuated the model wherein a majority of people still want to believe in the nuclear family, while ratifying changes it underwent that reject concomitant values. This is further exacerbated by the abundance of information and its broad dispersion by mass media.

Computer technology is adding another dimension to the life of individuals. This is happening at a time when more and more people are looking back to a sustainable pattern of family life and trying to revive it as a result of the experiments of the 1970's, which engendered other substitutes for the nuclear family. A powerful catalyst, such as information-communication technology, can contribute to eliminating an important function of the family: its memory retention.

The ever-increasing abundance of information actually threatens individual privacy. Within the family, this output of technology impacts negatively on domestic relations between family members. Internet and e-mail, as personal extensions of the individual, are highly demanding and time consuming. They serve as a factor that can mitigate family cohesion. This fact attests to the wide range of specific interests members of the family can develop with many other individuals outside of the family environment who exist only on the screen but are nevertheless influential. This raises the question of the useful expansion of inter-communications or the intrusion of dissenting opinions or beliefs. Efficiency of information is also another issue, particularly how it specifically permits sound decision-making within the family.

Concomitantly, individual rhythms and perceptions of time pervade family life since each member is influenced by a differential acceleration of time, leading to a de-synchronization of the family. This uneasiness apparently results from the distinct pace of each family member in absorbing the rapid technological changes. As individuals gain diverging views and interests due to their own distinct channels of information and communication, these views and interests tend to prevail over intra-family values. As a result, each member is inclined to have his or her own agenda and becomes detached from the community. Common residence becomes the only valid characteristic of the family.

Because of increasing facilities in communication, individual mobility has definitely been encouraged. Travels, whether personal or professional, have become part of contemporary family life. Home and work do not have to rely anymore on proximity. Family members can be located hundreds of miles apart due to the necessity of the work place but will always be in instant communication with each other. As a result, the notion of residence as a major characteristic in defining a family is waning.

Technology, which allows for the possibility of accumulated knowledge, seems to compete with formal education. For some time now courses in mathematics or related disciplines have been programmed on television. Schools, benefiting from the personal computer, resort increasingly to the same sources of versatile canned knowledge. Lack of systematization in the transmission of knowledge exposes the younger generations to a risk of hiatus in their education. Easily accessible information competes with formal teaching. The new generation desires quick answers, and electronic technology tends to eliminate the need for books and a lasting systemic view of a subject. Dictionary-type learning tends to supplant the encyclopedic approach. Self-teaching through computer courses has its advantages. Nevertheless, the drawback is that the student, being alone, must be motivated at all phases due to the absence of guidance and authority of a teacher. Passivity and inconsistency can be hindrances to a successful outcome.

For years, educational systems in developed countries have been urged to relate to the requirements of the industry at large in the teaching of skills. Now, with the ever present changing socioeconomic conditions, the immediate problem is how to prepare people who are likely to adapt their specializations to the changes in current knowledge and applications. The ability to adapt surpasses specialization as education becomes a continuous process of conversion and readjustments.

Everybody is aware that family can assume a great diversity of forms and that practically all of these, in various proportions, coexist in developed societies. In order to constitute and sustain a family, a few steps are necessary: encountering the "right" partner, marrying, having children, rearing them, establishing a family life, sustaining a family style, and surviving. In previous times, people lived in a closed world with restricted possibilities of meeting a marital partner. This meeting space has now expanded beyond expectations. First, technological breakthroughs on the ground and in the air have allowed people hundreds of miles apart to encounter each other. Growing flows of national and international migration have brought together people who previously had practically no chance of being connected. The wide extension of employment to women multiplied the probability of exposing male workers to a mixed gender environment. Telephone communications eased contacts. Even matrimonial agencies are now able to devise individual profiles of their clients and to match them with the hope of harmonizing their union. One could expect that given the convergence of all these factors, the number of marriages would soar, yet that is not the case. On the contrary, the numbers of marriages have plummeted in developed countries. It seems that a few elements took part in this reduction of modern family constitution. One of these is the continuous increase in life expectancy. Young people are confronted with a longer probability of life than were previous generations, while facing an ever-changing society. Young people seem unable to anticipate their future since they have more choices and it becomes more difficult to select a mate. Cohabitation has increased dramatically in many developed countries, as these societies have become more accepting of such arrangements.

Conclusion

The form of a family is only the outer shell. It is their interaction, interdependence, role, responsibility to each other, and the person within that really matters. Thus, a family is made up of people who respect each other and the children under their care and control. There is love, caring, and mutual support among all of the family members, as well as emotional and economic security, discipline, and responsibilities. A family should be a safe haven for all of its members, a place where the can go and know they are loved and cherished for who they are. Of course, families have internal tensions and few ever achieve perfection. But we should work to enhance and promote positive family relationships.

Medical and scientific technological developments are beneficial and represent otherwise immense progress in the field of human endeavor. The only issue with this group was how to manage these technologies. Technological interventions on human beings were seen as beneficial and positive; therefore, the main issues revolved around the safety and success rate of certain procedures.

The second group refused such a narrow approach to the analysis of the overwhelming issues facing society as a result of the use and development of technology in the field of human reproduction. Beginnings of life issues are important and fundamental in their own right, but they are also important because technology imposes itself not just at the beginning but at the end of life as well. Practices like euthanasia are just one dilemma raised by technology at the end of life. The Royal Commission on Reproductive Technology questioned the technological agenda and its control of our decision-making ability and even our language, but the voices of the Indian people and their points of view were not even heard.

Our ultimate challenge as a technologically developed society in this decade and the next will be to realize how technology affects the educational, cultural, political, and human structures and systems that have been the basis of our knowledge and actions for the past century. Only when we recognize technology's power to shape our actions and think about our roles and place within the community, will we be able to regain control of technological changes and make them sensitive and subject to our human agenda.

We must recognize the reality that we already live in a technological society with modern conveniences in our homes and offices, from microwaves to television sets to computers to fax machines and cellular telephones, and that we are surrounded by technological tools that have become a necessary, even indispensable, part of our daily lives. We must accept that these technologies shape our daily lives and relationships. We must use these advancements because if we refuse we will be left out of the loop. Faxing or emailing a letter is much more quick and efficient than mailing a letter, but because it is so much faster we are expected to send fax or email more letters. Because there are laptop computers readily available, we can have a computer anywhere we go, at home, on the plane, or in the car. We can spend our whole lives interacting with a machine.

We need to be aware that technology forces more, not fewer, choices upon us and that the choices we make as a result have a tremendous impact on our ability to make other, even different, choices in the future. We must realize that the frenetic pace we have set for ourselves in our professional and day-to-day lives including all things technical and technological has meant that hectic living is now the norm. We need to recognize that our work life is part of our home life and that one complements the other—we need to rethink our priorities. It is all part of an indivisible whole including our social environment. Spending too much time on our professional or work life will cause our personal or home life to suffer. There was once a time when this was obvious and even frowned upon. Today it depends on how we as individuals adapt to the situation, especially within the family. When the family goal is well defined and individual family members work in achieving the family goal, technology of varied types can be very helpful. When the individual is alienated from the family because of convenience, technological advancements are not so positive. Therefore, technology has both the qualities of having a positive and negative effect on family life. Family members need to be aware, sensitized, and educated enough regarding possible adverse effects of technology. They should use technology judiciously for its benefits only and not be pressured into using it in ways that will have a negative impact on family life.

References

Meter, M. A. (1995). Technology and the family. *Canadian Home Economics Journal, 45(1), 25-33.*

Nagrajan, K. (2001, January). Where are we? *Women's Era,* 44-45.

Sharma, N. (2001, January). Changing role of women and its impact on the family. *Women's Era*. 51-54.

United Nations, UN Workshop on Technology and Families. (1998, October 6-10). *The technological revolution–Opportunities and challenges for families [Background Paper].* http://www.un.org/esa/socdev/family/Meetings/FamTech/FamTecBk.htm.

5

Family Stresses and Quality of Life

K. Vijayanthimala

Stress is a normal part of family life and to some extent follows a developmental sequence. However, the cumulative effects of stress are harmful to individual family members and the family unit. Indian women face more stresses in their life than ever before as they try to balance family and work. Hence, there is urgency in educating women to confront and counteract stress in order to have a more stable and satisfying family life. This chapter discusses various types of stressors experienced by families today, and the most common causes of stress. It further provides information gleaned from a study concerning the role of marital satisfaction in confronting stress among thirty marital couples. Some coping skills are outlined that may help family members manage stress more effectively, including some for employed women who have multiple responsibilities and a strong commitment to both work and family.

The family is the basic social institution needed to meet the structural and functional requirements of society. In traditional Indian society there was no dispute regarding the nature and contribution of the family. However, given the cataclysmic changes that have occurred towards the end of the 20th century, the very concept of family in India has been challenged (Kumar, 2001).

The causes of family stress in modern day India are many. First and foremost, the disintegration of joint families and the mushrooming of nuclear family systems have brought a host of new stresses and strains. The members of the family are no longer participating in the production, distribution and protective functions of the family as they were doing earlier; in fact, most of these functions are now being done by professionals and outside agencies. Priorities in family life have also changed. The role of the family in determining individual status has been minimized. Though people still cherish family life, material success has become equally important, and it is the successful person who is more respected today and not the older one (Hari Kumar, 2000). However, there needs to be a balance between the old habits, behavior, expectations and attitudes with that of the new ways of life. It is because everything is out of balance that family stress is rampant.

Family values are also changing rapidly in modern society. Marriage was once a sacrament, and sex was encouraged among the married couples. Presently though sex has been redefined as biological need, and many men and women are tempted to indulge in sexual gratification outside of marriage (Kumar, 2001). Divorce, separation, and broken homes are becoming all too common in contemporary India. Rapid declines in the moral fiber of society, and clashes in values between the older and younger generation, lead to greater stress and conflicts in families.

The needs of family's today are many. People tend to spend more and more time in recreation centers even if they are costly.

Families with means view recreation as prestigious and necessary, and they are willing to pay for it. Gradually, however, this involvement leads to a lack of parental supervision and control (Harikumar, 2000). Diversification and specialization in various careers and disciplines, including the educational field, testify to the undue stress on individuals for career advancement. Hectic schedules of work, long distance commutes in cities, transportation problems, and the pressures of modern day work environments to be productive, require a great deal of physical and psychological attention. This can eventually take its toll on people and families (Baliga, 2000).

Expectations regarding women in contemporary India are high. The world demands radical changes in lifestyle and challenges traditional roles and rules in the family system. There is also a social climate that encourages the masculinization of women and a narcissistic self-love that hopes to demolish the last vestiges of patriarchy and establish a new order of superwomen (Bell, 2000). A large majority of women, particularly those who work, desire to have a co-partnership with their husband. They expect a large measure of happiness and demand personal gratification with regard to their emotional, physiological, social and economic needs in and outside of marriage. They put more emphasis on their privileges than on their obligations (Hari Kumar, 2000; Kapur, 1970; Sharma, 2001). Working women are either consciously or unconsciously expecting more authority; however, their husbands do not want to lose the traditional male concept of domination over the family. This often leads to conflict in marriage. In addition, the roles in the working woman's family are rather intermingled due to the uncertainty of prescribed roles for husband and wife in today's society. Even for women who do not work outside the home, roles can be ambiguous and the demands great (Bahl, 2001).

Developmental Roots of Stress

Early childhood experiences can have a powerful influence on how people deal with stress. For example, children raised in orphanages or in neglected homes may have elevated levels of glucocorticoids and 'hot' responses to stress later in life (Adler, 1999). A garden neglected by the gardener produces weathered or stunted plants that can never be productive or reach their true potential (Sharma, 2001). On the other hand, children raised in an atmosphere of love, affection, and security report less stress in their lives (Adler, 1999). Thus, "home" environment probably more than any other factor, plays the greatest role in children's behavior and development.

The present day family in India is facing numerous crises that are contributing to emotional disturbances, insecurity, anti-social behavior, and a host of other difficulties. Simply put, modern families are under stress like never before. Stress, like hunger and thrust, is an inescapable part of life, and not all stress is bad (Norfolk, 1978). However, mismanaged stress, or stress that piles up over time, can and often does have debilitating effects (Desai, 1993). Stress has been defined as the non-specific response of the body to any demand made upon it. Based on experiments carried out on non-human subjects, Hans Selye proposed the theory of general adaptation syndrome (G.A.S) or the biological stress syndrome. This syndrome consists of three stages: A: the alarm reaction; B: the stage of resistance; and C: the stage of exhaustion (illustrated below). These three stages are analogous to the three stages of man's life: childhood (with its characteristics of low resistance and excessive response to any kind of stimulus),

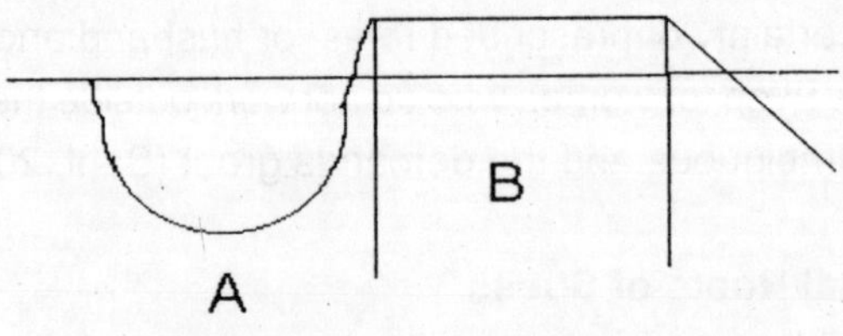

Three stages of General Adaptation Syndrome

adulthood (during which adaptation to most commonly encountered agents has occurred and resistance is increased) and finally, senility (characterized by irreversible loss of adaptability and eventual exhaustion) ending with death.

Stress is the state of an organism where it perceives that its well-being is endangered and that it must direct all its energies to its protection. Wolff (1968) views stress as a dynamic state within an organism in response to a demand for adaptation. In yet another usage, stress is defined as a class of conditions, producing disturbances within the individual based on a continuum of stimuli (Desai, 1993). One conception of stress then is that it is the physiological or psychological response an individual has to an environmental stressor. Yet another definition of stress is that it "..... occurs when pressure exceeds perceived ability to cope" (Cooper & Palmer, 2000). It is a response to a stimulus that places excessive psychological or physical demands on a person, and to which he or she is unable to cope with in their normal way of life. The stressor is an external event or situation which is potentially harmful (Loganathan, 1993).

Stressors may be 'Nuestress' (Nue means neutral) where the stress response is necessary for day to day adaptability of man to his environment; Distress (prefix 'dis' —implying bad or negative feelings) where the stress response is unfavorably and potentially disease producing; 'Eustress' (prefix 'eu' implying good or healthy feelings abbreviated from euphonic) where the stress response is favorable (Desai, 1993). Positive and negative stressors are antecedents to the experience of stress (Matteson & Ivancevich, 1979). Positive stressors are defined as events which ".....produce a state of challenge coupled with disruptive pleasure". Negative stressors are defined as those events, which "..... produce excessive and undesirable constraints or demands on the individual" (Bhagat, et al., 1985). Stressors can be classified as follows:

1. Environmental stressors such as weather, noise, temperature, traffic, etc.
2. Stressors in the family such as role conflict, role ambiguity, work overload, divorce, separation, marital problems, financial challenges, death, extramarital sexual relationships, etc.
3. Stressors in the work environment, social, or cultural environment, including hierarchy, deadlines, competition, pressure to achieve or produce, etc.
4. Social stressors such as a lack of acceptance, limited group cohesiveness, inadequate social support or an absence thereof, conflicts in the group, etc.

Stress can manifest itself in numerous ways. It may create physiological, psychological, and behavioral responses (Loganathan, 1993). Physiological responses may include: frequent colds and other respiratory infections, increased perspiration, tense muscles, rapid heartbeat, breathlessness, pain in the chest, indigestion, diarrhea, constipation, increased blood sugar, etc. If stress persists it may lead to ulcers, hypertension, headaches, fatigue, and heart attacks. Prolonged stress has also been linked to cancer. Psychological responses include problems with concentration, lower confidence, insecurity, jealousy, guilt, suspicion, anger, depression, reduced self-esteem, and a host of anxiety disorders. Persistent unresolved stress can also contribute to suicidal tendencies, substance abuse, eating disorders (including bulimia and obesity), and other self-destructive behaviors. Stress can also increase conflict in relationships, lower one's sex drive, and contribute to problems at work such as tardiness, absenteeism, and a lack of productivity. Over the long haul it can also contribute to fundamental changes in one's personality (Desai, 1993; Loganathan, 1993).

What important is not so much the event that causes the stress but the way the individual perceives the event (Nesmith,

1999). No environmental event can be identified as a stressor independently of its appraisal by the person (Lazarus, DeLongis, Folkman, & Gruen, 1985). Moreover, some stress in people's lives is better than no stress, for stress can be and often is growth-promoting. Thus, the objective is not to abolish stress but manage it. When it is allowed to get out of control, it can lead to sickness, low levels of performance, and even premature death. Indeed, some individuals have a much higher tolerance for stress than others (Norfolk, 1978).

In recent years, the effects that so called "stress hormones" have on the human machine have intrigued researchers. These substances are released by the adrenal/suprarenal glands, a pair of small glands perched on top of the kidneys that act in response to stress (Austin-American Statesman, 1999). It is essentially a response to danger in two distinct phases. The first of these, which involves the sympathetic adreno-medullary axis (SAM), is the familiar fight or flight response. Immediately blood pressure is raised, as well as heart rate and glucose in the blood. The second phase of the stress reaction kicks in five to ten minutes later. Here, the hypothalamic pituitary adrenocortical axis (HPA) appears to be more closely associated with emotional and intellectual stress. An excess of these hormones can become toxic, and glucocorticoids also suppress parts of the immune system. In short, stress can have a profound impact on our bodily systems and health (Adler, 1999).

Marital and Family Stress

Family stress has been defined as a state of tension that arises from an actual or perceived demand which calls for an adaptive response (Boss, 1983). In one sense it is a disturbance in the steady state of the family. Research on family stress has traditionally been concerned with the influence of normative life events over the life cycle on family members and the family as a whole. The events include birth of a child, having children first go off to school, graduations, marriage, mid-life and old age challenges, and death of a family member. Most of these stressors are temporary, and as soon as one perceives that the situation has changed and is no longer dangerous, the person's stress level begins to dissipate, although often gradually more than suddenly. Another type of stress are those associated with unpredictable or non-normative life events (e.g., sudden illness, injury, or death; job loss or transfer; infidelity or divorce; incarceration; etc.). These "bolts from the blue" often have more deleterious effects than normative life events. Still another type of stress includes the more minor daily hassles (or strains) that pile up or accumulate over time (e.g., chronic illnesses; bullying at school; working in an unfulfilling job; ongoing marital, sibling or parent-child conflicts; daily driving or commuting in city traffic; etc.). These daily hassles, if not successfully cope with, managed, or eliminated, can eventually take their toll on individuals and families physically, emotionally, and relationally.

Previous studies conducted in India have shown that women (especially professional women) report more stress than do men (Kumar, 1986). Interestingly, Indian women also report that it is difficult to succeed in their careers in a male dominated world (Kumar, 1986). Social scientists have proposed that individuals who have multiple obligations (e.g. home, work, and community) experience more job- related stress and conflict than individuals without multiple demands (Steven & Cox, 1996). Moreover, women generally report a high degree of stress in their lives (Walters, 1993). They seek mental health care more frequently than men do for stress-related difficulties, even though the problems often do not meet specific diagnostic criteria for mental disorders. In a study of healthy midwife women in the United States, stress was most strongly associated with health of all variables investigated either positive or negative (Thomas, 1995).

On the other hand, the majority of Indian women do not report that the conflict between work and home, and role overload, are major sources of stress in their lives. In fact, one study showed that females were better capable of handling stress than males, and that they reported little or no stress in their lives (Anjuly, 1997). However, women's increasing participation in outside of home employment, and the consequent growth in the number of dual-earning families, is creating a new dimension in Indian marriages. Along with this increase, there have been significant changes in the economic and social status of women. Hence, contemporary Indian families are besieged with internal and external stresses – many of which are contributing to less satisfaction in marital life (Vijayanthi, 1991). Yet, Indian woman have an uncanny ability to handle pain and emotional pain, as well as to love and sacrifice for their husbands and families (Malkani, 1999). This indeed helps keep the family united and adaptable.

Summary of a Current Investigation of Stress in Indian Families

A recent study was conducted that focused on the relationship between stress and marital satisfaction in Indian families. Sex differences among couples were also examined. The following section summarizes the intent of this study, the procedures employed, and the results obtained. The sample consisted of 30 couples working in different institutions and organizations (e.g., colleges, universities, hospitals, offices) in Berhampur City of Orissa State.

Measures and Procedures. Data were collected on two self-report measures, in addition to demographic information. One scale used was the Dyadic Adjustment Scale (DAS) developed by Spanier (1986). The DAS consists of 32 questions, with several subscales, that assess decision-making, handling of finances, marital happiness, areas and causes of differences, utilization of leisure, attitudes toward separation and divorce, attitudes towards job, sexual satisfaction, and preference of dual roles. The other measure used was Adler's (1999) assessment of stress. This scale has 10 questions that are each individually scored. The demographic questionnaire contained questions related to age, education, occupation, organizational affiliations, marital status, years of marriage, years of work experience, number of children, and so forth. These scales and questionnaires were given to each person in the marital relationship, and the purpose of the study was explained. Couples were assured of anonymity and confidentiality in completing all of the measures.

Major Findings. Table 1 includes means, standard deviations (SD's), and t values with regard to differences in variable scores between men and women.

Table 1. Means, SDs, and t values for Men and Women in Relation to Marital Satisfaction and Stress.

		Men		*Women*		
Sl. No.	*Variable*	*Mean*	*SD*	*Mean*	*SD*	*t*
1	Marital satisfaction	119.5	10.8	114.0	13.9	1.3
2	Stress	15.2	3.4	17.2	4.1	2.1*

*p<.05

The results indicated that women reported slightly less satisfaction in their marriages than men, although the difference was not statistically significant. However, women reported significantly higher levels of stress then men. It may be that women report more stress because of their multiple roles, including wife, mother, job or career, housekeeper, and community citizen. Women consider marriage as a desirable goal, but in many educated homes today they feel some conflict between home and job/career responsibilities. In addition, husbands' attitudes of non-cooperation and non-acceptance with regard to women's gradual change from the traditional roles have prevented them from realizing the strain that their wives experience in carrying out their many roles, thus contributing to increased marital stress and conflict. The correlation between marital satisfaction and women's stress in the current study was negative (r =-0.22; p<.05). However, in the case of men it was small and non-significant (r=.01). In sum, the results of the study suggest that women are more predisposed to stressful events than men in the family and react to a wider range of inside stressors due to role obligations and compulsions. There is little doubt that couples are in great need of marital preparation, education, enrichment, and support in today's society. The development of certain skills is central to this task. These include the development of communication and coping skills, health and wellness habits (e.g., adequate nutrition, exercise, relaxation, meditation, yoga, massage, positive visualization, etc.), social skills (e.g., cooperation, empathy, and other prosocial skills), mental skills (e.g., thinking, analyzing, and problem-solving skills), emotional skills (e.g., managing negative emotions like anger, fear, anxiety, worry, jealousy, temper, frustration, etc.), and personal management skills (e.g., time and money management; spiritual resource development, etc.).

Stress and Resilient Families

All families experience stress, but some manage stress much more creatively and successfully. These families have been referred to as "resilient families" (Walsh, 1998). Resiliency refers to a family's ability to respond to a crisis in a constructive way, and to eventually bounce back after adversity. Resilient families use an array of stress management strategies. For example, resilient families:

- Develop a realistic perspective toward stressful situations.
- Avoid blaming others for creating stress within the family.
- Deal with the stressful situation early and head on.
- Express emotions but keep them under control.
- Maintain good physical and mental health of individual family members.
- Establish warm, cordial and loving relationships within and beyond the family.
- Maintain healthy boundaries within and beyond the family.

- Use humor as a tool to reduce stress and maintain a positive outlook on life.

In sum, resilient families also develop certain strengths such as commitment, open and honest communication, and flexibility in response to stress. They tend to view difficulties as challenges and opportunities for change rather than as experiences that should be avoided (Norfolk, 1978). Indeed, the most important need in Indian marriages and families in the twenty-first century remains the development of strong and bonded relationships that can withstand the pressures and rapid changes that characterize modern life. Family Life Education's ultimate mission is simply this: To Build Stronger and Healthier Marriages and Families. Hence, the time for it has surely arrived, not only in India, but in all countries of the world.

References

Adler, J (1999). Stress. *Newsweek,* New York, June 14. 58-63.

Anjuli (1997). *Effect of stress in relation to organizational effectiveness.* B. A. Fieldwork, Dept. of Psychology, M.S.University, Baroda.

Baliga, S (2000). Enmeshed in careers. *Women's Era, Dec. (2),* 12-14.

Bahl, T (2001). Home makers can be stressed too. *Women's Era, Jan (2),* 28-31.

Bell, E (2000). Women of the new millennium. *Women's Era, Jan (1),* 12-18.

Bhagat, R., Mcquaid, S., Lindholm, H., & Segovis, J (1985). Total life stress: A multi-method validation of the construct and its effect on organizationally valued outcomes and withdrawal behaviors. *Journal of Applied Psychology, 70,* 202-214.

Boss, P (1983). *Family stress management.* New Delhi: Sage Publications.

Brown, S.P., & Cox, E.L. (1996). A meta analysis and review of organizational research on job involvement. *Psychological Bulletin, 120*(2), 235-255.

Cooper, C., & Palmer, S. (2000). *Conquer your stress.* Hyderbad: University Press (INDIA) Ltd.

Desai, T. P. (1993). Stress and mental work load: A study in an industrial organization. *IJIR, 28*(3), 258-269.

Etzion, D., & Pines, A. (1986). Sex and culture in burnout and coping among human service professionals: A social psychological perspective. *Journal of Cross-Cultural Psychology, 17*, 191-209.

Ghadially, R., & Pramod, K. (1987). Stress, strain and coping styles of female professionals. *Indian Journal of Applied Psychology, 26* (1), 1-18.

Hari Kumar, A. (2000). Family, sex and globalization. *Women's Era, Jan (2),* 33-34.

Kapur, P. (1970). *Marriage and working women in India*. New Delhi:Vikas Publications.

Kumar, U. (1986). Indian women and work: A paradigm for research. *Psychological Studies, 32*(2), 147-160.

Kumar, R.B. (2001). The crisis of the family in the new millennium. *Women's Era, Jan (2),* 80-83.

Lappe, L. (1975). In the treatment of choice selecting stress skills to suit the individual and the situation. In N. Loving & D.A. Tubesing (Eds.). *Job stress and burn out*. New Delhi: Sage Publications.

Lavee, Y., Shlomo, S., & Ruth, K. (1996). The effect of parenting stress on marital quality: An integrated mother-father model. *Journal of Family Issues, 17*(1), 114-135.

Lazarus, R., Delongis, A., Folkman, S., & Gruen, R. (1985). Stress and adaptational outcomes: The problem of confounded measures. *American Psychologist, 40,* 770-779.

Loganathan, M. (1993). *Stress management: Behavioral skills management (Reading material)*. Hyderabad: NIRD, 131-136.

Malkani, V. (1999). *Spirituality made simple*. New Delhi: Sterling Publishers (pvt) Ltd.

Matteson, M., & Ivancevich, J. (1979). Organizational stressors and heart decease: A research model. *Academy of Management Review, 4*, 347-357.

Nesmith, J. (1999). *Its not the years, it's the mileage.* Austin, TX: American Statesman, August (15), U.S.A.

Norfolk, D. (1978). *Execute stress-strategies of survival.* London: Associated Business Programmes Ltd.

Selye, H. (1956). *The stress of life.* McGraw Hill, New York.

Sharma, N. (2001). The changing role of women and its impact on the family. *Women's Era, Jan (1)*, 20-24.

Spanier, G.B. (1976). Measuring dyadic adjustment: New scales for assessing the quality of marriage and similar dyads. *Journal of Marriage and Family, 38*, 15-29.

Thomas, S.P. (1995). Psychological correlates of women's health in middle adulthood. *Issues in Mental Health Nursing, 16*, 285-314.

Vijayanthimala, K (1991). Income and marital satisfaction. *The Journal of Family Welfare, 37*(2), 24-27.

Walsh, F. (1998). *Strengthening family resilience.* New York: Guilford Press.

Walters, V (1993). Stress, anxiety and depression: women's accounts of their health problems. *Social Science and Medicine, 36*, 393-402.

6

Child Abuse in Indian Families

Sucheta Priyabadini

Family is the primary agent in the transmission of culture to the child. When parents intentionally or unintentionally abuse their child, the development of the child is threatened. This chapter focuses on the importance of parent/family life education in preventing child abuse and neglect (CAN) in India – a phenomenon that occurs mostly in the family system. Indeed, knowledge and awareness on the part of parents is a prerequisite for the provision of adequate psychological and emotional support for their children. CAN is also examined in lieu of issues associated with stress, coping, resiliency, risk and vulnerability.

Children are generally innocent, vulnerable and dependent on their parents. Unfortunately, for many children in India, childhood is altogether different. Each day countless children are becoming the victims of abuse one form or other. Children have limited resources of their own to combat traumatic experiences. Moreover, exposure to "western thinking" has brought about changes in attitudes towards traditional methods of guidance, discipline, and other child-rearing practices (Mullati, 1995; Sinha, 1984, 1988). However, because traditional attitudes have not been completely abandoned, many parents alternate between permissive and strict (authoritarian) child rearing, thus creating anxiety and confusion in children and making them more vulnerable to behavioral or emotional disorders (Bharat, 1997). Unknowingly, many parents are abusing their children by using severe punishment and being inconsistent and arbitrary. Parent's who mistreat or abuse their children have been described as individuals who have trouble prioritizing and weighing their needs against those of the child's and receive little support in making appropriate choices (Justice & Justice, 1976). Often these parents manifest an odd picture of both selfishness and impoverished self-image. A child who is scolded harshly for the smallest mistake may grow up into an adult who fears taking initiative.

Child abuse and neglect is becoming increasingly common in India. Some contributors to CAN include low socio-economic status, low levels of literacy, malnutrition, cultural customs and taboos, socio-economic inequality, lack of social justice, and gender biases. Child support is a critical concern for both regional and national policy makers. In India the concept of family is sacred, and abuse often happens because of ignorance. Family life is deeply embedded in the community as friends, neighbors and relatives share responsibility for children's lives and well being (Carson & Chowdhury, 2000). In spite of modernization, family always has been considered as the foundation of Indian society. Children and adolescents are given a special place in the family and community, and interdependency, support and nurturing across the generations are uniquely valued in the Indian family system (Madan, 1990, Simhadri, 1989). Parents and extended family members continue to be the primary socializers of children in ways that are no longer evident in many regions of the world, and parents and adult children tend to maintain close ties even when great geographical distances separate them (Gupta, 1987; & Shukla, 1994). It is, therefore, a necessity for parents to acquire knowledge, not only about different aspects of physical and psychological development of the child, but awareness about different types of child abuse and its remediation.

Child abuse in the family often manifests itself in the physical maltreatment of a child or adolescent. Examples of physical abuse include thrashing, shaking, choking, kicking, burning or throwing objects at the child. However, in reality there are a variety of types of abuse occurring today. These include:

- Physical abuse
- Social abuse
- Sexual abuse
- Verbal abuse
- Emotional abuse
- Situational abuse
- Educational abuse
- Drug abuse etc.

Child neglect has to do with physical, emotional or psychological impoverishment; i.e., when the basic necessities of life are denied by a parent or caregiver. Indifference, forgotten promises, and withdrawal are all inappropriate behaviors that are damaging to children who may feel they are not worth their parents' concern and care. In the long run, neglect of a child and/or ongoing verbal/emotional/psychological abuse may be the most damaging (Garbarino & Eckenrode, 1997).

Sexual abuse includes sexual contact with a child, including incest, rape, inappropriate touching, obscene language, or using a child for sexual photographs, films or prostitution. It is estimated that one in every ten children is sexually abused in India, and that every other hour a child is raped (Ravi Kumar, 2003). Further, according to Lois J. Engelbrecht, founder of the Center for the Prevention and Treatment of Child Sexual Abuse (CSA), ".....Over 50% of children in India are sexually abused, a rate that is higher than in any country". In many cases the offender is a person known and trusted by the child. Emotional or psychological abuse, on the other hand, has to do with a pattern of behavior on the part of the parent or caregiver that is geared toward attacking a child's sense of self (i.e.., his/her value, worth, competence, or belongingness). Examples include refusal or inability to express love, conditional love, cocooning and smothering, denying the child opportunities to develop as a separate individual, being used as a pawn by warring parents, witnessing alcohol or substance abuse (especially on a regular basis), and witnessing violence between parents and parents and other family members. Emotional/ psychological abuse also includes parental/caregiver behavior that involves constant criticism, unjustified balance, refusal to acknowledge the child and their achievements, refusal to praise, refusal of parents to agree with or support each other when dealing with children, or unpredictable behavior on the part of parents.

Some Causes and Correlates of Child Abuse

India is diverse in terms of history, culture, language, religion, socio-economic status (SES), caste, and creed. In modern India the family has been increasingly recognized as instrumental in providing unique contributions to the social and educational competence of children (Priyabadini, 2001). Family interactions and parenting styles vary greatly with regard to religion, culture, SES, and geography. However, the stresses and strains of everyday life in families can be remarkably similar. Some of the major problems and challenges in contemporary Indian society that contribute to child abuse are discussed as follows:

Stress: Stress is often found to be a major factor in child abuse. Sources of stress can include financial difficulties, loss of a job, social isolation, marital problems, economic and resource limitations, natural disasters, inadequate parenting skills, serious illness, death, and substance abuse, to name a few. Sometimes there is a crisis or a series of crises that trigger child abuse. In addition, some children are at higher risk for abuse, including children under the age of six, children with physical or emotional handicaps, adopted children, and hyperactive or emotionally disturbed children. Some children may even provoke abuse in an attempt to get attention (Chadwick, 2003).

Ignorance and Lack of Parenting Education: Parents play the main role in the social, emotional, intellectual, and moral development of their children (Stedman, 1969). However, ignorance about child-rearing patterns can negatively affect the child's development. Use of physical punishment, especially if it is not carefully controlled and used sparingly, can not only demoralize children but lead to further aggression that can easily escalate into abuse. Moreover, parenting that is too permissive can encourage dependence and an egocentric view of the world. Since some child abuse occurs because of sheer ignorance, parents in modern India are in dire need of alternative modes of child guidance and discipline, as well as knowledge of children's development throughout adolescence and beyond.

Poverty: Lower SES families in India, which make up a major segment of the population, lack many of the basic necessities of life. Children may not get proper food, clothing and shelter. Extreme poverty compounds the problems. Sandeep and Pushpa (1981) have reported that mental retardation in children is more prevalent in poverty-ridden homes. Many of these children from an early age take on the responsibility of the family and are often forced to be child labourers. They work long hours in deplorable conditions. It is estimated that India has 20 millions bonded labourers, 35% of whom are children under the age of 14. These are mainly individuals in villages who are poor are often forced to take loans to feed their family to meet their basic needs. When the loan is not paid back, families (including children) are forced to work as bonded laborers as a way to repay the debt. Furthermore, in the Indian scenario, ritual prostitution (Devdasi) and child trafficking are quite prevalent. Other correlates of poverty, such as illiteracy, are also often associated with child abuse in India. Illiterate parents (knowingly or unknowingly) may expect their children to do well in academics so they can elevate themselves and the family. However, a lack of ability or opportunity on the part of the child to learn may frustrate some parents to the point of abusing their child.

Achievement Pressures in Middle and Upper Social Class Families: Competition in the educational sector can put immense pressure on children and youth to excel in school, and occupational success in India is closely linked to educational success. Often rigorous tutoring of the child begins from the tender age of three in order to get insure the child's admission to school. In some families, a high level of parental involvement can contribute to parent-child conflict and emotional turmoil, thus affecting children's self-esteem and motivation to learn (Lareau & Shumar, 1994). For many children in SES secure homes today, childhood is filled with responsibility and pressure to achieve. Educational success is believed to be closely associated with occupational opportunities in the future, as well as family status and well-being. When children or adolescents fail to meet parents' expectations, abusive behavior sometimes follows. Pressures for academic achievement can easily encourage school failure. Attempting to force children at early ages to learn specific academic material or develop specific skills may produce negative attitudes towards learning in general, with serious long-term effects evident in increased dropout rates and high rates of cheating (Harris, 1986; Elkind, 1982).

Family Size: As family size increases, parents find it more difficult to devote individual time, attention, and assistance to each child. Menaghan and Parcel (1991) found that larger families generally present less optimal home environments for children. Other studies have showed that larger numbers of children in the family were generally associated with constrained parental nurturance of and stimulation for children (Bradley & Caldwell,

1986; Haveman, Wolfe, & Spaulding, 1991; Menaghan & Parcel, 1991; Parcel & Menaghan, 1990; Rogers et al., 1991; Steelman & Powell, 1991). Families with five or more children in particular may be at higher risk for physical child abuse, with the risk increasing as children are added to the family. This may be because larger families are typically more stressed and chaotic, with both human and material resources often being stretched and limited.

Gender: Given the general preference for male children in India even today, girls are particularly at risk for abuse and neglect. Parents often treat the boys more affectionately than girls, and girls are more likely to experience all types of discrimination. Some girls develop extreme submissiveness, lack of self-confidence, or hostility towards parents and others who practice favoritism. Anandlaksmy (1993) and Khullar (1993) point to the existence of different realities for boys and girls in India, including the rights and duties of boys and girls, what they are expected to do, and opportunities for learning and self-expression. Girls face many more taboos and are susceptible to a host of double-standards in India. The family, then, can become a breeding ground for parental abuse towards female children and neglect of their physical and emotional needs, especially in resource-limited families.

Consequences of Various Types of Child Abuse and Neglect: Abuse and negative reinforcement from parents can have an array of negative effects on children's development and behavior. Chadwick (2003) summarizes the common consequences of physical child abuse as follows:

Physical abuse is manifested by a variety of physical symptoms, many of which may require medical attention. Some of these include: bald spots in the hair, human bite marks, and unexplained bruises and welts on the face, lips, mouth, chest, back, buttocks or thighs. They may be in various stages of healing, form regular patterns, and resemble the shape of the article used to inflict harm. There may be unexplained burns, especially on the hands, feet, back or buttocks. Other burns may include rope burns on arms, legs, neck or chest; or patterned burns resembling the shape of an electric burner or iron. There may be broken bones or unexplained fractures to the skull, nose, face, arms or legs. Such fractures may be multiple and in various stages of healing. Cuts and bruises may be evident around the mouth, lips, gums, eyes and genitals. School teachers may notice that these signs regularly appear after a student's school absence. Children who are physically abused may be accident prone; unable to tolerate physical contact or touch; show fear of adult contact; feel apprehensive when other children cry; exhibit aggressiveness, withdrawal or extreme compliance; feel afraid to go home; complain of soreness; move awkwardly; exhibit destructive behavior to self or others; arrive early to school or stay late as if afraid to go home; wear clothing that covers the body when not appropriate; or run away from home.

Neglect may be evident from poor growth; failure to thrive; consistent hunger; low weight and a host of other health-related problems; distended stomach; poor hygiene; lice; inappropriate dress; a consistent lack of supervision, especially for prolonged periods or in dangerous activities; unattended physical or medical problems; or abandonment. The behavioral signs of neglected children include stealing or begging for food; persistent fatigue; listlessness or falling asleep; frequent school absence or tardiness; destructive behavior; dropping out of school; and/or substance abuse. Educational neglect includes allowing a school aged child to commit the act of chronic truancy or having inattention to a special educational need of the child and doing nothing about it.

Sexual abuse may be exhibited through difficulty in walking or sitting; torn, stained or bloody undergarments; bruises, bleeding, pain, itching or sensitivity around genitals or anal areas; stomachaches; sleep disturbances and nightmares; bedwetting; or sexually transmitted diseases. Children who are sexually abused may feel depressed or isolated; be reluctant to participate in certain physical activities; perform more or less well than usual in school; have difficulty in concentration; withdraw, fantasize or exhibit infantile behavior; appear to cry for no reason; develop eating disorders of substance abuse; develop poor peer relationships; possess an usually high level of sexual knowledge; act sexually provocative; show fear of or seductiveness towards the opposite sex; engage in prostitution; report sexual assault by an authority figure; become pregnant; run away from home; or attempt suicide.

Children who are verbally or emotionally abused may experience speech disorders; lags in physical development; failure to thrive (especially in infants); asthma; severe allergies; ulcers; substance abuse; or hyperactive/disruptive behavior. They tend to have a poor self-concept and low self-esteem. They may also become clinically depressed and manifest various disorders, including generalized anxiety and obsessive-compulsive disorder, psychosomatic disorders, adjustment disorders, and acting out.

Children who experience any type of abuse may or may not talk about being abused. If they do, it is crucial that adults listen closely and take them seriously. These signs don't always indicate abuse, but it is best to find out. Children who are sexually abused may keep the abuse a secret for various reasons: they may think no one will believe them; they may have been told by the perpetrator that something bad will happen to them or their loved ones if they tell; they may feel embarrassed or ashamed; or they may be too young to have the verbal skills to talk about the abuse. They may also protect an abusing parent or family member from being found out so that family relationships are maintained and family dignity in the community is preserved.

Suggestion for Families in Preventing Child Abuse

The widespread prevalence of child abuse the damage is causes to children and families is not sufficiently acknowledged by legal professionals, educational institutions, academicians, and especially families themselves. Indian families today, because of urbanization and westernization, face a complex set of problems.

In many families there is an absence of clear and consistent role models for the child beyond his or her own parents. In addition, partly due to safety reasons, parents are becoming more restrictive of their children in having free time to interact with peers, either at school or in the neighborhood. This not only reduces children's social network but also tends to instill feelings of fear and distrust (Carson & Chowdhury, 2000).

The most common abuser of children is someone familiar, such as parent, another relative, or a close family friend. It is less common for children to be abused by strangers in most societies, including India. Abusers often have low self-esteem, poor control over their emotions, and a lack of close family and social support. Although most children who are abused do not grow up to be child abusers themselves, retrospective reports of child-abusing adults reveal that they were usually abused earlier in life. Thus, in recent years researchers have emphasized specific behavioral styles that are transmitted across two or three generations in the family. Parents who are abusive individuals and whose disciplinary techniques involve explosive behavior are more likely to rear antisocial, impulsive children. When these children grow up, they tend to be less effective disciplinarians and poorer monitors of children's behavior; hence, their children are more likely to carry on these family traits and patterns with their own children. However, as Brooks (1996) indicates, such problems can be reversed when parents learn how to show love, concern, and nurturance towards the child.

Government policy makers, non-government organizations, and educators in various domains have been trying to advocate against child abuse India for several decades. However, the family plays a pivotal role in curbing child abuse. Awareness about child abuse should be inculcated in children during their early childhood years so they can learn to report abuse when it occurs. Patterns can be reversed, although not easily, even after abuse has occurred. When individuals are treated for problems associated with child abuse, there can be positive results (Sharma & Chadd, 1990). However, when the client returns to family, often there is a regression to earlier patterns of behavior and functioning, for while the client has changed, the family has not (Davar, 1998, 1999; Sethi & Manchanda, 1978). Hence, it is important to focus on the family as the primary unit of education and intervention. Providing family life education for families not only helps them learn but also receive support and encouragement from professionals and other families in the community alike (Aken & Riksen-Walraven, 1992; Khera & Kherde, 1986).

Conclusion

All children have the right to a safe and secure environment in which their dignity is nurtured and their capacities developed to the fullest (Singh, 2002). Indeed, the major cause of trauma and mental illness in India's children today is some form of child abuse or neglect. The shame, secrecy and silence surrounding child abuse needs to be made more public. The sources and consequences of child abuse are clear. There is an urgent need to direct our efforts toward balancing priorities for children in the home, school, and community. The national campaign against child abuse is also breaking the myths and social stigma associated with abusers and helping to provide alternative support systems for families. However, far less attention has been paid to educating individuals and families about child abuse and neglect, especially with regard to prevention. Children form a constituency that does not have much power in society and whose needs we are not conscious of when setting up structures that help to protect them (Vrushali, 2002). Indian families today could benefit tremendously from parent training (e.g., positive discipline and behavior management practices, effective communication with children and youth) and basic information about child/adolescent development and health maintenance (Carson & Chowdhury, 2000).

Parenting in India is no longer an amateur business; i.e., something to be picked up in a haphazard way. A society which gives total responsibility to professionals as service providers is one which has lost the ability to educate and care for its own children (Bernard Van Lee Foundation, 1986). However, parenting and family life education may be the number one enemy of child abuse and neglect. Policy-makers should develop strategies that help and support this type of education at the local, state, and national level, and lay training and volunteerism should be at the heart of such programming efforts. Family life education is guided by the principle that all human beings have the right to develop their full potential to the full, to carry responsibility for their own deeds, and to be valued as individuals. Counseling services, spiritual guidance, and legal assistance are also important for families today. These provisions must occur initially at a grassroots level. Citizens need to be made aware that one of the best ways to eradicate a social malady such as child abuse is to encourage knowledge and behaviors that threaten its very existence (Ravi Kumar, 2003). This is a cooperative effort that includes parents and professionals working together for positive change in their communities.

References

Aken Van, A.G. Marcel, & Walraven-Riksen, J. (1992). Parental support and the development of competence in children. *International Journal of Behavioural Development, 15*(1), 101-123.

Anandlaksmy, S. (1993). Personal Communication at the Workshop on Children's Environment, Bernard Van Leer Foundation, New Delhi, India.

Bernard Van Leer Foundation (1988). *Children and Community: Progressing through Partnership.* Summary Report and Conclusions of Tenth International Seminar with the Cooperation of the University of West Indies, Kingston, Jamaica, 14-24 November.

Bernard Van Leer Foundation. (1986). *The Parent as Prime Educator: Changing Patterns of Parenthood.* Summary Report and Conclusion of the Fourth Western Hemisphere Seminar with the Cooperation of the Ministry of Education, Republic of Peru, Lima, Peru, November 7-16.

Bharat, S. (1997). Family socialization of the Indian child. *Trends in Social Science Research, 4*(1), 201-216.

Bies, J.D. (1972). Environmental influence on problem solving ability in three demographic groups. *Dissert. Abstr. Intern (1973). 33A* : 4038.

Bradley, R., & Caldwell, B. (1986). The relation of infants' home environments to achievement test performance in first-grade: A follow up study. *Child Development, 55*, 803-809.

Brooks, B. Jane. (1996). *The process of parenting.* London: Mayfield Publishing Company.

Carson, D. K., & Chowdhury, A. (2000). Family Therapy in India: A new profession in an ancient land? *Contemporary Family Therapy, 22*(4), 387-405.

Daver, B.V. (1999). *Mental health of Indian women: A feminist agenda.* New Delhi: Sage Publications.

Elkind. D. (1982). Misunderstandings about how children learn. *Today's Education*, 24-25.

Garbarino, J., & Eckenrode, J. (1997). An ecological approach to theory and practice. In: Understanding abusive families. San Francisco: Jossey- Bass Pub.

Gupta, A.K. (1987). *Parental influences on adolescents.* New Delhi: Ariana Pub. House.

Haveman, R.Wolfe, B.L. and Spaulding, J. (1991). Educational achievement and childhood events and circumstances. Demography, 28, 133-157.

Haris, A.C. (1986). *Child development.* New York: West Pub..

Isenberg, J. (1987). Societal influences on children. *Journal of the Association for Childhood Education International, 63*(5), 341-348.

Khera, J.K., & Kherde, R.L. (1986). Real architect of the child's destiny. *Journal of Home Science, 24*, 1-12.

Khullar, M. (1983). Personal communication. Workshop on Children's Environment. Bernard Van Leer Foundation, New Delhi, India.

Lareau, A, & Shumar, W. (1994). A Study on individualism in family-school policies. *Educational Policy*, 25-39.

Madan, G.R. (1990). *Social welfare and security*. New Delhi: Sage Pub.

Mc Elroy, M. (1982). Consequences of perceived parental pressure on the self-esteem of youth sport participants. *American Corrective Therapy Journal, 36*(6), 164-167.

Menaghan, E.G., & Parcel, T.L. (1991). Determining children's home environments: The impact of maternal characteristics and current occupational and family conditions. *Journal of Marriage and the Family, 53*, 417-431.

Mullati, L. (1995). *Families in India: Beliefs and realities. Journal of Comparative Family Studies, 26*(1), 11-25.

Priyabadini, S. (2001). Role of Mother in Educational Achievement and Social Development of Children. *Unpublished Doctoral Thesis*, Utkal University, Orissa.

Ravikumar, M. (2003). India's guilty secret. *Indian Express*.

Justice, R., & Justice, B. (1976). *Families who abuse: The relationship between patricide and child abuse*. Synergy Book Source

Rogers, S.J., Parcel, T.L., & Menaghan, E.G. (1991). The effects of maternal working conditions and mastery on child behaviour problems:Studying the intergenerational transmission of social control. *Journal of Health and Social Behaviour, 32*, 145-164.

Sandeep, P., & Pushpa, M. (1981). Deprivation and cognitive development in children. *Child Psychology, 14*(2), 47-54.

Sethi, B.B., & Manchanda, R. (1978). Family structure and psychiatric disorders. *Indian Journal of Psychiatry, 20*(3), 283-288.

Sharma, S., & Chadd, R.K. (1990). *Mental hospitals in India: Current status and role in mental health Care.* Delhi: Institute of Human Behaviour and Allied Sciences.

Shukla, M. (1994). India. In K. Hurrelmann(Ed.), *International handbook of adolescence* (pp.191-206). Westport, CT: Greenwood Press

Simhadri, Y.C. (1989). *Youth in the contemporary world.* Delhi: Mittal Pub

Singh, G., & Muskaan, S. (2002). The campaign against child sexual abuse. Pune: *IAWS Newsletter,* July.

Speck, R.V., & Attneave, C.A. (1973). *Family networks.* New York: Pantheon.

Steadman, D.J. (1969). A comparison of ratings by mothers and teachers on the preschool attainment records of 17 five-year-old children. *Exceptional Children, 35*, 488.

Steelman, L.C., & Powell, B. (1991). Sponsoring the next generation: Parental willingness to pay for higher education. *American Journal of Sociology, 96,* 1505-1529.

A child must be made to [illegible] both [illegible] attitude. Parents must close the gap between the [illegible] and the [illegible] of self acceptance. Instead of [illegible] the child, parents must [illegible] those characteristics (especially temperament). Parents must be aware and even vigilant of any indication of psychopathology no matter how minor it may be. This will help them to plan remedial measures so that bad habits or faulty behaviors do not develop into a habit. Sometimes it may also require a major change in the child's social environment.

The child's most important needs required for happiness are feelings of achievement, acceptance, and affection. These basic needs must be met at every stage and level of development, and the child must feel secure and content with his family around him. Firm, consistent and loving discipline, taking into account the child's expanding ability for self-discipline should instill in him social and moral values to serve as guidelines for socially approved and self-approved behavior. In the present era, the lines between parent-child relationships are becoming blurred, with each one trespassing another's territory. While the closeness is good, it has been observed that each individual needs a certain amount of privacy. Parents must stop being over-indulgent and over-involved as it hurts the child's development of independence and belittles the ego. The child must be taught to do things himself, develop success factors like persistence, thoroughness, accuracy, curiosity, originality, leadership, pride in achievement, and creativity in his thinking. Parents must provide him or her with opportunities for success, especially soon after a failure to avoid the development of a "failure complex". When misbehaviors do occur, the focus should be on the behavior and not on the child. Thus, responses

7

Effects of Family Life on Child Mental Health

Aparajita Chowdhury
and
Indumati Patnaik

"A child is young only once, and only for a short time. So much depends on the home and the social environment and the way these influence the child's physical and mental development."

This is an age of tremendous growth of knowledge and rapid social change. Over the past 50 years more scientific and technological advances have been made than in all of previous recorded time. For many people this pace of change is simply too fast, resulting in what has been termed "Future shock". Many investigators have raised the question of whether the human organism is equipped, either physiologically or psychologically, to cope with the supercharged rate of change in our "manic society". There are limits to the resilience of the human organism to change, and such limits apply to both the complexity and the rate of change. When these limits are exceeded, the results can be detrimental to both individuals and groups. This phenomenon is found to be more present in the lives of children and adolescents than in adults of contemporary India. Indian youth today are under tremendous pressure psychologically to adjust to parental expectations and societal competitiveness. The child copes with these challenges for "better" or for "worse", and the successfulness of adaptation is largely contingent on the family system. This chapter discusses the crucial role of the family in nurturing and maintaining the mental health of the children based on an exploratory study done on 800 preschool and school-age children in the State of Orissa. The investigation revealed that family stresses including the father's behavior towards the mother, parental conflict, faulty food habits, inconsistent child rearing, sibling comparisons, and pressure to excel in educational and social situations contributed significantly to the poor mental health of children. The author also discusses some preventive approaches for maintaining good mental health of children within the family.

Children in contemporary society are hurried and confused, as are their socializing agents. They are asked by socializing agents to mature, both physically and mentally, much before "Mother Nature" permits them to. This leads to a severe conflict in the child's natural growth pattern and thus leads to maladaptive behavior. The following comment by Murphy (1962), based on her intensive and long range studies of children, is directly relevant: "Seldom do we think of the child as a small human being, carrying on his own struggle to make sense out of life, to meet his own needs, to master the challenges presented by life-but differing from adults especially in the proportion of newness to which he is exposed". Today the very concept of childhood is eroding through the institutionalization of early learning and social environments that deprive children of their right to discover, create, and invent independently by imposing education which is unrelated to their development and interests (Suransky, 1982). The culture of peer cooperation is diminishing with children spending less time with friends and more time with machines such as televisions and computers. Children are also exposed to violence, desensitization, and brutalization of sexuality through the media. The effects of accelerated social changes in India are evident due to the fact that all socializing agents of children are experiencing a period of conflict and crisis that is immensely stressful. Most decision-making in families is based on inadequate information, and too often action taken by parents toward their children is simply a reaction to the present emergency rather than part of a coherent plan for the future. Contemporary life is extremely stressful with family tensions are heightened in numerous ways. Many mothers are working outside the home, resulting in not enough high quality day care for young children. Many children today are therefore being deprived of proper care, while parents feel guilty about neglecting their children. There is less spiritual and moral direction given to children compared to the past, and the traditional support of the extended family and community is loosening. All of these influences put children and youth at risk for a host of mental and emotional disorders.

Children, contrary to popular belief, suffer from mental and behavioral disorders as much as adults do. Most mental health problems in children are evident during 5 to 15 years of age as their social environments widen. According to the Census Report for the Govt. of India, in 2001 India's child population was around 400 million and about 14% of these children suffered from distress caused by maladaptive behaviors. That accounts for around 56 million children in India. These numbers call for immediate action to do something for maintaining child mental health. Given the process of development, it is not surprising that these disorders are known to wax and wane, such that some afflicted children improve as development unfolds, perhaps as a result of healthy influences while some may develop full-blown forms of a disorder. Children hold a very important position in the society physically, but they are the most neglected group, mentally. Their critical socializing agents play a very important role in balancing the act of buffering and exposing the child to learned effective coping skills to face the future. As the government promises to commit to providing children with a poverty and violence free life with their rights secured and protected, doubts arise about the government's integrity and persistence on this issue. It is like a time bomb, with each minute moving India nearer to a severe disaster. What will the world be like when the majority of people are unhappy and maladjusted, especially the children who are the future citizens of the country?

Understanding Mental Health

An understanding of mental health and mental functioning is important as it provides the basis on which to form a more complete understanding of the development of mental and behavioral disorders. Scholars from different cultures have had various definitions of mental health but all agree that the concept of mental health includes subjective well-being, perceived self-efficacy, autonomy, competence, inter-generational dependence, and self actualization of one's intellectual and emotional potential, as well as other factors. According to Dennerstein, Astbury and Morse, in a 1993 World Health Organization (WHO) report, mental health has been described as *"the capacity of the individual, the group and the environment to interact with one another in ways that promote subjective well being, optimal development and use of mental abilities (cognition, attention, and relational), the achievement of individual and collective goals consistent with justice, and attainment and preservation of conditions of fundamental equality."* The importance of mental health has been recognized by WHO since its origin and is reflected by the definition of 2001 health as *"not merely the absence of disease or infinity (not understanding why they used this world so don't know if it is right or not) but rather a state of complete physical, mental and social well being."* In recent years this definition has been given sharper focus by many due to huge advances in the biological and behavioral sciences. These in turn have broadened our understanding of mental functioning and of the profound relationship between mental, physical and social health.

Today it is known that most illnesses or disorders, mental and physical, are influenced by a combination of biological, psychological and social factors. While physical disorders are evident to the eye, mental health problems are not but may cause greater distress to the person, his/her family, and the immediate social environment. Untreated or ignored, mental health problems can magnify into proportions from where there is no returning, especially in today's society where there are enough distractions available to make matters worse. Mental health is an extremely vast field and encompasses everything and anything that is not physical. After it was understood that children are not little adults, mental health in children has been seen from a different perspective. There exist different problems which are typical of children and if left untreated could lead to mental disorders in adulthood. They include problems like childhood schizophrenia or autism, hyperactive or hyper kinetic syndrome, unsocialized aggressive reaction, overanxious and withdrawal reactions, speech and language disabilities, specific learning disabilities, conduct disorder, and developmental delays. Child psychologists have further grouped these behaviors into three broadband areas: 1) Internalizing or over controlled behaviors- includes withdrawn and emotionally sensitive behaviors; 2) Externalizing or under controlled behaviors- includes behaviors such as excessive activity and aggression and; 3) Other problems, which include developmental delays such as encopresis, enuresis, sleep and eating problems. These are referred to as over-controlled and under-controlled behaviors by those who believe that they reflect problems in the development of self-control. To acknowledge the increasing sophistication of older children, the problems are referred to as "emotional and behavioral problems". It is possible and quite common for different categories of problems to occur in the same child thus suggesting that the problems may have a common underlying basis.

Role of Family in Maintaining Children's Mental Health

In order to help a child grow up into a normal and healthy adult, certain conditions must be present in their environment. Just as food and water are needed for physical development, certain needs of the child have to be fulfilled for a healthy social and emotional development. A child needs love, affection and recognition to develop feelings of security and confidence. These developments can only take place when the environment is prime for enhancement. When the social environment fails to meet the needs of the child, the child feels insecure, and fails to learn appropriate skills to adjust to the environment. As a result, the child faces stress, which develops into unnecessary tension, anxiety and fear. This leads to maladjustment on the part of the child and the development of emotional disturbances or mental health problems.

The family is frequently regarded as the most influential agency in the socialization of the child, and is the most basic and universal group found in all the strata of the society. It provides the child a link between continuity and change and is a major source of nurturance, emotional bonding, and socialization. It also plays a significant part in maintaining the physical and psychological integrity of the individual over a period of time. The family is best conceived of as a complex system involving interdependent functioning among members. Research indicates that several functioning factors of the family affect the frequency of different mental disorders. They are (i) family composition, (ii) type of child rearing, (iii) sex of child, (iv) birth order, (v) social class, and (vi) male dominance in the culture. Any modification in structure or behavior of a single-family member can affect the whole set up. The structure of family develops interpersonal conflicts regarding child rearing thus leading to child's maladjustments and scholastic difficulties. These issues are more evident in the families of today as they go through a period of transition. In this transitional phase of Indian families, the child is often torn between age-old traditions and modern norms. Families do not function in isolation. They are influenced by the larger social environments in which they are embedded. The extent to which these environments support or stress the family, affects its role as a socializing agent of the child.

Numerous studies reveal that the family has a tremendous psychosocial influence on the life of the child. The interaction between members is of profound significance in determining the individual's mental attitude and behavior in society (Gomez, 1975; Radhamani, 1975; Shetty, 1975). Socialization within the family has been frequently viewed as a process by which parents shape the behavior of children or as a process of mutual shaping. Child rearing practices, patterns of discipline, inter and intra familial relationships, type and structure of family, and the mother's educational and occupational status are all vital predictors of mental health of children in Indian families. Inconsistency of child rearing practices, ambiguity in role models, change in status or role, and/ or empowerment of women have led to children who have a higher incidence of hiding feelings and nervousness. Khatri (1970) points out that traditional child rearing practices have the ability to make a child dependent and submissive. He also argues that the female child is particularly vulnerable to mental health problems because of early experiences. Ramanujam (1976) states that emotional needs of the child are always considered secondary. Kakar (1978) suggests that the Indian children have a prolonged infancy and it fosters dependency. In spite of the fact that the families are patriarchal, the mothers play a vital role in shaping children's mental health through their constant presence. The presence of grand parents and extended family like uncles and aunts, siblings and permanent domestic help also contribute to the mental health of children. The interaction and emotional relationship between the child and family, especially parents, shapes the child's expectancies and responses in subsequent social relations, Although the family is seeing major rearrangements in its ties, family relationships still remain the most intense and enduring bonds and hence play an extremely vital role in shaping the mental health of a child.

At any age however, the effectiveness of parents as agents of socialization depends on their emotional relationship with the child, the type of controls they attempt to extend, the appropriateness of the controls to the age and personality of the child, and demands of the situations (Macoby & Martin, 1983). In a classic study, Baurmind (1967), identified and classified children into three categories according to their interaction styles – energetic-friendly children, conflicted-irritable children, and impulsive-aggressive children. She then observed their parents behavior and found that authoritative parents had children who had positive psychosocial development. These parents were not intrusive and permitted children to have enough freedom. They imposed restrictions in areas where they had greater knowledge or insight than the child. In general, high warmth, moderate restrictiveness, responsiveness, and attentiveness to the childs needs on the part of the parents led to the development of self-esteem, adaptability, competence, internalized control, and popularity with peers. On the other hand parents of conflicted-irritable children were rigid, power-assertive, harsh, and unresponsive to the child's needs (authoritarian). The child had less control over their environment and received few gratifications which resulted in unhappy, conflicted, and neurotic children. Permissive parenting, in spite of reasonably affectionate relationships, develops problems in children due to lax and inconsistent discipline. This results in uncontrolled and impulsive behavior in their children. A fourth parenting style that is disengaged parenting, where the parents are motivated to do whatever is necessary to minimize the costs in time and effort of interaction in the child (Maccoby & Martin, 1983). Such parents are parent-centered rather than child-centered, and this is associated with the recent egocentric social movement that emphasis's the primary importance of personal satisfaction in social relations. Some parents who are under severe stress (marital discord, relationships gone sour) also act similarly (Hetherington, Cox, & Cox, 1982). In the case of children, such parenting leads to impulsivity, aggression, noncompliance, moodiness and low self-esteem (Block, 1971); Locks, Horst & Horton 1980; Martin, 1981). Such children also show disruptions in cognitive development, achievement, and school performance (Pulkkein, 1982; Seegmiller & King, 1975). Marital harmony amongst parents and spousal support are related to responsive, competent parenting in both fathers and mothers (Cowan & Cowan, 1983; Crnic et al. 1983; Feldman, Nash & Aschenbrenner, 1983). Parental conflict on the other hand is related to aggressive or delinquent behavior in children and unpopularity with peers (Emery, 1982; Hetherington et al., 1982). Conflict appears to be more destructive to children than extreme permissiveness or authoritarian disciplining styles. Boys are more susceptible to the negative effects of family disharmony than are girls (Block, Block, & Morrison, 1981; Heterington, et al., 1982; Rutter, 1977). Children also have an impact on the relationship between their parents. Temperamentally difficult children, deviant or handicapped children impose additional stresses on parents and may break up an already fragile marriage.

Most families today have a total of two or less children. Economic constraints don't allow families to have more than two children. In cases of single-child families, interaction between parents is extensive but social contacts and the importance of sibling relations is lost. The only child has been regarded as a "*spoilt brat*" combining undesirable symptoms such as dependency, egoism, lack of self-control and emotional disorders. Research findings also suggest that the only child does not have to adapt to ultimate displacement and competition with siblings, hence the only child, like first-borns, has low anxiety, is more assertive, has higher self-esteem, and is socially adaptable. Second-born children are less family, and more peer-oriented as they find relatively little satisfaction from companionship of the older siblings or from parents. They accomplish less in life and are less successful academically and vocationally than older siblings. (Koch, 1960). Last born are the babies of the family and "*bear unmistakable signs of the fact that they are the youngest*" (Adler, 1930). Their personality characteristics resemble those of firstborn like dependency. They also exhibit afflictive need, lack of self-confidence, lack of frustration tolerance, resentfulness, defiance of authority and a tendency to be troublesome.

Size of family also effects mental and behavioral health of children. Indian families mostly prefer one child or two children, with small family setups. Large families mean extended families where there are elderly grandparents, or uncles and aunts. In the one-child families, the child is often a spoilt brat or 'mice'. G. Stanley Hall (1907) describes it as; "*Being an only child is a disease in itself. He can't be expected to go through life with the same capacity for adjustment that the child reared in the family with other children has.*" The only child families have less rigid discipline, which encourages him to be selfish and self-centered. The parental expectations are unrealistically high and the mother's personality is more affected by the child's performance than the father's. She also suffers from role deprivation sooner than other mothers. Parents in these families are willing to make financial investments to give the child every opportunity and advantage and they expect

100 percent results. In contrast to one-child families, small families with two or more children are more democratic, and the parent child relationship is warm and wholesome. Most of such families are economically secure and give children enough opportunities (more to the first born) to prepare for adult life. But these families also tend to put pressure on children to live up to their expectations. There is at least one parent available for each child thus building self-confidence and self-assurance. There is the existence of sibling rivalry and a competition for parental attention, affection, and approval which can be very damaging to their self-control. In spite of the unfavorable traits, small families have more positive effects on children than negative effects.

Extended families are more likely to have friction that is severe and more persistent than that present in the family unit. This is due to differences in needs, interests, aspirations, and values among family members. Economic and financial pressures on the family due to the presence of elderly relatives (i.e., grandparents) often lead to marital conflict and contradictory demands on the child. The relationship between parents and grandparents can serve as models for behavior. However, differences in child rearing practices, and disciplining techniques by extended family members can lead to maladjustment on part of the children. Children in large families appear to be interactive and adjusted, as a general rule. Children usually identify with uncles or aunts and get additional support from grandparents.

Roles played by father, mother, and the child affect mental health to a large extent. Changing roles and responsibilities, especially involving the mother, affect children a lot in the Indian setting. How the mother feels about the role she plays and how well she participates and accepts it has a direct effect on the child. The role of the father in child rearing now includes increased co-operation and willingness to help the spouse with work around the home, as compared to the past. The role of the father and the mother must be balanced and devoid of social assumptions, with the final result aimed at good mental health of the child and of family members.

The need to understand the role of temperament in the present context (family as a socializing agent) is necessary as most parents are unaware of the subtle yet vital role played by it in the child's mental development. The role of temperament (or aspects of emotionality) in children is that it regulates social behavior and reflects behavioral tendencies rather than behavioral acts. It is biologically determined and becomes increasingly complex as the child grows into adulthood. It refers to individual characteristics and shows complete continuity through which the expression can be modified. While cognition and intelligence have been researched to a great extent, research into temperament is a recent phenomenon. Thomas and Chess (1977) have described nine dimensions of temperament, namely activity level, rhythmicity, approach or withdrawal, adaptability, threshold of responsiveness, intensity of reaction, quality of mood, distractibility, attention span and persistence. These dimensions were grouped in different combinations to describe the child as "easy" "difficult" and "slow-to-warm" depending on the traits. Buss and Plomin (1984) considered temperament as inherited personality traits which appear early in life. They described temperament along three dimensions of emotionality, activity and sociability.

Rothbart (1986) suggested that each dimension of temperament has a different developmental time frame and Goldsmith et al. (1987) proposed that temperament comprised individual differences in the primary emotions which are present at birth, such as distress, fear and anger. In the Indian context, ancient Indian texts have referred to adult personality traits as being innate pre-dispositions (sanskara). The trigunas (satvik, rajasik and tamasik temperaments) are present in every individual but only the dominant one is said to color the personality. Children's temperament and child-rearing practices in the family are interacting forces and can be studied effectively in the dynamic process of interaction.

Impact of Present Day Families on Children's Mental Health

A study by Patnaik (2003) on 800 preschool and school-age children in the eastern state of Orissa, India, was conducted to find out the contribution of family as one of the socializing agents in the mental health status of children. Results of the study revealed that the prevalence of mental health problems among these children was about 14.8% as indicated both by parents and teachers, and further corroborated by the investigator. The most highly reported behavioral problems in preschool children were externalizing problems, especially in case of boys; whereas, internalizing problems were more evident in elementary school children. In regard to the family demographic variables contributing to the poor mental health of the children in this study, it was found out that the children having mental health problems were mostly from either very small or very large families. The family stressors that were the main cause of mental health problems among these children included the lack of a good parent-child relationship (specially with fathers), poor father-mother relationships, parental conflict over child care, faulty food habits on the part of the children, excessive love, inconsistent discipline, sibling comparison on the part of the parents, and excessive pressure to excel in educational and social activities. Further, high parental expectations and ambition were also found to be the main causes of maladjustment among children. Moreover, parents were found to be over-indulgent and extremely possessive about their children and tried to met each and every demand of their children. It was typically observed that the parents over-attentiveness of their children was very much "adult-centered" not "child-centered", which may have created problems for their children.

Results from the investigation (Patnaik, 2003) further showed that parents prefer their children to spend more time with the machines like the television and computer, rather allow them to spend time with their friends, peers, or neighbors to learn and develop human skills and behavior properly. The majority of parents failed to realize the importance of human interactions and establishing relationships with others outside the family. Further, Indian families have the traditional values of considering the grandparents as assets for the whole family. Unfortunately, results from this study indicated that the participants (i.e., parents) were unaware of the significant contribution of grandparents to their grandchildren. Even if grandparents were staying with the grandchildren, their services were not used for the benefit of the grandchildren. No longer were the wisdom and experience of elderly people in our families alued and used. Rather, grandparents were considered as old and too traditional to be of benefit in today's families.

Another striking revelation of the study (Patniak, 2003) was that the lack of parenting skills was at least partially responsible for children's behavioral problems. Immaturity, ignorance, and incompetence on the part of the parents contributed greatly to the poor mental health of the children, especially when they are young. Findings indicated that proper family intervention consisting of parental counseling, education, and, in some cases, play and behavioral therapy for the affected children were very successful in enhancing the mental health in our families.

Moreover, it was noted that children from financially and educationally good backgrounds also had mental health problems and their social stressors were more like "*silent killers*" because the child was not prepared to face them (Patniak, 2003). Children from this stratum of society may be "*cocooned*" in comfort both physically and socially which can leave them "*bare*" or vulnerable psychologically. Parents, teachers, peers, media and other socializing agents are ill-equipped to deal with the gap between physical comfort and psychological starvation, and thus the child's mental health can be affected in this process.

Apart from all scientific and technological developments, parents still were found to be helpless in taking care of their children (Patniak, 2003). The absence of social support factors was seen to be a major contributor to this problem. Most fathers and especially mothers were not prepared for childbirth and child rearing, although it was thought of as a natural product of marriage between two human beings. The basic know-how of the development of a child was seen to be lacking amongst new fathers and mothers. In spite of high incomes, educational and occupational status of parents, parent-child relationships were observed to have strains. Maternal stress and less physical involvement of the father were two factors responsible for such strains on the child's psyche. Grandparents and siblings had positive effects on children's mental health, thus implying that having them around would do more good than bad. Less reliance on domestic help for work that could be easily handled by the parents and child prevented the child from learning habits and behaviors (from the domestic help) that were not socially approved. Those children suffering from mental health problems were generally from families that displayed an unorganized style of parenting, where over-protection and over-indulgence combined with punitive ness and permissiveness prevailed in the environment, thus confusing the child. A balance between firm discipline, extreme love, care and compassion were seen to be vital factors for bringing up mentally healthy children. Marital harmony and general agreement between parents and other members in the family, especially regarding child rearing practices and the child's issues, were seen to be positive predictors of healthy mental status of children.

Children need not only a healthy mind, but also require a healthy body. Proper eating habits should be developed early with a balance of traditional and modern styles of food preparation and handling. Further, proper exercise and allowance for play time is important, as is stimulating activities for development of creativity, and less involvement with television, computers and video games. A child must be made to accept himself or herself, including both positive and negative traits, in order to have a healthy mental attitude. Parents must close the gap between the real and the ideal in order to provide the child with self-acceptance. Hence, early experiences of the child are extremely vital for the foundation of self-acceptance. Instead of criticizing the child, parents must accept the undesirable traits of the child and teach him/her to make efforts to change those characteristics (especially in temperament). Parents must be aware and even vigilant of any indication of psychopathology, no matter how minor it may be. This will help them to plan remedial measures so that bad habits or faulty behaviors do not develop into a habit. Sometimes it may also require a major change in the child's social environment.

The child's most important needs required for happiness are feelings of achievement, acceptance, and affection. These basic needs must be met at every stage and level of development, and the child must feel secure and content with his family around. Fair, firm, consistent and loving discipline, taking into account the child's expanding ability for self-discipline should instill in him social and moral values to serve as guidelines for socially approved and self-approved behavior. In the present era, the lines between parent-child relationships are becoming blurred, with each one trespassing another's territory. While the closeness is good, it has been observed that each individual needs a certain amount of privacy. Parents must stop being over-indulgent and over involved as it hurts the child's development of independence and belittles the ego. The child must be taught to do things himself, develop success factors like persistence, thoroughness, accuracy, curiosity, originality, leadership, pride in achievement, and creativity in his thinking. Parents must provide him or her with opportunities for success, especially soon after a failure to avoid the development of a "*failure complex*". When misbehaviors do occur, the focus should be on the behavior and not on the child. Thus, responses such as, "I don't like your behavior right now," rather than "You are being bad" separate the child from the behavior. The child is not bad, just the immediate behavior. Also, statements that provide choices can help develop a sense of consequences for misbehaviors in the child, while the parent is still giving corrective guidance. An example would be, "You can either stop fighting with your sister or you can sit in the 'time-out' chair in the corner. The choice is yours."

Children need friendly, accepting parents, to be enjoyed and to do things with them. However, with work pressures and other stressors, many parents find it difficult to spend time with their children. Parents may need to make special efforts to create quality time with their children, and also with themselves to maintain a healthy marital relationship. It is always better to chat enjoyably for 15 minutes, than to spend an hour playing grumpily. Fathers should be involved in these special times with their children, particularly during playtime. Boys especially often look upon fathers as role models. Girls look upon mothers as role models. Mothers provide for companionship in more ways than just spending time in daily routines. Children need their mothers physically and emotionally, round the clock. With mothers today playing an active role out of the home, their companionship becomes all the more important. For working mothers, choosing the right daycare and exposing the child to daycare workers are very important aspects in their busy work schedule. Most children attend preschool and crèches, but many stay at home and are taken care of by their grandparents or other members of extended family. Grandmothers are often considered as experts and young mothers can not only get advice but also comfort from their presence. Today's new mother is turning to her doctor for professional help because she is so used to technological changes in her life. Advances in the knowledge of medicine are replacing age-old tradition. But as stated earlier, results from Patnaik's study (2003) found that children usually thrive better in the presence of grandparents both physically and emotionally, and they are a major supportive factor in the child's life. The presence of siblings is also a very positive supportive factor in the process of socialization especially as they provide the first building blocks of friendship particularly in absence of peers. The concept of a "*one child*" family may not be good psychologically for either parents or the child. The presence of uncles and aunts helps children grow in a nurturing environment with lots of love and attention from different socializing agents and teaches him/her early rules of socialization. Parents must develop cordial and healthy relations with other critical socializing agents like school personnel, friends, etc., because children model parental behaviors.

Conclusion

Parents today appear to be highly ambitious and over-expectant of their children. They may set unrealistic goals for their children and themselves, which leads to improper mental health and maladjustment. Parents also may be overindulgent in their child rearing practices, and are sometimes extremely possessive of their children. They may attempt to meet each and every demand of the child in order to keep him/her happy. Less attention, though, is paid to the mental health aspects of child development. Indifference, especially on part of mothers, has been found to be a major predictor of mental health problems. Apart from meeting all physical needs, mothers must also attend to the child's psychological needs (like sitting together, spending quality time playing together, being the child's friend, and sharing thoughts, etc.). Mothers who spend large amounts of time watching T.V. and talking to friends may be depriving their children of vital time together. Likewise, fathers who come home from work tired and stressed may neglect their children. Children reared in such environments may not develop strong relationships with their parents, and thus could go through adulthood lacking the psychological foundation such relationships foster.

Some parents may lack knowledge about child rearing practices and overall child development, which could lead to inconsistent discipline. Excessive maternal stress, marital disharmony and over expectations on part of parents can lead to punitiveness towards the children. Findings from the Patniak (2003) study suggested that fathers made up for loss of companionship, while some mothers emotionally blackmailed their children to perform well or finish up daily chores by providing excessive love and material gifts. This sudden shift between punishment and permissiveness, confused the children and led to development of problem behaviors.

The upbringing of children in large families where everyone contributed in child rearing resulted in children being confused and extremely pampered, thus suggesting that children need consistent discipline and permanent role models to follow in order to learn proper behavior. It was observed, however, that the presence of three to four adults at home had extremely positive effects on mental health children. This was especially evident in families where grand parents were available (Patniak, 2003).

The role of grandparents is generally considered to be negligible, but findings from Patniak (2003) suggest that they have a huge impact on the mental health of children, as they serve as buffers for their grandchildren in times of stress and strain. In spite of conflicts in relationships at home, grandparents showed extreme love and care for grandchildren, and they assumed various roles that parent did not have the time to perform. They also imparted moral values into the young minds of the future generation so that their legacy continued. Grandparents are an asset, and nothing in the world can replace them and their experience and knowledge. Children loved their grandparents (sometimes more than their parents) for their loving support, care, and affection. Presence of siblings was seen to do more good than bad in the mental health of children. Only children had more problems than children who had aggressive or dull siblings. The presence of siblings involved healthy jealousy, taught lessons on social interactions and developed the concepts of sharing and caring with others.

The concept of the "*only child*" family may be necessary financially but not psychologically; one child at home appeared to create more problems than several children (Patniak, 2003). Parents with more than one child tended to be less possessive, less expectant and less indulgent rather than concentrating all their efforts on one child.

Finally, it has been concluded that family demographic factors are not predictive of resiliency to mental health problems. Parent's commitment to children gives the family a sense of coherence, and out of such experiences children learn to make sense out of life and motivate themselves to achieve well in future. Children must receive familial support, both physically and mentally. Proper adult role models (either parents or other adults) are extremely important to make the child feel confident in his/her ability to build other strong relationships in future. Most families would benefit from support from other sources in times of increased stress so as to buffer the child from the adverse effects of psychopathology. Such support systems could be in the form of school-community resources (supportive school programs, sibling counseling), family resources (religion, inner language, family commitments and external family interaction), social systems resources (link between the individual and groups), and external resources (volunteer groups, social service organizations, and counseling services).

Mothers need to be informed about child rearing practices because they are prime targets for educational intervention on subjects relating to marriage, pregnancy and infant care. This intervention has to be imparted by institutions, because traditionally as girls, they cannot have a dialogue with parents or family members about such subjects. During pregnancy, both parents must attend preparatory classes or read books on childbirth, child rearing, child development patterns and the importance of early and consistent discipline. Both parents need to contribute equally to the child's development. They must also learn to leave bad habits behind and behave properly as they will be imitated as role models by their children. Most grandparents should be intimately involved with child rearing, because nothing can replace them. The aged are not a spent force, they are a treasure house of knowledge. They are not to be sidelined; they are to be mainstreamed. These flowers may be faded, BUT they still remain sweet.

References

Adler, A. (1930). *The education of children.* New York: Greenberg.

Baurmind, D. (1967). Childcare practices anteceding three patterns of preschool behavior. *Genetic psychology Monograph, 75*, 43-88.

Block, J. (1971). *Lives through time.* Berkeley, CA: Bancroft Books.

Block, J.M., Block J., & Morison, A. (1981). Parental agreement – disagreement on child rearing orientation and gender-related personality correlates in children. *Child Development, 52*, 965 - 974.

Cowan. C. P., & Cowan, P. (1983). A preventive intervention for couples during family formation. Paper presented at the meetings for the Society for Research in Child Development, Detroit, April.

Crnic, K.A., Greenberg, M.T., Ragozin, A.S., Robinson, N.M., & Basham, R. (1983). Effects of stress and social support on mothers and premature and full term infants. *Child Development, 54*, 209-217.

Emery, R.E. (1982). Inter-parental conflict and the children of discord and divorce. *Psychological Bulletin, 92,* 310-330.

Feldman, S.S., Nash, S.S., & Aschenbrenbier, B.G. (1983). Antecedents of fathering. *Child Development, 54*, 119-135.

Gomez, K.C. L. (1975). Unpublished D.P.S.W. Dissertation. NIMHANS, Bangalore.

Hethington, E.M., Cox, M. & Cox, R. (1982). Effects of divorce on parents and children. In M. Lamb (Ed.), *Non-traditional families.* Hillsdale, NJ: Erlbaum.

Kakar, S (1978). Popularity, intelligence, economic status and academic achievement. *Indian Journal of Psychiatry; 45*, 233-37.

Khatri, A. (1970). A personality and mental health of Indians (Hindus) in the context of their changing family organization. In E.T. Anthony

& C. Kougernik (Eds.), *The child and his family: Vol. I.* New York. John Wiley and Sons

Koch, H.L. (1960). The relation of certain formal attributes of siblings to attitudes heed towards each other and towards their parents. *Monographs of the Society for Research in Child Development, 25*(4).

Locks, R.B., Horst, L., & Horton, P.J. (1980). Family interaction patterns associated with self-esteem and pre-adolescent girls and boys. *Merrill-Palmer Quarterly, 26,* 203-217.

Macoby, E.E. and Martin, J.A. (1983). Socialization in the context of the family: Parent child interaction. In E.M. Hetherington (Ed.), *Socialization, personality and social development (Vol. 4): Handbook of child psychology.* New York, Wiley.

Martin, J.A. (1981). A longitudinal study of the consequences of early mother-infant interaction: micro analytic approach. *Monographs of the Society for Research in Child Development, 46* (3).

Murphy, L. (1962). *The widening world of childhood.* New York: Basic books.

Patnaik, I. (2003). *Effect of critical socializing agents on the mental health of school children.*Unpublished Ph.D. Thesis, Department of Home Science, Berhampur University, Berhampur, Orissa.

Pulkkein, L. (1982). Self-control and continuity from childhood to adolescence. In P.B. Baltes & O.G. Brim (Eds.), *Lifespan development and behavior (Vol. 4).* New York: Academic Press.

Radhamani, R. (1975). *International patterns in family of anxiety patients.* Unpublished D.P.S.W. Dissertation, NIMHANS, Bangalore.

Ramanujam, B.K. (1976). Psychoanalytic perspectives of personality development in India. *Samiksha 32*(3), 47-68.

Rothbart, M.K. (1980). Longitudinal home observation of infant temperament. *Development psychology, 22,* 356-65

Rutter, M. (1977). Individual differences. In M. Rutter & L. Hwersor (Eds.), *Child psychiatry: Modern approaches* (pp. 3-21). Oxford, England: Blackwell Scientifc.

Seegmiller, B.R. & King, W.L. (1975). Relations between behavioral characteristics of infants, their mother's behaviors, and performance on the Bayley Mental and Motor Scales. *Journal of Psychology, 91*, 99-111.

Shetty, G. (1975). *Hysteria in childhood: A study of phenomenology personality and family interaction*. Unpublished D.P.S.W. Dissertation, NIMHANS, Bangalore.

Stoodley, B.H. (1952). Mother role as a focus of some family problems. *Marriage and Family Living, 14,* 13-16.

Suransky, V.P. (1982). *The erosion of childhood*. Chicago: University of Chicago Press.

Thomas, A. and Chess, S. (1977). *Temperament and development*. New York: Bruner/Mazel.

8

Management of Family Resources For Strengthening Family Life

Sanjukta Das

Family resource management is the primary activity of the family life management system. This chapter discusses the types of family resources available and factors involved in educating families about resource management, with suitable examples provided. The focus in family resource management education today is on family decision making processes and the goal directed behavior of family members in improving their quality of life. This is done through values clarification and other organizing activities that help families use their resources effectively.

"Resources are assets - anything owned as accessible that has exchange value that can be used to accomplish goals." - Rice & Tucker

The heart of family life education is helping families learn new ways to cultivate and use available resources to attain their goals more effectively. The field of family resource management has much to offer in this regard. Motivation, information, and creative thought are human resources that have the power to increase the usefulness of other resources and thereby enhance satisfaction in families. Decisions and opportunities determine the quality and quantity of resources that are available and appropriate in meeting the family's needs and helping them achieve their goals. Resources are necessary to solve management problems, and both the conscious and unconscious use of family resources has an enormous impact on the quality of family life.

Little has been written about the importance of resource management in modern day Indian families, how this is linked to the health and well-being of family members, and how families can be educated about the wise and intended use of the resources they have. Moreover, many families are not able to identify all of the usable resources available in their own lives. Thus, the family resource management component of family life education helps families (and professionals who work with families) understand the various kinds of resources available to them on both a micro and macro level, and how to cultivate and use these resources to enrich their lives.

The Concept of Family Resource Management

The concept of family resources can be defined in the following way. "Resources are the means available for reaching goals, maintaining standards and solving problems." - Hogan and Buchler, (1984).

Family resource management includes problems, values, goals, standards, resources, decisions and plans. Resource management is not a static concept but consists of a combination of dynamic processes. For example, the concept of "problems" is included in the process of problem recognition, problem definition, and problem solving. The concept of "values" is part of the process of values identification, values prioritization, and values mediation, as well as standard setting and standard maintenance. Other processes that are part of family resource management are described as follows.

Classification of Family Resources:

The purpose of classifying family resources is to increase awareness among family members about the number and kinds of potential resources that are available to them in attaining family goals. These resources are summarized in Table 1 below.

Table 1: Classification of Family Resources

Resource classification	*Some examples*	
1. *Human Resources:*		
Cognitive resources	Knowledge	Creativity
	Judgment	Initiative
	Perception	Adaptability
Affective resources	Attitude	Consideration
	Trust	Friendliness
	Taste	Motivation
Psychomotor resources	Work habits	Manners
	Typing	Communication
	Child care skills	Carpentry skills
Temporal resources	Clock time	Past, present and future calendar time
	Pace	
	Psychological time	
2. *Economic Resources:*		
Income	Wage	Commission
	Dividends	Royalties
	Pension payments	Interest
Wealth	Owned home	Automobiles
	Furnishings	Stocks, bonds,

(Contd.)

(Contd. Table-1)

Resource classification	*Some examples*	
		possessions
Employee benefits	Appliances	Compensation plans
	Insurances	Unemployment
	Retirement programs	Vacations
	Pensions	
Credit	Cash loans	Charge accounts
	Mortgages	Service credit
	Installment purchases	
3. <u>Environmental Resources:</u>		
Physical environment,	Soil	Animals
Natural tangible	Minerals	Rain
Surroundings	Plants	Terrain
Non-tangible surroundings	Air	Light
	Sound	Temperature
	Space	Sunlight
Immediate Surroundings	Work space	Living space
	Rented apartment	Yard
Social environments	Family, nuclear	Friends
Social organizations	and extended community	
	Assistance leagues	
	YMCA	
Economic institutions	Stores	Hospitals
	Super markets	Banks
	Stock markets	Laundries
Political institutions	City, country, officials of State. National Government, Voting rights, Laws	
Community facilities and services	Police, Water, Sewage systems, Fire protection, Religious places, Recreation centers, parks	

Human Resources: Human resources are all the means that are vested in people that can be used to meet demands.

They include personal characteristics such as intelligence, ingenuity, creativity, sensitivity, delicacy, optimism, decisiveness, perseverance, dedication, health, energy and time. Time is considered a human resource and refers not only to "clock-time", which everyone possesses in equal amounts, but also to a person's characteristic methods of assimilating and perceiving the passage of time.

Economic Resources: Economic resources are things that can be used for exchange or barter. Examples include money, credit, investments, fringe benefits, wealth, land, labor, stock and capital. As a resource, money includes not only monetary receipts from all sources, but its characteristic patterns and frequency of flow to the family. Wages, commissions, interest, dividends, tips, royalties and pensions are money income resources, but savings and investments are wealth. Income is earned, wealth is accumulated.

Environmental Resources: Environmental resources may be either physical or social. The physical environmental resources include two types of surroundings – natural tangible and less tangible surroundings. The former are the elements of the environment and climate that can be perceived by the sense of touch, such as soil, rain, terrain and minerals. Less tangible surroundings are the elements of the environment and climate that cannot be touched but include those that can be measured such as air, light, sound, temperature and humidity.

The remaining resources that people manage have been classified as social environmental resources. These are social organizations, economic institutions, political institutions, and community facilities and services.

Characteristics of Family Resources

All resources have certain characteristics. Knowing the major characteristics of family resources may help family members become more aware of personal resources. Further, understanding the nature of each characteristic of family resources will surely increase the usefulness of resources in the family. These are briefly outlines as follows.

Useful: The definition of resources itself is indicative of this characteristic. All family resources have 'utility' which has to do with the satisfying power of the family members. Utility means value, worth, applicability, and productiveness for a definite purpose. The usefulness of a family resource is determined by the family member's knowledge of how to develop and use the resource to attain family goals. Example: A new computer program has little usefulness until the owner learns how to use the program and does so for the management or solution of everyday problems.

Limited: The second way in which resources are alike is that they are all limited. Actually, resources become important in proportion to the degree to which they are limited. The inevitability of these limitations must be accepted. Example: Before the busy homemaker can make and carry out plans that will work, she who constantly complains because her work is unfinished everyday, compared to her friend at the day's end, must actually accept the fact that no one can push time backward. Limits, like the uses of available resources, must be assessed in relation to specific goals.

Interchangeability: Interchangeability of resources is exhibited through conversion, interdependence, and creation. All resources are interrelated to the extent that one may be substituted for or interchanged with another in the quest of attain goals. Example: When a person is unable to buy the level of living desired due to lack of money, the person may be motivated to develop other resources that can be sold to earn money to buy the desired things to improve his or her life-style.

Transferability: Not all resources are transferable. Time may be used to accomplish tasks for other people, but no one may give any portion of their personal time directly to others.

Human energy has similar characteristics, and some environmental resources, such as air, may not be transferred easily. However, an individual's time, energy and abilities may be used to work for an employer in exchange for economic resources. This is the principle that underlies market work – "work for pay". These are transfers in kind of resources for other resources. Example: Parents provide their children with food, housing and education while the children are growing up, and the children may later provide the parents with personal care, housing and medical attention in the parents' old age.

Alternative Uses: Alternative uses for family resources characterize their inherent "re-source ability". As the term suggests, they may be used in different ways. For example, wood may be used for buildings, for heat, or for objects of art. The special qualities of given resources determine their value for the different uses to which they may be put. Alternative uses of manufactured or highly processed items may be limited since these items are directed toward specific purposes. However, the potential for alternative uses is a general quality of more basic resources, either material or human. The transforming of basic material resources into processed goods for consumption involves the application of knowledge, skills, energy and tools. What occurs is the incorporation of needed characteristic designed to be useful for particular purposes. This adaptation of resources occurs as managerial actions within the household, just as it does as a part of the manufacturing process. In sum, when family members are aware of the characteristics of the resources available to them, they can recognize more readily the varied uses and constraints of resources in creating desired life styles.

Management of Family Resources –

Family resource management means that family goals can be achieved through conscious choice and application of resources in the management system. Although all resources can be managed; i.e., used to satisfy the purpose of building life style and improving the quality of life, it should be understood that an improved life style is not the same thing as having more possessions. Too many possessions can become constraints on mobility, travel, safety and other goals. The ways in which family resources are used is as important as the assets themselves in determining the quality of family life that people can achieve. *It is not always what a person has but what the person does with available resources that count most in management of family life.*

Although resources may not be always completely controllable, it is possible to exert limited control over all resources. For example, it may not be possible to add a foot to one's body height through management, but some height may be added through improved health care and body posture. The amount of energy required to accomplish home tasks can be reduced through the choice of housing with adequate storage and convenient arrangement for work in the kitchen.

Within the constraints of present technology, people cannot exert complete control over the weather or other environmental factors, but technology has made great strides in that direction. Air cooling and heating make homes, offices and automobiles more comfortable. Smog devices on cars and filters on airborne waste emissions of industry can decrease eye and respiratory irritation from polluted air.

Resource manageability makes it possible for family members to focus on the development of one resource at a particular time, as in the case of an athlete learning to walk again after a severe accident. People living together in the family tend to develop a style of resource use. Some people emphasize use of time and energy to construct desired products. Others automatically think of monetary resources to exchange for desired products. Some people think first of the relationships involved and emphasize finding a joint response to needs.

Kamal and Asha, for example, are oriented towards use of both human and non-human resources to achieve their goals. Asha and her husband, Kamal, have been a model couple in the eyes of their friends. She is an attractive teacher and he an Engineer. Both have spent many years and rupees developing the skills needed to succeed at their chosen career. They helped each other during the course of their education. Each took a part time job with a small salary, while the other concentrated on course work. When they were eventually settled in their jobs in the same town, it looked as though they would finally be able to enjoy living. They purchased a place to construct their dream house. Together they planned, designed and supervised the work of their own house. At first they spent many hours on these tasks after work. It had taken all their savings, but as both had good salaries, they felt, they could afford their dream house. They had contacted a good architect-cum-house decorator, brought several antiques to decorate their house, and read books on gardening to acquire sufficient knowledge to maintain a beautiful garden in front of the house. Now after careful handling of all their resources, making all the right decisions at the right time, they are enjoying living in the beautiful house, much to the envy of the neighbors.

Management of family resources also makes it possible to predict, with some degree of accuracy, the outcomes of resource use. Conditions of weather can be predicted to some extent so that precautions may be taken against extremes of wind, temperature, and rain. Span of life has been extended through discovery of treatment for communicable diseases and preventive medicines, although one has to seek help when they need it. Creating and transforming one's resources into another are functions of the management system. Converting raw foods into appetizing meals is one example of the management of resources.

The Process of Family Resource Management –

The processes involved in family resource management are problem solving, decision-making, choice, and decision implementation. Management is an adjustment process that begins and ends with change. The decision makers either must respond to changes in the environment that require deliberation, or the desired changes are initiated by the decision makers and later affect the environment. Although problem solving, decision making and decision implementation are part of the adaptation that characterizes resource management, other processes listed as follows are also part of this picture.

- Problem solving, decision making, choice and decision implementation.
- Valuing, standard setting and standard maintaining.
- Goal identifying, agreeing and prioritizing.
- Resource producing, allocating, consuming, conserving, investing and exchanging.
- Information accessing, processing and sharing.
- Planning, organizing, facilitating and implementing.
- Coordinating, controlling, checking, adjusting, evaluating and innovating.
- Communicating, integrating, negotiating, mediating.
- Leading, motivating, supervising, learning and socializing.

In sum, family resource management views the family as a problem-solving group where management is a means of engaging some of the most prized qualities of life.

Management Applied to Specific Family Resources–

Specific family resources that are required to achieve a reasonable level of harmony and satisfaction are time, energy and money.

TIME: A constant rush in our lives today implies that we tend to suffer from a host of problems due to tension. In fact, we are clueless about how fast the time flies. There is a pressing need, therefore, to know how time should be effectively managed within family. Today, time is one of the most important aspects of our lives. Money can buy almost everything except time. It is one of the major factors that can cause stress in individuals. If we are highly stressed people today, it is only because we have so little time for the multitude of tasks that await our attention. Time is one of life's great equalizers. It is a unique resource that everyone throughout the world has in equal amounts as long as the person lives twenty-four hours a day.

If a person could manage only one personal resource and still keep control of life, time would be that resource. Use of time directly affects the use of other resources, such as money, energy, space and even knowledge. ***"Time planning is life planning"***. However, "time management" is a misnomer since people cannot refuse the next hour coming to them or make up the last 15 minutes that have been misused. Despite this deficiency, time management is a convenient phrase that is used to mean the management of activities within a time frame.

Regardless of the situation, either at work or at home, people can apply certain concepts and techniques to gain control of their time. Cormier defines time management as "gaining control over what you do, when you do it, how you do it, and why you do it." Time management requires some understanding of the nature of time and how it differs from person to person, in spite of its finite management. It is crucial to the well-being of families.

Time Perceptions: The phenomenon of time seems so natural that once people have developed a perception of time, they have difficulty understanding that other people could perceive time differently. In actuality, people differ widely in their orientation to time within and between cultures as well as families, and these perceptions affect their behavior in many ways. Different perceptions and uses of time can be a major source of conflict and confusion in families.

Measurement of Time: Formal time management helps people synchronize their activities with those of others. For example:

A person who wants to consult a physician will call to schedule an appointment for a specific time in the future. The receptionist may schedule the meeting the following Tuesday at 5 p.m. The appointment is based on the understanding that those involved know when Tuesday is and understand the meaning of the term 5 p.m.

While people's personal sense of time helps them become oriented to reality, clock time is useful to co-ordinate and synchronizes events with other people and other places inside or outside the family. Learning about time is a gradual process, and the formal measurement of time is the last in a series of time related learning. Time is a concept that is understood gradually and as a resource, is measured, and can be both subjectively and objectively understood within family and workplace. Perception of time as a manageable resource can give order and direction to life in general.

The Process of Managing Time: The ability to control time in relation to goals increases in importance as people try to shape their life styles to include more and more activities. In today's world larger numbers of women are working outside the home, higher proportions of college students are dividing their time between jobs and studies, increasing numbers of men are spending more time in family integrative activities, and dual-career couples are commuting great distances to provide themselves with challenging work. The complexity of life today places increasing emphasis on using time effectively.

A general goal of time management is the conservation of time to match needs and wants, and to gain greater satisfaction from life's activities. Time plans should, therefore, reflect personal, professional and household goals. Based on these goals people determine activities to be included in the day, week, month, or year for which they are planning. The one-minute goal setting concept is a useful technique for daily planning and will work as well for longer-range goals. The processes involved in managing time are:

1. Planning: Time plans have to be centered on inflexible activities – those that occur at fixed times. Inflexible hours wield considerable power over the time when other activities may be scheduled. Work hours for adults and school hours for children are usually the primary activities that provide structure to people's days. Inflexible activities are logically scheduled first and related activities such as arising, dressing, eating breakfast and leaving for work are paced by the time for arriving at work or school. Since many people require a specific number of hours of sleep, the time they must arise to reach work on time determines their bedtime. Scheduled events in a typical family's day add to the framework that imposes order, or sometimes chaos, on life. However, a time plan cannot accomplish miracles. It must be pointed out that neither it, nor a money budget, nor any similar device, is more than a technical aid in the wise management of a resource. A daily time schedule can be no more effective than the concepts of management behind it. If careful consideration has been given to the relative values of disposition of time within the family, it will be reflected in their daily schedule. If such consideration has not been given, the schedule may defeat its own purpose. Whatever may be the techniques adopted for making use of time judiciously, learning to manage time within the family situation is important.

2.Controlling: Though much has been written about the techniques of making time schedules and forms, including suggestions for writing them down, there is little in the literature about controlling time plans in action. Certain points included in the original time plan can be used as factors of control. This does not mean that if they are in the plan it will be carried out successfully. It simply means that they make certain types of control possible. Controlling a time plan in action is much aided by the development of a time sense, and by devices such as breaking down household schedules/chores into parts for scrutiny, checking frequently and soon enough to make adjustments possible, and including catch-up periods.

3.Evaluating: In evaluating the management of time, as other resources, goals and values must be considered. As they vary, so do the methods of evaluation. Evaluation enters into making and carrying out plans, as well as reviewing the results. As time and work plans are carried out, there is constant evaluation of performance and checking of accomplishments to be certain that things are going about as planned. If time runs short, or if adjustments must be made in the days work, the evaluation of many factors enters into the decisions that must be made. Conscious or unconscious evaluation of one's use of time and accomplishments shapes and improves new plans. Evaluation is a flexible mental tool in time management, which can be very well incorporated within family life management.

4. **ENERGY:** "Energy" is the source of all activity, even though it is unseen; it is the potential to do all types of activities. Energy management is more difficult and complex than time management. We can always count on 24 hours a day when making time and activity plans, but we never know how much energy can be counted on to carry them out. The amount of energy that each individual family member has for work and other activities (inside and outside the family) depends on genetic heritage; physical, mental, and emotional health; and a number of other factors. In addition to this inherent constitutional energy, most people have large resources of latent energy that can be mobilized when required.

Family goals are important in energy management of individual family members because they determine how much and what kind of energy should be mobilized. In making daily, weekly, monthly, or yearly plans, two questions should be asked: (1) How much energy should be spent in pursuit of a particular goal? And (2) How much is its attainment worth to people in the family? If the cost in energy required to meet the family's goals appears too high, different goals may be set. It is essential to decide family goals within the supply of available energy among the family members, with enough energy left for enjoying and participating in other family as well as community activities.

Planning energy use: When discussing time management, time and energy planning are inseparable. Managing energy is similar to managing time. It involves the making of activity plans, as well as carrying them out and evaluating the results. In time planning, one's clock or watch helps measure time expenditures. In the case of energy planning, knowledge of the energy costs of different activities, family member's skills and abilities to turn out work, and the effects of fatigue, all help measure energy expenditures. Through experiences the family learns how to work out well-balanced, energy-spending patterns that are based on the store of energy available from day to day.

Controlling: Motivation plays an important role in carrying out all activity plans, including those having to do with energy management. High motivation makes more energy available for the tasks at hand, and helps control fatigue costs resulting from work. Motivation can be increased among family members by developing more favorable attitudes toward household activities, by making work situations more comfortable and attractive, and by stimulating greater interest and goal consciousness on the part of the family as a whole.

Developing skills in fitting activities of daily living into the minutes and hours of the day conserves emotional and physical energy and stimulates greater efficiency in household work. Skills of this kind lead to greater mental flexibility in the management of energy and in carrying out activity plans. The "work simplification" method, which had to do with the effective use of the body in household work, and the skillful performance of homemaking tasks, are tools which enable a homemaker to conserve time and energy so that it will be available for other interests and activities.

Evaluating Energy Management: Evaluating energy management consists largely of questions related to a person's fatigue and body mechanics. There is a dearth of quantitative data for evaluating the use of energy and avoidance of any type of fatigue that is "safe" to accumulate. According to Gilberth, fatigue ought to be overcome within a 24-hour period. If it mounts too early in the working day, it is considered something of a danger signal, whatever its type. According to one writer, "a worker should not feel tired more than one-fifth of the working day".

Asking oneself the following questions will help to evaluate success in utilizing one's store of energy.

Do I think of the use of energy in terms of the goals I wish to attain?Do the energy costs of any homemaking tasks seem too high?Am I using my energy effectively?Have I worked out a well-balanced energy spending pattern for both my homemaking and my other activities?What homemaking activities do I like best?What do I dislike & why do I dislike these activities?How can I change my attitudes towards these activities?What tasks are most tiring and why?Do I tire easily?Do I recognize the type of fatigue I frequently experience?Does it make me want to stop work?What can I do to relieve fatigue?Do I use effective methods of work to avoid fatigue?Have I learned to relax and rest?

MONEY: "Money" – a scarce and precious resource these days – should be treated with respect and care. There is a saying, "Take care of the pence and the pounds will take care of themselves." This is a good sermon on thrift and teaches us that every little saving will soon make up a large amount. This great quality of saving can be cultivated only if we keep our eyes on our expenses and regulate them carefully. Spending and saving are the financial lessons learned from the family, particularly one's parents.

Money problems in the family often begin with prices rising almost everyday and incomes not keeping pace. If requests for help are an index, many families are conscious of the need for learning how to manage their money. Since the majority of consumer goods today must be purchased, families apparently recognize that better management of income may provide more of the goods desired.

The Planning for Money Use: Budgeting – frequently considered the whole of money management – is in reality only the first step in the financial planning process. Since money management has not always been presented in a manner which is psychologically sound, the word *budget* has unpleasant connotations for many. Financial experts agree that leaving money management to only one member of the family is a dangerous policy. It is essential that both husband and wife know exactly their credit and debit. The family finance plan – the budget – is part of the way of life of the family using it and is based upon an understanding and agreement made by both husband and wife. Briefly stated, the method is one of analysis of family needs and resources available to meet demands of making decisions on what is important, and of working out a plan for the use of money in accordance with the analysis.

Controlling and Evaluating: As so often is the case, these two activities go hand in hand, and this is true in managing money as well. As with all types of management, plans are unlikely to be carried out successfully unless some control is exercised. This is particularly true with a complex plan such as a 'budget'. Control in family financial management is usually of two types: first, checking to see how well the plan is progressing, and second, adjusting when and where necessary by all the family members.

Evaluation of the use of money should be in terms of the family's goals. Are these goals being achieved, or is progress being made towards their achievements? Evaluation of the use of money is particularly important because so many of the satisfactions which families desire today are purchased with it. As was noted in the discussion of making budgets, the finished plan tells a great deal about the family, since no interest can be represented without the use of economic resources. In the evaluation stage the families must not only decide whether their planning and their control achieved the family goals which they had set out to attain. The must also decide whether or not these goals are as satisfying as they had expected.

Use of Family Resources–

Because resources have alternative uses, choices must be made among goods to determine their most satisfying uses by family members. Money can buy many things, including personal items, but can also be used for family essentials such as paying for child care services or tuition for children's education. Money will also buy healthy foods, as well as wholesome fruits and vegetables. Time may be used to earn income to keep an orderly home, gain education, enjoy reading, participate in family recreation or develop hobbies. However, family resources can be used in two different ways – through allocation or exchange.

- **Allocating Resources:** Allocation is the process of assigning family resources to various places, situations, or processes in order to attain family goals. For example, if a family has a goal to have the dining table set in a particularly attractive way for special guests, they may turn to the family member they think is the most artistic and ask that person to decide what centerpieces, dishes and arrangements should be used. This is allocating a fairly intangible personal, non-economic resource that is artistic ability. This is the kind of resource that is used, but not consumed or used up, because the individual who has the artistic ability has just as much — and perhaps even more — after setting the table.

Another example of resource allocation can be observed in a family which has a member who is discouraged or depressed. In some families this type of situation may not be considered a problem and might be ignored. But other families would consider this a problem and set the goal to take time to help and marshal other family resources as well. In these situations, resources such as tenderness, patience, compassion, understanding and nurturance would be called upon.

Sometimes allocation is a process of carefully dividing resources among alternative goals. At other times, allocation is done almost unconsciously. Time and money are limited family resources for most families, so they are usually portioned carefully among the many desirable things a family wants to accomplish. Few families, on the other hand, have thought about dividing up the drinking water from the kitchen. They generally assume there is more than enough to meet everyone's needs.

• **Exchange Resources:** Exchange resources are the process of transferring one resource for another resource. Usually exchange does not in itself accomplish a goal, but we do it because we think that the exchange will help both parties attain their goals. For example, when we apply for a job, we are offering to exchange our resources of time, energy and expertise in return for a salary. We do it because this is an efficient way to accomplish goals like getting food, clothing and shelter. If we tried to allocate our time, energy and training directly towards getting food, shelter and clothing, most of us would find ourselves hungry, cold or poorly clothed, and may be all three.

• **Use Enough Resources to Accomplish Desired Goals Without Wasting Resources:** How much is enough? When the cost of family resources is greater than the benefit it confers, it is too much. When the supply is abundant, resources are often considered permanent and indestructible. This type of attitude that may lead to waste. Even when resources are scarce, there can be a lack of consumer knowledge and careless preparation on the part of the family members of precious resources.

Most people do not make explicit decisions to consume finite resources, such as energy, at some level or up to some amount. Rather, people engage in activities of their choice, presumably to meet particular goals, and they consume energy in the process.

- **Protect Those Resources on Hand:** Family resources that are protected will last longer than those that are treated carelessly. Equipment that is not kept clean and in good repair will soon become rusted and sluggish in operation. Clothes require immediate mending to prevent tearing during wear and laundering.

- **Balancing Choices Concerning Resources:** Achieving balance among family resources used to reach family goals increases the chances of living a well-balanced life. People must determine what represents balance in their own lives and assign resources to each area if they wish to achieve balance. Gross and Crandall (1967) conclude that the important factor in achieving balance among family resources is not an equal or even a specific distribution of resources among interests; rather, it is insistence that all resources be represented. Balance is needed among personal, family and community interests. Consciously allocating resources to these facets of life can improve this balance in families.

Factors Affecting Management of Family Resources

Family life management would be simple if it were possible to set goals, learn theories and standard practices, and simply program them into effect. However, many factors in addition to resources affect management. These include:

Value, Goals and Standards: The value, goals and standards people hold motivate them to deal with current situations and seek solutions to problems. These are internal motivations, and along with external demands they lead people to make decision regarding the use of specific resources. Example:

When people value education and commit to the goal of attaining a Master's degree, they are also committing themselves to the use of many resources – five or six years of time past high school and many calories of energy for studying and moving from building to building for classes. A collage education is costly in economic resources. Most of all, human capabilities are committed to concentration, study and research to achieve the grades that have become standard for proof of knowledge achievement.

The goals people set are important because they determine the quality and quantity of resources needed to achieve satisfaction. Regardless of the source of motivation behind goals, they do influence which resources will be used to reach the desired objectives. Attitudes that determine choices between such things as luxury and comfort, asceticism and self-indulgence, and stability or flexibility of expenditures, are reflections of people's feelings regarding the use of resources to achieve goals and what is to them a satisfying life style. Standards are attitudinal and reflect the quality of people's goals. They reflect what people believe as well as the desirable qualities or minimum acceptable characteristics of what they want.

Resourcefulness: Improving satisfaction from living requires resourcefulness. Baker defines resourcefulness as "the ability to recognize and effectively use resources". Before resources can be used to the family's advantage, it needs to be recognized and assessed in relation to the wants they can satisfy. Deacon and Firebaugh indicate that resourcefulness is one of the highest of human capacities. They describe resourcefulness as the ability to analyze, synthesize and reformulate varied insights and experiences creatively into new approaches to situations. When young children need materials for a kite, a parent will often find materials and use technical knowledge to build a kite that will fly. The parent uses social knowledge to enlist the children's help in building and decorating the kite and in mediating who will fly the kite first.

Decision-Making Style: The resourcefulness with which people view their resources and the pattern of goal seeking they typically employ contributes to their decision style. Decision-making is essentially a process of choice or resolution of alternatives. Decision making style is the typical habitual process of what an individual considers and does when making choices and the time frame utilized in resolution. Some people seem to get a rupee and a half's worth of living out of every rupee they spend. Others achieve far less. Some people frequently use facilities of the community, whereas others seldom think of parks for recreation or community services for assistance with problems. Some people's decision-making style is based on identifying all available relevant resources before acting. Other people concentrate on processing information relating to individual/family goals. Some prefer to use human resources to achieve their goals whenever possible, habitually choosing inputs of time, energy and psychomotor skills instead of monetary resources.

Stock and Flow of Resources: By now it should be obvious that people have many kinds of resources and that the amount of each may vary widely from one person to another. When people live together and share resources, some resources are increased and others are decreased. The managerial process changes the nature of the family's stock supply of all resources on hand at a particular time. The resource stock of a group is the management system's reservoir for action. As resources are used to supply daily needs and wants of the group, the supply of one resource is exchanged for another, is consumed, or is increased through its use. This ebb and flow of resources in and out of the resource stock is referred to as the flow of resources. The size of the resource stock makes a difference in the goals that may be attained. Housing and household goods compose the major material assets of families. In the management system, housing and household goods were goals before they became assets. This is true with many resources.

Factors of income and credit affect resource use by limiting or expanding purchasing power, or by making possible investments that bring greater family security. The supply, frequency and certainty of income flow to a family affect the allocation of other resources to provide for needs and satisfy wants. Although the group's goal influences how both economic and non-economic resources will be used, the quality and quantity of material possessions to serve the family are also affected by the economic resources available.

Income may serve as a goal to one person, as a resource to others, and as a constraint to yet others. Income does not guarantee happiness, but it can oil the wheels of satisfaction. Its instrumental value should be recognized and utilized, not only to bring personal satisfaction to its possessor, but also to produce a better way of life for all humankind.

Family Heritage: Heritage is legacy and tradition passed down from one generation to another. It is the family status or lot acquired by a person through birth-rank or position in the family and in the social environment. Family status and tradition within a group determine not only who will control the resources – who will make the decisions – but also the quantity and quality of the family group's resources that will be devoted to each family member. Family heritage is an influential factor in transmitting values and establishing approved ways of satisfying family wants. Asian families traditionally devote considerable time and effort to honoring the oldest family member, because their culture encourages respect for the elderly. Management patterns are thus influenced by the aged. Time is set aside by each family member to spend with the elderly. Their judgement is sought, and resources are devoted to their comfort and honor.

Family Life Cycle: The family life cycle is a comparatively new concept, which recognizes that the ebb and flow of family resources and demands upon them follow rather characteristic patterns during the lifetime of a family. It is important to understand the family life cycle for effective handling of resources at any stage, and for predicting the probable flow of resources from stage to stage. Adequate solution of family problems at each stage influences the success of later stages. The early beginning stage of the life cycle (i.e., marriage), though short, is highly significant. Managerial habits that will last for many years are formed at this time. The furnishing of a home may extend over a long period, but its major impact upon the family typically occurs in this first stage.

The expanding stage of the family life cycle begins with the birth of the first child and ends with the last child leaving home for university or work. When the costs of rearing a child from birth to 18 are summarized, the total is surprisingly large. However, it is a small amount when compared to the potential resource to the nation, which these young people represent. In the expanding stage, education of their children is a primary responsibility of parents, despite the fact that a large part of formal education today is provided at public expense.

The contracting family has assumed increasing importance, due to the large number of persons in this age group and the increased duration of the period itself. In this stage, major problems in the family stem from cessation of accustomed work, with negative effects upon income and the use of time. They also come from failing health and strength of family members.

Socio-Economic Status: Although in a democracy people tend to ignore the existence of social classes, there is without question an observable difference in the lives of families in India based on their socio-economic status. Despite the obvious imperfections of most attempts to analyze and compare status groups, the observed differences have significant implications for the ways in which families use all their resources to achieve their family goals. Ordinarily an individual's use of resources will be greatly influenced by his or her own status group in the family, and also the family's status in the society. In a higher class family, the standard of living is constantly upward moving. Hence, it is not surprising that many families, consciously or unconsciously, choose upward mobility as a goal. For example:

Dinner-related patterns vary widely for the three classes:

- In the lower class family, members tend to eat the meal prepared by the mother or sisters whenever they wish.
- Middle class dinners involve more formal procedures, with a set time for all family members present with assigned duties.
- Upper class families dine more formally than the other groups. Servants serve the dinner and no member of the family leaves during mealtime.

Size of Money Income: Another factor in determining the use of family resources is the size of the family's income. Although size of income is not the sole determinant of either standard of living or socio-economic status, it is closely related to both. People do not often select a standard of living far beyond what their income is, and the amount of their income may be determined by those occupations typical of their socio-economic group. While size of income affects the use of all family resources, most of the information available stresses the effect of size upon distribution of income among the various budget categories.

Guides to Increasing Satisfaction from Family Resources to Enrich Family Life

An overall objective in the use of family resources is to get the greatest satisfaction from them. Help in doing so is Elizabeth Hoyts' well known fourfold guide to maximize satisfactions in order to enrich and strengthen family life. These are:

- Increasing supply of family resources.
- Knowing alternative uses of family resources.
- Increasing utility and expanding appreciations.
- Balancing choices among family resources.

Increasing Supply of Family Resources: In order for a family to increase its available resources it must be aware of its total assets. Frequently, families are unaware of the total supply of the variety of resources available to them, particularly the less tangible or less obvious ones. It is unfortunate if family goals which might have been easily achieved by using all available resources are laboriously achieved through the use of only a few.

An example of the latter might be a woman who is compelled to work outside her home, but because of limited resource – knowledge, she has no way of caring for her four-year old daughter until she learns from a friend about an inexpensive nursery school for the children of working mother maintained at a nearby settlement house.

Another example is Mrs. Bimla who, because of limited energy, skimps on all other expenditures to provide elaborate labor. Saving equipment in meal preparation thus deprives other family members of some desired goods.

The entire family could have been challenged by the mother's need for help, and drawing upon many resources, could actually have achieved more satisfying results. The father might have improvised some labor-saving devices, and family members might have offered to shoulder some of the responsibility for meal preparation. Further, the mother might have seen opportunities for saving energy by simplifying menus and becoming "motion-minded" in preparing them.

This example has more to do with increasing family resource supply than its total income level. A change in attitude on the part of family members may also represent an increase in family resources available for reaching a desired family goal. It is often less easy to increase the supply of energy than to pursue other resources.

Knowing Alternative Use of Family Resources: Alternative uses of family resources raises the question of how family members become aware of alternative choices. In some cases, becoming acquainted with alternate uses of resources may call for a long-drawn out search, as when children from middle income families spend many days and weeks discussing with friends, teachers, and counselors what to look for and where to apply given their economic resources. On the other hand, to a person who has no money barriers and grown up in a family with brothers and sisters who have gone to college or have opted studies before him, many of these alternatives are already known. Yet, to assume that only the same alternatives are available to him as were to his siblings or relatives may be an example of not maximizing his satisfactions through understanding alternate uses of resources. The present guide assumes a knowledge or consideration of a sufficient number of alternatives so that the most satisfying use can be selected.

Increasing Utility and Expanding Appreciations: Not only may a general resource such as money have alternate uses, but some specific goods embody many possible uses. The selection of such goods increases utility. For example:

Mrs. Roy has selected one dress which she wears on many different occasions, without raising the brows of her friends. The beautiful bowl of oven china that she has purchased from the exhibition is now used for a casserole dish, for salad, for fruit, or even for decorating flowers for her dining table

The use of time to get a book from the library and then read it may open doors to new and growing interests, for example, a book on gardening, which is of utmost interest to the reader. The same amount of time given to watching a favorite television program may not open the doors to new interests.

Balancing Choices Regarding Family Resources: Most thinking people agree that a satisfying life must represent a synthesis of varying elements. One commonly speaks of a well-balanced life, although the elements involved are not present in equal or in known amounts. The important factor in a satisfying family life is probably not an equal or even a specific distribution of resources among interests, but rather an insistence that all be represented.

For example, a "butter" cake is made from flour, sugar, baking powder, fat and eggs. One may make a richer cake by increasing the amount of fat, or a less rich one by decreasing the fat, but other ingredients must be varied to maintain the necessary balance. If one omits fat completely, then no "butter" cake can be made. Therefore, the balance among the ingredients may vary according to the product desired or the resources available, but a product quite different and often unsatisfactory will result if all necessary ingredients are not represented. Macfie stresses the importance of balance among interests. He intimates that various interests serve as checks and balances upon each other, and further, that balance in itself provides some degree of satisfaction.

Family Resource Management as Integral to Family Life Education

Contemporary Indian families face a number of challenging issues, some of which arise from the social and economic environments in which they live. Parents find it difficult to develop good interpersonal relationships with children/adolescents when economic resources are insufficient to provide for the basic needs of safety and comfort. It is challenging to be patient and tolerant in communicating with a family member when one is exhausted from working two jobs to make a living. Parents are currently realizing that the commonly shared goals of making a living, creating a comfortable home, maintaining healthy bodies and minds, finding some enjoyment in life, and encouraging growth and development are family goals that are harder to achieve with the resources available in current economic environments. Many well-paying production jobs in India have been lost in recent years, and jobs in the service economy are providing lower incomes, thus making it hard to maintain a normal family life.

The income available for families affects not only their current level of living but also the investments that can be made in learning new skills or acquiring new competencies. If families can also take advantage of their community resources, time, abilities, talents and material things available, they can then often accomplish their goals. The problem-solving and decision-making competencies that are needed to meet these challenges are becoming increasingly more important in the complex and rapidly changing family/social environment in which Indian families live.

Because the purpose of family life education is to help individuals and families develop their capacities as family members and meet their needs for family living over the life span (Arcus, 1990), family life educators are needed to provide family resource management education. This can be accomplished through assisting others in identifying value conflicts, prioritizing goals, and developing resource awareness and alternative-mindedness about resource uses, as well as strengthening the family's decision-making competencies.

Education for family resource management had its historical origin in the discipline of Home Economics (now commonly referred to as Home Science in India) and was unique because of the learning environments provided for students. In the early days home economists realized that the mental processes of management needed to be implemented in action for the most effective learning to occur. They had already discovered the ".....new realization that learning needed to be subjective and experiential, and that learners needed empowering involvement in the body of knowledge and its application" (Allen & Crosbie-Burnett, 1992). The foundational belief supporting this realization was that they considered both classroom and laboratory experiences to be a necessity for learners of all ages.

The scope of family resource management education must be broadened to ensure the mutual survival and well being of all members of the human family. There are a few examples in the literature on family resource management education of programs that include a global resource perspective. The challenges for future educators are in learning how to create "teachable moments" that will result in major attitudinal and behavioral changes. But questions remain. How, for example, do we develop a curriculum that assists students in understanding the cumulative effects of family decisions on the natural environment? How do we help students realize that environmental quality is more than a question of quality of life; it is often a matter of life and death? Finally, how do family life educators incorporate family resource management into an already full curriculum or program and infiltrate their communities with this valuable knowledge and skills? These and many other challenges need to be carefully considered by concerned citizens and professionals who are involved, formally or informally, in any type of family life education.

Conclusion

Family resources are the tools and talents with which people build lifestyles and attain family goals. When used in family goal attainment, family resources are assets. When left unused or underdeveloped, they become constraints on the potential accomplishments of people and their living companions. Family resources are human, economic, material, and environmental. Families need to be aware of the total resources available to them and how to cultivate and nurture them to their benefit the the benefit of others.

The salient characteristics of family resources that assist in their management include utility, limitation, interchangeability, transferability and alternate uses. Family resources must be available in the place they are needed and at the time needed if they are to provide service. The inherent characteristics of family resources allow people to adjust resource use to life goals and the current demands of their environments. Principles of resource allocation are reminders that some natural resources are scarce, and that too many personal possessions can become a constraint on the very life style that the resources were meant to improve.

Factors affecting the use of resources have been explored in this chapter, including the family life cycle and stock and flow of resources. Guides to increasing satisfactions in the use of family resources include the understanding of their interrelatedness, along with the possibilities of alternate use; the principles of increasing utility and expanding appreciation; and the achievement of balance among interest.

The focus in family resource management education is on the internal dynamics of family decision making processes and on the goal directed behaviors of families in improving their quality of life. These include decision making, valuing, planning, communicating, and organizing activities to guide the use of family resources. Through family resource management education, individuals and families are assisted in gaining some degree of control over the events of their everyday living, to mobilize resources towards their values and central life purposes, and to address their changing goals and concerns over the life span. Thus, the component of family life education helps families to prioritize goals, develop resource awareness, address value conflicts, and strengthen decision-making capacities.

Family resources are important because they are the building blocks of management. The way they are used influences the health and well-being of the family. Family resource management is concerned with facing situations and opportunities that may change the status quo, threaten achievement of desired standard of living, or offer challenges for personal growth. Family resource management addresses perplexing situations that involve doubt, uncertainty, or difficulty and call for a choice of action that can lead to a successful adjustment and even a solution. It values the family as a problem-solving group where management is a means of engaging some of the most prized qualities of life.

References

Burr, R.W., Day, D.R., & Bahr, S.K. (1993). *Family science*. Belmont, CA: Brooks/Cole Pub. Co.

Decan, R.E., & Firebaugh, F.M. (1981). *Family resource management: Principles and applications.* Boston: Allyn & Bacon.

Duggal, G. (2001). Managing your money. *Women's Era, 28*, March (Second), New Delhi: Delhi Press Patra Prakashan.

Gross, I.H., & Crandall, E.H. (1967). *Management for modern families.* New Delhi: Sterling Publishers (P) Ltd.

Karpel, M. (1986). Testing, promoting and preserving family resources: Beyond pathology and power. In M. Karpel (Ed.), *Family* *resources: The hidden partner in family therapy* (pp. 174-234). New York: Guilford.

Nickell, P., & Dorsey, M.J. (1991). *Management in family living.* New Delhi: Wiley Eastern Limited.

Pell, E.C., & Cohen, E.P. (1995). Parents and advocacy systems: A family system approach. In M.C. Wang, M.C. Reynnold, & H. J. Walberg (Eds.), *Handbook of special and remedial education: Research and practice* (pp. 371-439). New York: Elsevier.

Poddar, T. (2002). Effective time management. *Women's Era, 29*, April (Second), New Delhi: Delhi Press Patra Prakashan Ltd.

Rao, J. (2001). Save for a rainy day. *Women's Era, 28*, March (First), New Delhi: Delhi Press Patra Prakashan Ltd.

Retting, D.K., Rossman, M.M., & Hogan, M.J. (1993). Educating for family resource management. In M.E. Arcus, J.D. Schvaneveldt, & J.J. Moss (Eds.) (pp. 161-184). *Handbook of family life education: The practice of family life education.*

Rice, S.A., & Tucker, M.S. (1986). *Family life management* (6th ed.). New York: Macmillan Pub.

9

Population Explosion and Family Planning Measures in India

N. Jayapoorani

Population explosion stands as the single greatest barrier to India's progress and development. The need for controlling the population through various family planning measures and education in India is essential for the general welfare of the country. This chapter sheds light on the population growth trend in India and explains family planning programs that are being adopted by our government to hold population growth in check. Understanding the significance of population explosion and its impact on family life is discussed at length.

Population Explosion: Demography, Causes, and Consequences

During the past few decades there has been a worldwide concern about the growth of population of the world, and especially of developing countries such as India. Development of any country essentially means the ability to attain material progress, as well as its capacity to satisfy the demands of her people for a better living. Rapid population growth reduces per capita income, deteriorates the standards of living, limits family savings, increases unemployment, results in high prices, retards industrialization, lowers production, contributes to poor health, illiteracy, ignorance, and diseases; leads to a fall in standards of education, housing and health; creates environmental problems; and has a negative impact on social services and the social security system. In sum, population explosion has an immeasurable effect on the individual, family, and the nation at large.

According to the provisional results of the 2001 Census of India, which began at 00.00 hours of March 1, 2001 as the reference date, the population of India stood at 1,027,015,247 comprising 531,277,078 males and 495,738,169 females, thereby making India the second largest country in the world after China to exceed the one billion mark. India's share of the world's population is 16.7 per cent. The percentage of growth of the last decade as a whole has declined from 23.86 during 1981-91 to 21.34 during 1991-2001. Population growth slowed to an average rate of 1.95 percent a year in the past decade from 2.16 percent registered in 1981-91. The lowest growth rate was recorded in Kerala at 9.42 percent, followed by Tamil Nadu at 11.19 and Andra Pradesh at 13.86. Andra Pradesh showed the sharpest decline among all major states which averaged 10.34 percent. Haryana, Bihar, Sikkim, Nagaland, and Manipur have shown an acceleration in population growth. The first census of the second millennium presents a very positive picture. Literacy rates have increased creditably in the past decade, the sex ratio has improved, and the population growth rate has slowed down. Population of our country has increased by about 181 million persons between 1991- 2001. This is more than the estimated population of Brazil, the fifth most populous country.

The country at present has 57 more persons per square km as compared to 1991. Almost two thirds of the population lives in states and union territories. The increase in literacy in the past decade has been the highest ever. Literacy rates have improved for both men and women, and the rates among the population seven years and above now stands at 65.38 percent. The corresponding figures for males and females are 75.85 and 54.16 percent, respectively. The figures show that three-fourths of the male population and more than half of the female population are literate. Literacy rates have improved considerably in the traditionally less developed states. Rajasthan, Orissa, and Madhya Pradesh have shown a literacy growth rate of 15 to 20 percent since 1991. The average exponential growth rate has declined from 2.14 percent in 1981-91 to 1.93 percent today. The number of females for 1000 males is 933. In the 1991 Census this ratio was 927. The highest sex ratio has been reported in Kerala. This state's sex ratio is 1058 females for 1000 males. Haryana registered the lowest sex ratio of 861 among the major states. The sex ratio in the 0-6 age group was 945 in 1991 and declined to 927 in 2001.

India's fertility rate and infant mortality rate have remained at very high levels, primarily due to object poverty and widespread illiteracy, especially among females. Total fertility Rate (TFR), or average number of children per mother, is still at 3/4 level (1993), which is far greater than the ideal number at replacement level (2/1 children). In rural areas the total Fertility Rate (TFR) is still 3.7 children, which is 36 percent higher than the urban TFR of 2.7. Infant Mortality Rate (IMR) is still very high. It was 78.5 deaths of infants per 1000 live births. The under age five mortality rate was 109.3 deaths per 1000 children born during 5 years preceding the survey (1993). In India, infant mortality and total fertility are intimately connected, so we need to first reduce IMR before the TFR level can be expected to decline. This calls for a multi-pronged global strategy to check population growth. The world's six billion inhabitants include over one billion young people aged 15-24, the largest such group ever. Due to sheer numbers, young people's reproductive behavior, life style choices, consumer habits, and impact on the environment will largely determine the future of the planet.

Causes of Population Growth in India

The principal reason for the recent rapid rise in India's population (as in much of the developing world) is a sharp fall in the death rates, primarily due to improvements in health care. The availability of vaccines and their accessibility to the poor, total or near eradication of certain deadly diseases, an increase in food availability resulting from a rise of food production, and the development of distribution networks, have contributed substantially to the decrease in mortality. As a result, the gap between birth and death rates has widened, thus leading to high growth. The decline in mortality rates in developing countries like India has been much faster than those in the developed world; hence, there has been a much greater acceleration of population growth.

Most developed countries today have fertility rates that are near the replacement level; i.e., the population replaces itself and does not expect to increase in the near future. The developing countries, generally, have high fertility rates and exponential growth. Some countries, most notably China, have been successful in lowering fertility to a replacement level, but in other countries fertility rates continue to be high and the growth rapid — some over three percent per annum. India has experienced some fertility decline but is far from reaching a replacement level. Thus, its growth might be defined as somewhere between moderate and high. A population continues to grow for some time even after its fertility comes down to replacement level. This is a phenomenon referred to as "momentum of population growth".

In India the life expectancy was only 20-25 years at the beginning of the century, but it is nearly 60 years today. There have been improvements in the availability of food, consumer goods, housing, health care, and so forth. So why then should we be concerned about population growth in India? It must be noted that the improvements in living conditions have taken place not necessarily because of population growth, but because advances in technology have made it possible for the earth to support such a large population at a high level of living. Moreover, the rate of growth in the past was small, generally below one per cent, per annum. It was possible for science and technology to advance sufficiently to raise the standard of living of the growing population. How, demographers wonder about what the future will bring. Can we expect further notable advances to help production can keep pace with the rapidly growing population? This is the concern for all at this time in history.

Effects of Population Growth

The consequences of population explosion are complex. In developing countries, rapid population growth increases the need for more food being produced on smaller and smaller areas of land which is already suffering from over use. The problem of feeding millions of people is a monumental task. Basic requirements such as clean drinking water, adequate housing, available health care, sanitation and hygiene are difficult to meet for a great number of India's citizens. There are also problems of marketing and transporting food and other consumer goods, raw materials, capital equipment, and the like. Public expenditures are frequently diverted to welfare activities without creating any tangible assets. The rapid growth of population also tends to depress people's per capita income, lower their standard of living, lowers the rate of capital formation. A very large part of the available capital and resources has to be spent for duplication of facilities for day to day life, and for production and procurement of food, shelter and clothing for the growing population. For example, the per capita availability for food grain in the country in the year 1971 was 542 gms/day. This figure decreased to 478.5gms/day in the year 1979.

It was further reduced to 495.5 gms/day in the year 1981 and 436.5 gms/day in the year 1983.

Some of the specific correlates or outcomes of population growth are briefly discussed as follows.

Food: During the period 1968-1981 the population in India increased somewhere between 161 and 181 million people. However, food production increased only by a total of 30.35 million tones, in spite of tremendous efforts taken. The rate of growth of food production was only 2 or 3 million tons per year, as compared to 14 or 15 million in population growth. If each person is to receive the minimum quantity of food grains at an annual rate of 215 kg early in this new millennium, 230 million tons of food grains would have to be produced annually. However, this is over 30 percent of the current production, which is very difficult to achieve. This is true for all major foodstuffs, including milk, edible oils, rice, and sugar.

Inadequate and improper food intake contributes to nutritional deficiencies and a host of other problems. According to a survey conducted by the National Nutrition Monitoring Bureau, only around 40 per cent of the children in India have diets which can be considered adequate, and it has been estimated that around 45 to 50 million children below five years of age subsist on a diet that is totally inadequate, particularly in terms of energy. In 1989, 59.6 percent of families in India had at least one member suffering from Protein Calorie Malnutrition (PCM), and it is believed to be worse today. In short, the gap between the population growth and the required food supply is widening and causing serious concerns to all.

Clothing: The per capita availability of cotton cloth has been steadily declining in recent years.

Housing: A great majority of the rural population in India lives in backward and blighted areas and in conditions that have minimum amenities. In cities, population pressure has resulted in over crowding and ever-expanding slums. India's urban population will soon be the largest in the world. Planning for this urban population will be the difficult task. Nearly 61 to 72 percent of the population is forced to live in single rooms, including cities such as Delhi (61 percent), Calcutta (71.9 percent), Bombay (72.3 percent), Madras (67.5 percent), Ahmedabad (65.3 percent) and Kanpur (62.3 percent). Problems of air and water pollution, as well as and urban decay, have thus emerged and are adversely affecting the quality of life of the nation.

Education: After Independence, only 52 per cent of Indians were literate (male, 63.86 and females 39.42). By the year 2015 there will be only standing rooms in the schools and colleges. Although the directive principles of state policy in the Indian constitution indicate that states would strive to provide free and compulsory education to all children up to the age of 14 within a period of 10 years, it has not been possible to achieve the above goal despite a network of 8.5 lakhs schools and 34.9 lakhs teachers.

Employment: The number of job seekers on the live registers of employment exchanges increased from 34.34 lakhs in 1969 to 178.38 lakhs in 1981, 262.70 lakhs in 1985, 301.31 lakhs in 1986, and 304.95 lakhs in 1987. Today the union Government has put the total number of educated unemployed at an astronomical 45.37 lakhs. Nearly all sociological studies of the militancy in Punjab have pointed out the high incidence of educated unemployment as the catalytic factor for the spread of terrorism.

Problems of Urbanization: The concentration of an over growing population in the country's mega cities poses serious problems. These include but are not limited to excessive crowding, sprawling slums, pollution, transport problems, inadequate basic services, environmental degradation, rising crime, and exploitation of certain groups that leads to strains in the political and social fabric of the community. The rapidly expanding slums lack even the most basic provisions of housing and sanitation. The traditional family and social structures are crumbling, and where parental discipline is breaking down, children are prone to be in the streets, using drugs and stirring up violence.

National Income: The national income has increased at about 4.5 per cent per annum in recent years, but the per capita income has increased at the rate of 2 per cent per annum only. This difference is due to the growth of population at the rate of 2.5 per cent per annum.

Farmland and Forestry: Large areas of existing farmlands are depleted in India which can no longer grow enough food to feed the people who live there. From the per capita land availability of 0.60 hectare in 1971, it came down to 0.41 hectare in 1988, and this was further reduced to 0.33 in 2001. Higher population density has led to more intense use of farmland and is the sole cause of increased soil erosion, degradation and deforestation. India has lost half of its tree cover in the last forty years. Large scale deforestation now occurring at the rate of 1.5 million hectares per year would make India virtually forestless in 2050.

Industrialization: Industrialization has changed the chemistry of the earth's atmosphere and contributed to acid rain, holes in the Ozone layer, and climatic change. Some of the damages done in the environment are irreversible within human time table. Environmentalist Barry says that population growth is responsible for 24 to 31 percent of the environmental degradation.

The Concept and Significance of Family Planning

India is the largest functioning democracy in the world with the second largest population on 2.4 per cent of the world's land area. The population In India is increasing by approximately 18 million every year. Recognizing that the planning of families would enhance individual health and welfare, the Government of India was the first in the world to initiate a comprehensive family planning program in 1951. In keeping with the democratic traditions of the country, family welfare programs seek to promote, on a voluntary basis, responsible planned parenthood through independent choice of family welfare methods best suited to the acceptors.

Family planning is a very important component of population control. The status and roles of men and women have changed over the past several years. Thus, the goals and expectations of marriage partners also have changed in terms of the timing, number and spacing of children. Traditionally, it has been the wife/mother who stayed at home and cared for the children, even if she had previously been employed outside the home. A new trend had emerged which is the result of the dramatic movement of married women and mothers into the world of work and careers. Children, however, are costly in terms of the time, energy, and money expended on them, and many couples have realized the value of having a small family, spaced in a way that will not interfere with the wife's employment outside the home. Effective family planning is critical to those marriages where the wife's employment is essential for the economic well-being of the family.

There are several compelling reasons why family planning is desirable. One has to do with protecting the health of the mother and children. Births to mothers who are too young or old, or births that are too close together, create extra health hazards to both mothers and children. Becoming a parent is a significant, irrevocable, and stressful event that requires preparation and considerable adjustments. Timing is especially important, since childbirth has a major impact on the individuals involved. Thus, the birth of a child to an unmarried 17-year-old may generate a personal, social and economic crisis, whereas a planned birth to a happily married 28-year-old would certainly not have similar effects. The psychological impact on the mother and father are lessened considerably if parenthood is chosen and welcomed. Family planning is necessary for the good of the marriage and the family. Having children imposes strains on the marriage. Yet, a majority of teenage coupes have a baby within one year after marriage. Not only do young couples begin having children at an early age, but they also have more children. The more they have, the greater the strain on them and their marriage.

The Government's Effort in Popularizing the Notion of a Small Family

At the time of India's independence there were but a few health facilities serving the common people. The past five decades have witnessed significant investments in developing a network of health centers all over India. Through this vast infrastructure of sub-centers, primary health centers, and community health centers, the government has been playing the role of a facilitator by providing family planning services for the people to plan their families. The family planning program in India started with a very cautious approach. The first five year plan launched in 1952 emphasized field research with a view to identifying values, norms, customs and beliefs concerning childbearing. Since then this program has undergone several revisions.

In 1971, India played an important role at the UN world population conference at Bucharest. One of the results of the world population conference was the declaration of national population policy in India in April 1976. Some of the more important features of the National Population Policy of 1976 are:

a. Increase the age of marriage from 15 to 18 years for girls and from 18 to 21 for boys.
b. Freezing of the population figures at the 1971 level until the year 2001 for purpose of representation in the National Parliament, as well as for allocation of central assistance, devolution of taxes, and so forth.
c. Link a part of central assistance to the states for their development with their performance in family planning.
d. Give greater attention to girls' education.
e. Provide a proper place for population education in the total system of education.
f. Involve all Ministries/Departments of the Government in family planning programs.
g. Increase monetary compensation for sterilization.
h. Institute group awards as incentives for various organizations

and bodies representing the people at local levels, including Zila parishads and Panchayat Samities.

i. Create closer associations among voluntary organizations, particularly those representing women, with the implementation of family planning programs.

j. Enhance research related to family planning.

k. Make greater use of motivational media, particularly in rural areas, for increasing acceptance of family planning.

In the 1970's the policy was welcomed by all sectors of society. Its implementation was taken up in all States in right earnest. The many programs invigorated the climate in the country in favor of family planning. Leaders of public opinion came forward to help the Government in promoting the family planning movement. Development departments of the Government started sharing responsibilities with the health and family welfare infrastructure at all levels in a more effective manner. Women across the country also united in many ways. The climate created by the new family planning program encouraged them to come forward with the demand that they should have their rightful say in planning the birth of their children. People on the whole started feeling that it was important that they should plan for their families. Appropriate messages were designed for them through mass media and interpersonal communication messages, which were in tune with the country's cultural ethos and the requirements of a vibrant society moving forward towards a better future.

However, not all was well. There were allegations that some malpractices had crept in while implementing the programs under the National Population Policy of 1976. So in June 1977 a new policy was created. In pursuance of the new policy to eliminate coercion, all measures, as well as rules and regulations, which had the slightest element of compulsion or coercion, were dropped and the welfare approach to the problem was increasingly emphasized. The wider policy of family welfare covered education, health, maternity and child care, family planning, and nutrition. It was also emphasized that the change in the name from family planning to family welfare was a reflection of the Government's thrust towards promoting the total welfare of the family and community. Many of the other measures outlined in the National population Policy declared in 1976 were retained. These included the following:

1. Raising the minimum legal age at marriage for girls to 18 and for boys to 21
2. Taking the population figure of 1971 till the year 2001, in all cases where population was a factor, as in the allocation of central assistance to State Plans, devolution of taxes and duties and grants- in-aid.
3. Accepting the principle of linking 8 percent of the central assistances to State Plans with their performance and to success in the family welfare program.
4. Plans to popularize the family welfare program and use of all media for this purpose.

Methods Adopted for Encouraging Small Families

There are several types of contraceptive methods in use today that provide families with the option and technology for having a small family. These methods range from those considered to be medically safe and effective to those viewed as ineffective and potentially harmful to one's health. In addition, the various methods of birth control vary considerably in terms of their advantages, disadvantages, and financial cost. The major objections which people may have about using any particular contraceptive method, and whether or not they will actually use that method, relate directly to the perceived advantages, disadvantages, and costs involved. They also have a lot to do with the family's religious and cultural background and personal set of values and beliefs. A method is more likely to be avoided if it is perceived to have the disadvantages of being difficult to use or unnatural; if it interferes with the spontaneity and enjoyment of sexual intercourse by requiring that the partners take time during foreplay to apply the method; if it is too costly; or if it has too high a failure rate.

Common methods of birth control are discussed under the following headings:

Chemical methods such as the pill which alter the body's hormone balance to prevent pregnancy.

Barrier methods such as the diaphragm, creams and jellies, foams and condoms, which prevent the sperm from entering the women's uterus by providing an impenetrable shield.

Action methods such as surgical sterilization, withdrawal (coitus interruptus), rhythm, and lactation (a woman nursing a child), none of which provide an artificial barrier or introduce a chemical into the body, and all of which require some kind of effort on the part of the male, female, or both partners to prevent a pregnancy.

Inter-Spousal Communication Concerning the Use of Modern Contraception

The national family planning program has undergone major restructuring during the part two decades. The introduction of female family planning workers at the grassroots level to supply modern contraceptives free of cost has been the major intervention responsible for the success of the program. Additionally, health centers have been built at the lowest level of administration for providing basic family planning services. Strong motivational campaigns and mobile clinics are held regularly to motivate and provide couples with various contraceptive methods in order to increase the chances of them having a smaller family. The mass media, including TV, radio, newspapers, and village drama groups, are utilized to inform people about the benefits of family planning.

Research has shown that inter-spousal communication in Bangladesh has changed in recent years from general conversation about family planning to method specific or objective specific interaction.

Population Education as a Means to Family Planning

With only 2.4 percent of the world's land area, India is supporting 16 percent of world's total population. Thus, we need population education to inculcate the responsibility of reproductive behaviors among the younger generation of the society who will be the future parents and future leaders of the country.

Population education is the process by which the participant investigates and explores the nature and meaning of population processes, population characteristics, causes of population change and the consequences of these processes, and characteristics and changes in one's self, family and the world. UNESCO identifies, "Population Education" as an educational program to develop in the learners, with goals that include:

a) Understanding the inter-relationship between population and quality life.
b) Responsible attitudes and behavior towards population issues.
c) Skills in making rational decisions about population related matters.

The UNESCO workshop of 1970 defined population education as an educational program which provides for a study of population in the family, community, nation and the world with the purpose of developing in the student's rational and responsible attitudes. The objectives of population education are to develop awareness and understanding about:

i) Population situations (national and world)
ii) Basic demographic concepts and theories
iii) Processes of population change
iv) Concept of equality of life in different socio-cultural settings
v) Interrelationship between population change and different aspects of quality of life at the micros and macros levels
vi) Consumption explosion and its implications on quality of life for others
vii) Human reproduction and family welfare

viii) Population, plans, policies and programs

Population conditions of our country which include birth rate, death rate, growth rate, sex ratio, density, life expectancy, rural-urban distribution, the total dependent population, optimum growth rate, zero growth rate, population explosion, etc., form the contents under demography. Ecological and social factors include aspects such as pollution of air, water and land and the effect of these on people; depletion of natural resources due to population increase; urbanization such as over crowding and pollution; and other such factors. Malnutrition, nutritional needs of various vulnerable groups, meeting nutritional needs within available means, the need for improved food production, etc., all fall under the rubric of nutrition education. Included are poor health and low quality health facilities resulting from population growth, the spread of diseases, increased mortality, and concomitants of population increase such as increased illiteracy and child labor. Also inherent to the concept of family planning's emphasis on small families is the definition of what a small family is; the advantages to the individual, couple, family and nation of small families; the relationship between late marriage and child bearing and a small family; the comparison of expenditure per month of a large sized family and a small family; and the relationship between morbidity and size of the family. Basic human physiology and the reproductive system of males and females, as well as biological factors affecting the population growth of the family, are also emphasized.

About 50 percent of India's populations are below 18 years of age. This age group should not be allowed to enter the reproductive stage without proper orientation to the population problem. Secondly, the marriage age is exceptionally low in India as compared to that of many other countries. Hence, population problems and planned parenthood should be topics that are an integral part of the secondary school curriculum. This type of education should extend through the university level as well, but more importantly it should be implemented at a grassroots community level through both the public and private sector.

Family Welfare Measures

Family planning program of the government was changed to family welfare programs which had to embrace all aspects of family welfare, particularly those which were designed to protect and promote the health of mothers and children. It became a part of the total concept of positive health and was integrated with other welfare programs that included nutrition, food, clothing, shelter, safe drinking water, education, employment, and women's welfare. The family welfare program seeks to promote, on a voluntary basis, responsible and "planned parenthood" with the one child norm (male or female) through independent choice of family welfare methods best suited to acceptors.

Another threatening phenomenon to family life in India is AIDS, where India ranks near the top in prevalence but average or worse in terms of AIDS awareness and education. STD's are also affecting all aspects of economic, social and cultural life, and lack of knowledge and the reluctance of great numbers of people to use condoms are largely responsible for the spread of these diseases. Since 1986 when the first case of HIV infection was detected in the country, the Government of India has taken several steps to educate people about AIDS and STD's, but there is still a long way to go.

National Population Policy and Its impact on Family Life

The policy drafted by the Government of India (April 16, 1976) included the following measure with regard to restricting population growth:

- Minimum needs programs to alleviate poverty.
- Family planning as a tool to check population growth.
- Increasing of minimum age at marriage to check population growth.
- Importance of female literacy.
- Monetary compensation to induce acceptance of family planning.
- Participation of voluntary organizations in family planning

programs.

- Government's proposal to make sterilization compulsory.

According to Parsuraman (1994), family planning and population policy influences the structure and well being of the family. The mechanisms through which family planning and population policies affect families are:

- Increase in age at marriage for boys and girls, and delay in formation of new families.
- Delay in addition of new members to the family due to family planning practices.
- Relief to women from the burden of child bearing and provision to them of opportunity to enter gainful employment and activities.
- Indirect help to improve the survival chance of infants and children, and to a large extent help to allocate the family's scarce economic resources for the welfare of children.

In conclusion, it is well known that early marriage and child-bearing seriously undermine the health conditions and welfare of women and the newborn child. Current population policies aim at increasing the age at marriage of girls and help in enhancing the welfare of women in a variety of ways, but much more needs to be done. Further economic opportunities for women are central to family welfare. The social, economic, educational, and political empowerment of women will raise their decision-making capabilities and opportunities and help them protect and manage their reproductive health. These changes will have a positive overall impact on Indian society.

References

Amuja, R. (1992). *Social problems of India*. Jaipur: Rawat Pub.

Arul Selvi, K., & Nalina Devi, R. (1992). Population awareness of the animators of the mass literacy programme. *Research Highlights, 2* (2), 96-101.

Devadas, R.P., & Jaya, N. (2000). *Textbook on child development*: New Delhi: Macmillan Pub.

Jaya. N., & Premila, E. (1998). Creating awareness among rural adolescent girls towards small family norm. *Research Highlights, 8* (3), 128-132.

Jorgansen, S.R. (1986). *Marriage and family*. New York: Macmillan Pub.

Kamal, N. (1999). Interspousal communication on family planning as a determinant of the use of modern contraception in Bangladesh. *The Journal of Family Welfare, 45* (1), 31-33.

Kathija Beebi, P., & Velmayil, C. (1998). *Awareness on reproductive health and rights among young girls in Coimbatore district*. A Thesis Submitted to the Avinashilingam Institute for Home Science and Higher Education for Women,Coimbatore. In partial fulfillment of the requirements for the degree of M.Phil.

Kumari. P.V., Srinivasulu, J. (2001). Attitude of learners towards population education at CEC,Santh Nagar in Tirupati. *Indian Journal of Adult Education, January-March,* 5-10.

Macklin, E.D. (1983). *Contemporary families and alternate life styles.* New York: Sage Pub.

Ministry of Information and Broadcasting, India (2001). *Reference Annual.* Government of India: Minister of Information and Broadcasting.

Nalina Devi, R., & Padma, G. (1992). Attitude of slum women towards acceptance of small family norm. *Research Highlights, 2* (3), 168-172.

Nalina Devi. R, Sudha. J. (1992). Rural women's utilization of existing services for limiting family size. *Research Highlights, 2*(4), 266-270.

Nalina Devi, R., & Suganthy, J. (1991). Evolving and evaluating learning materials for neo-literals on population education, *Research Highlights, 1* (4), 290-296.

Ravindra Kumar, V.K. (1989). *Indian population control: A study of crucial aspects.* New Delhi: Anmol Pub.

Reddy, K.M. (1998). *Population and society in India*. New Delhi: Kanishka Pub.

Rice, F.P. (1990). *Intimate relationships, marriages, and families.* Mountain View, CA: Mayfield Pub.

Sharma, A.K. (1987). *Fertility and family planning in rural areas*. New Delhi: Mittal Pub.

Srinivasamurthy, A.D. (1981). *Investment allocation in Indian planning*. New Delhi: Himalaya Publishing House.

Sunitha, N.C., & Nalina Devi, R. (1992). Impact of population education teaching materials on animators of mass literacy programme. *Research Highlights, 2* (1), 6-11.

Suriakanthi, A. (1999). *An introduction to child development*. Gandhigram: Kavitha Pub.

10

Reproductive Health and Sex Education for Children and Adolescents

T. Banoomathi

The objective of the present chapter is to provide an overview of the realities of reproductive health scenarios in India. It is visible in the glaring spotlight of health statistics that death and illness from reproductive causes are highest among women. Enhancement of reproductive health is a notable contribution to the development of women, family, and the society at large. Guided by this goal, a comprehensive reproductive health care program which covers integrated topics such as pregnancy and safe motherhood, postnatal health, menstruation, reproductive cancer, sexually transmitted diseases (STD's) and acquired immunodeficiency syndrome (AIDS), menopause, and the need for sex education are discussed. Long-term solutions to prolong life expectancy in good health are also suggested in the context of family life education.

During the past few decades, there has been a reawakening that health is a fundamental human right, and it has become a worldwide social goal. Health is essential to the satisfaction of basic human needs and to an improved quality of life that it is to be attained by all people. Health is usually subjugated to other needs deemed to be more important, such as wealth, power, prestige, knowledge, and security; however, without health one can enjoy none of these. In addition to physical and mental health, issues relating to reproductive health have drawn national and international attention and concern.

The concept of reproductive health refers to the process in which reproduction is accomplished in a state of complete physical, mental, and social well-being, not merely in the absence of disease. According to Fathallah (1988), reproductive health means that people have the ability to reproduce and regulate their fertility, and women are able to experience pregnancy and childbirth safely. Couples have the choice to engage in sexual relations without the fear of pregnancy, while the outcome of pregnancy is successful in terms of maternal and infant survival and well-being.

The Platform of the Fourth World Conference on Women held in Beijing in September, 1995 declared that programs for the enhancement and education of women's sexual and reproductive health are notable contributions to the development of women's welfare and thereby to family welfare. But an overview of women's health status in India presents a sobering picture. It is distressing to note that, even in 21st century, death and illness due to reproductive causes are highest among women in India. Many women are in charge of housework and are also responsible for earning an income outside of the home. Inadequate support from the family and community can take a heavy toll on their reproductive health.

India is a male-dominated society, and reproductive issues are considered to be the responsibility of women. Therefore, awareness generation programs must include information on topics concerning family welfare. When women are given the knowledge that enables them to make informed choices about what happens to their lives and bodies, the entire family will benefit. Sociologically speaking, the issues of reproductive health are affected by other cultural issues, including gender sensitivity and the ability to communicate messages in the proper manner and environment. Women are generally prevented from interacting with healthcare workers by elders in the family. Elders usually hold the belief that workers in the health industry provide inaccurate information and attitudes about birth and family size to women because they are motivated by earning incentives for the fulfillment of government quotas, and that these workers are not actually concerned with the women's health care needs.

At the dawn of the 21st Century, women's reproductive health has become a human rights issue. In order to create awareness among women and their family members, it is essential to have a comprehensive reproductive health care program included in the education of children from school-age onwards. A program of this type should include:

- Pregnancy and Safe Motherhood
- Abortion
- Infertility
- Family Planning
- Postnatal Health
- Menstruation
- Prevention of Reproductive Cancer
- Preventive Care for Sexually Transmitted Diseases (STD's) and Acquired Immunodeficiency Syndrome (AIDS)
- Menopause
- Reproductive Health Care for Men
- Sex Education for Children and Adolescents
- Family Life Education in Schools

Pregnancy and Safe Motherhood

A healthy and fit body is the best possible place to implant and carry a fetus to term. Good prenatal and postnatal.care will contribute to the health of mothers and babies. A baby's health depends to a large extent on the reproductive health of his or her parents at the moment of conception.

Child bearing is physically, psychologically, and socially imposes additional health needs and problems on women. In developing countries, maternal mortality is a leading cause of death among women of reproductive age. Malnutrition and its concomitant problems of decreased body weight and height, poor weight gain during pregnancy, and low hemoglobin levels (anemia) are some of the causes of maternal mortality in India. Maternal deaths are also attributed to domestic violence, poverty, and gender inequality. Adhering to the following guidelines during pregnancy may lessen the risks to the growing fetus:

- The correct diet and exercise, as well as regular check-ups, are essential.
- Measuring height and weight gives a clue regarding the size of the pelvis.
- Routine urine tests will reveal protein levels, kidney infections or presence of gestational diabetes.
- Routine blood tests will reveal blood type, level of iron, immunity to certain diseases (e.g., rubella), and the presence of infections (e.g., hepatitis B or syphilis).
- An initial vaginal examination will help to feel the uterus and check for pelvic abnormalities.
- Tests of maternal serum level for alpha-fetoprotein (AFP) will indicate the risk of fetal abnormalities.
- Ultrasound can assess fetal maturity, prospective multiple births, delivery date, position and condition of the placenta, and fetal abnormalities. It will also reveal the fetus' position in the uterus, which may have implications for the delivery.
- If vaginal bleeding occurs, the doctor should be consulted immediately.
- Seek expert advice of a genetic counselor if either parent has experienced any of the following:

– A previous child was born with a genetic (e.g., cystic fibrosis) or chromosomal disorder (e.g., Down syndrome).

- A previous child was born with a congenital defect.
- Family history of mental handicap or abnormal development.
- Blood relationship between husband and wife.
- Maternal history of repeated miscarriages.
- Either parent is over 35.

Over the past few decades, women in India have taken greater control of their own health care needs. Children need parents who are healthy and responsible to provide them with adequate care and attention for proper development.

Abortion

Abortion is theoretically defined as the termination of a pregnancy before the fetus becomes viable, whether it occurs spontaneously or is induced. Women choose to have an abortion for a number of reasons. In India, induced abortions are more commonly seen for female fetuses then male fetuses. The following are the conditions under which a pregnancy can be terminated by choice:

- Medical
- Eugenic
- Humanitarian
- Socio-economic
- Failure of contraceptive devices

Abortions, whether spontaneous or induced, may lead to complications that could result in maternal morbidity and mortality. Complications that could occur during the abortion process include hemorrhage, uterine perforation, cervical injury, thrombo-embolism, and anesthetic complications. Side effects that could occur long-term following an abortion include infertility, ectopic gestation, reduced birth weight of subsequent fetuses, and maternal psychological complications. Abortions performed by unlicensed and unskilled individuals remain a threat to safe motherhood. Hence, the urgent need for strategies directed toward improving reproductive health care for women after abortion. Previously in India, decisions regarding abortion and childbirth were made solely by the male member of the household or by other family members, not by the woman herself. Now that women have more control over their health care, they need to be aware of the complications associated with abortion and be given a chance to decide for themselves accordingly.

Infertility

Many couples experience trouble with infertility despite technological advances and achievements in reproductive science. Nearly 10% of Indian couples suffer some degree of infertility, with the causes split about equally between the partners. The causes are many and varied, and some are easily amenable while others demand complex treatments. Among women, causes of infertility include: infection, damage to reproductive organs, hormonal deficiencies, and antibodies that kill sperm. Some of the causes of infertility among men include: testicular failure, low sperm counts, hormonal problems, sperm abnormalities, abnormal conditions of the testes, retrograde ejaculation, and blockage of the vas deferens. Medical science tries to assist the infertile couples through the following current reproductive technologies:

- Artificial insemination: Delivery of sperm from the husband or an anonymous donor into the woman's uterus during ovulation. Usually this method is followed when the sperm count is low or if the husband is sterile.
- In vitro fertilization (IVF): This requires collection of eggs from the woman and sperm from the man. The fertilized egg is implanted in the uterus.
- Gamete intra-fallopian transfer (GIFT): Sperm and eggs (gametes) are injected into the fallopian tubes before fertilization.
- Zygote intra-fallopian transfer (ZIFT): The fertilized egg (zygote) is placed in the fallopian tube.

  Surrogate motherhood is another option for couples in India, and very few legal complications have arisen from this form of assisted conception.

Family Planning

Family planning refers to practices that help couples attain certain objectives in their reproductive health care. These objectives include:

- Avoiding unwanted births
- Bringing about wanted births
- Regulating the interval between pregnancies
- Determining the number of children in the family

Contraceptive methods are preventive methods to help women avoid unwanted pregnancies. In rural India, delivery care and post partum family planning services still exist in primitive and traditional form. They are not well integrated into existing health services. Women who fail to obtain effective family planning counseling are at higher risk of unwanted pregnancies than does who de obtain counseling. Gender inequality issues still permeate Indian society in the 21st Century, and sexual selection has become a major social problem. National laws in India forbid sex selection, so this has lead to a dramatic increase in the rate of female infanticide.

Family planning is seen as a panacea to regulate the number and spacing of births in the context of positive sociocultural measures to improve the standard of living of families. Further, it also aims to educate and enlighten parents and to protect children and prepare them for constructive participation in societal development.

Postnatal Health

Postnatal care is imperative because it not only determines the child's ability to reach his or her development potential but also enhances the woman's health in the postpartum period. During the first couple of weeks after birth, many women experience depression. In India, the responsibility of child care often belongs solely to the woman. Postpartum depression can continue weeks or months after delivery, and it affects 40% of women to some degree. Symptoms include chronic lethargy, back ache, headache, poor appetite, loss of interest in sex, sleeplessness, tearfulness, and irrational fears about the baby's health. A healthy diet, rest, and exercise can help alleviate the symptoms. Severe exhaustion, another possible post-natal problem, may arise due to lack of potassium in the body. There is very little understanding and awareness regarding the care of lactating mothers in Indian society, which contributes to the increase in maternal mortality.

Whenever possible, mothers should breast feed their babies. Research has shown that mothers who breast-feed their babies on demand produce more milk than those who feed their babies at regular, but less frequent, intervals. Breast-feeding strengthens the bond between mother and baby and provides health benefits to them both. These benefits include:

- Uterine contraction, protecting the mother from postpartum hemorrhage.
- Breast shape is improved.
- Decreased risk of breast cancer.
- Onset of menstruation is delayed (lactational amenorrhea), reducing the chance of conception.
- Infant's immune system is strengthened.

During the postnatal period women benefit form a healthy diet, enough rest and sleep, gentle exercise, and treatment and advice from doctors. It is also important to avoid bottling up of emotions. Every woman should visit the doctor for a checkup which involves an internal examination of the condition of the uterus. The breasts and abdomen will also be palpated to make sure there are no abnormalities. Resuming leisure and sporting activities as a family is important to postnatal health and well-being.

Menstruation

The menstrual cycle is the name given to all the changes occurring in a woman's body each month in order to produce eggs. Hormones control the menstrual cycle; two major types are estrogen and progesterone. They are responsible for the development, growth, and maintenance of the reproductive system.

The worst symptoms of menstruation (i.e., period) include irregular periods (metrorrhagia), absent periods (amenorrhea), painful periods (dysmenorrhea) and extremely heavy periods (menorrhagia). Irregular periods may be caused by emotional upsets as well as physical disease or the onset of menopause. Absent periods not caused by pregnancy require investigation by a specialist. Possible causes could include: emotional upsets, anorexia nervosa, stopping the contraceptive pill, or even too much exercise. Painful periods are usually coupled with premenstrual syndrome (PMS). Extremely heavy periods should be reported to the doctor immediately. Any sudden change to heavier periods may suggest a serious problem.

Any vaginal discharge associated with menstruation requires medical consultation. Vaginitis (yeast infections) and sexually transmitted diseases can be diagnosed and treated by a doctor. Uterine tumors are common and require biopsy and treatment. The treatment of PMS consists of doses of progesterone, which reduce fluid retention, breast tenderness, headache, spontaneous bruising, nausea, and many of the associated emotional problems. Vitamin B_6 tablets, if taken from 3 days prior to symptom onset up to menstruation, are effective in relieving depression and headache. Self-help treatments found to be effective for painful periods include exercise, dancing, and curling up with the knees to the chest, or using a hot water bottle on the abdomen or lower back. Sometimes more than one treatment must be tried or used in combination, but a great measure of relief can usually be found.

Prevention of Reproductive Cancer

All sexually active women should have a full gynecological examination once a year. Breast cancer and cervical cancer are symptom-free in their early stages. The gynecologist examines the breasts and takes a mammogram (x-ray) with the purpose of detecting abnormalities that may give an early indication of breast cancer. A pelvic examination will reveal any abnormal growth, damage, or infection in the uterus, cervix, or vagina. A Pap test helps to detect precancerous cervical cells. Breasts undergo subtle and normal changes throughout a woman's life. All women, from puberty onwards should examine their breasts every month. Abnormal signs to look for include:

- A lump in the breast or local lumpy areas
- Unusual increase in the size of one breast
- One breast unusually lower than the other
- Puckering or dimpling of the breast skin
- Turning-in of the nipple
- Fluid emerging from the nipple
- A rash on the nipple
- Swelling of the upper arm
- Enlargement of the lymph nodes in the armpit

Breast cancer affects 1 in every 15 women and is the single most common cause of death in women between the ages of 35 and 54. Furthermore, breast and cervical cancer, if detected in its early stages before it becomes invasive, can be treated successfully. If left untreated they can be fatal.

Preventive Care for STD's and AIDS

STD's: STD's are becoming a major public health problem in India. STD's, also referred to as venereal diseases (a less-inclusive term), are transmitted predominantly by sexual contact via bodily fluids or skin-to-skin contact. STD's are caused by bacteria, viruses, protozoa, fungi, and ectoparasites.

The most prevalent STD is Chlamydia which causes infections of the urinary tract, rectum, and cervix. Chlamydia can lead to pelvic inflammatory disease (PID) in women, which is a serious abdominal infection. Other STD's in order of incidence are: gonorrhea, human papilloma virus (HPV/genital warts), herpes simplex virus (HSV), syphilis, and AIDS. Certain demographic factors and numerous social and behavioral factors are involved in the spread of STD's. These factors include population explosion, rural to urban migration, prostitution, broken homes, sexual disharmony, emotional immaturity, urbanization and industrialization, social disruption, changing behavioral patterns, and social stigma. The following guidelines minimize the possibility of acquiring a STD and maximize the chances of getting prompt treatment if one is acquired:

- Have regular medical check-ups
- Avoid having unprotected sexual intercourse
- Minimize the number of sexual partners
- Learn the symptoms of STD's

AIDS: AIDS is a fatal illness caused by a retrovirus known as the human immunodeficiency virus (HIV) which breaks down the body's immune system, leaving the victim vulnerable to a host of life threatening infections. Among the special features of HIV are that once infected, the person will be infected for life.

The main modes of transmission of the infection are by fluid transfer during anal, oral, or vaginal intercourse, transfusion with infected blood products, use of contaminated drug needles, and maternal-fetal transmission. The emotional, social, and financial consequences of HIV/AIDS can make coping with the illness very difficult for the infected individual and his or her family. Families have to make great sacrifices to provide treatment, relief and comfort to their sick family member. Realizing the gravity of the epidemiological situation of HIV in India, the Ministry of Health and Family Welfare has set up a network of surveillance centers called the National AIDS Control Organization (NACO) to track HIV/AIDS. For a healthy and prosperous family life, there is a grave need to obey life's traffic signals.

Fig. 13: Life's Traffic Signals

	Stop !! Engaging in unsafe sexual acts
	Caution !! Protect yourself from infected blood transfusions
	Go !! Lead a healthy life

The red color stresses on the need to stop participating in unprotected casual sex with multiple partners. Amber emphasizes the need to exercise caution during blood transfusion by using proper screening techniques, and green gives the go-ahead signal to lead a healthy life style by adhering to the above two rules. Though there is no known cure for AIDS to date, the quality of life could be improved to a great extent by strengthening family and social support and extending the reach of health care facilities.

Menopause

The cessation of menstrual periods marks menopause, signaling the end of a woman's reproductive ability. The end of menstruation can occur at any time between the ages of 36 and 56 years. Women suffer menopausal complications to different degrees. The three major physical symptoms are: hot flashes, night sweats, and loss of vaginal lubrication. All are believed to be caused by low estrogen levels. Hot flashes can occur frequently or infrequently during the day or night where a woman feels chilled, then extremely hot, then exhausted. Night sweats often cause insomnia, a reason in itself for exhaustion, irritability, and depression during waking hours.

Generally, from menarche to pre-menopausal period, estrogen enhances the development of female accessory sex organs, female secondary sex characteristics, menstrual cycle, pregnancy, multiplication of vaginal epithelium, water retention, and calcium deposition in bones. During menopause, as the estrogen production falls below reference values, it depresses the normal physiological functioning of the body. Cessation of ovarian function followed by an increase in cholesterol and triglyceride levels is the predisposing factor to heart disease.

One of the most troublesome symptoms for sexually active women is loss of lubrication of the vagina. The lining of the vagina also becomes thinner which may make intercourse uncomfortable. Women become more vulnerable to vaginal and urethral infections which can cause bleeding and ulceration of the vaginal walls.

During menopause, women's bones may become more brittle through the loss of calcium and estrogen. Other menopausal symptoms include: irritating dryness of the nasal mucous membrane, headache, palpitations, dizziness, weight gain, abdominal pains, swollen ankles, and loss of memory and concentration ability. Emotionally, menopause is a highly charged time. The end of child bearing can be emotionally traumatic for some women, particularly if menopause coincides with empty nest period (i.e., when children start to leave home). Yet, menopause can result in a change for the good. Positive thinking, modified diet, relaxation, yoga, and finding new interests are some ways to cope with the physiological changes occurring in the body. Women can now continue to enjoy a full sex life without the fear of an unwanted pregnancy.

Reproductive Health Care for Men

A man's sexual desire and performance will decline when he is constantly overtired, under extreme pressure, is under the influence of alcohol or drugs, or suffering from a debilitating illness. A comprehensive screening that tests blood pressure, heart and lung function, analyzes the blood for fat content and liver, kidney, and metabolic diseases, and tests urine for diabetes, should be able to detect any health problems that could be contributing to sexual dysfunction.

Aberrant sexual behavior in men can be the result of problems in the family environment. Family disharmony, lack of an outlet for normal sexual behavior, depression, fear, and complexes associated with the opposite sex are some of the causes for sexual deviations and reproductive health problems among men. Psycho-physiological disturbances can cause impotence and impair sex life. In family life, both partners must be supportive to avoid a breakdown in sexual relations.

Reproductive health is explicitly linked to the reproductive rights—a means to women's empowerment. Higher age at marriage, smaller achieved family size, increased educational attainment, elevated female status in society, and improved accessibility and better utilization of health services are plausible reasons for an encouraging picture of the reproductive health status of women in India.

Though still a developing country, India has made substantial progress in the field of health. The dramatic increase in life expectancy offers hope for a healthier, improved future. Increased longevity without increased quality of life is an empty achievement. Ensuring complete, appropriate, and prompt care is essential to promoting improved reproductive health and quality of life.

Sex Education for Children and Adolescents

Sex is a creative energy and plays a leading part in people's everyday lives. Sex penetrates the whole person as it shapes and constitutes a personality. The theme of modern psychoanalysis is that sex functions from cradle to the grave. In simple words, the child as well as the old man comes under its subtle influence. School-aged boys and girls have questions about body structure and function that are not generally answered in classroom texts. Their questions may center on the reproductive organs and on sexuality. It is important for parents and teachers to be aware that today's young children and adolescents are growing up in a culture that overemphasizes sexuality. Many of these children have knowledge, interest, curiosity, and experience that go beyond what is usually attributed to this age group. Television shows, commercials, and movies that boys and girls watch are openly sexually stimulating and they show patterns that may influence adolescents' own behavior. Articles in magazines discuss types of sexual behavior engaged in by adults and older adolescents both within and outside marriage. Norms and values of relationships between the sexes are openly questioned. Thus, the many pressures that children face at an ever-younger age make it imperative that school and home work together in the area of sex and family life education. All youngsters should be helped to obtain the knowledge needed to guide them wisely as they grow up.

Need for Sex Education: Modern science has revealed the importance of sexual knowledge, and as a result educators, physicians, and psychiatrists are devoting attention to the dissemination of correct ideas about sex and morality. The main purpose of sex education should be to help the child grow up in such a way that sex will be an enriching, not damaging, experience. Moreover, sex education allows the children to be more capable of giving and receiving love in all human relationships as they grow older.

Sex education aims at giving children healthy attitudes towards themselves and others so that when they are grown, they will be able to draw on these same healthy attitudes as a basis for living happily with others. Developing a healthy social attitude towards sex, and reducing sexual maladjustments in number and intensity is also a prime goal of sex education. The probability of overcoming sex-related obstacles in life will be more favorable if the instruction in sexual matters begins at home.

Ignorance born of a negativistic attitude towards sex has drastic effects on the minds of young adults, which can lead to a lifetime of bitterness, frustration, and even neuroses or psychological disorders. Hiding the truth in regard to sexual matters is not going to benefit younger members of society. There exists an urgent need for a coordinated and systematized effort to impart essential knowledge about sex to children, youth, and adults in India.

Contents of Sex Education: Sex is a major factor in individual behavior and development. Systematic sexual enlightenment has to be started from early childhood. A comprehensive program of sex education will include the following aspects:

- Information relating to the origin of babies.
- Developing knowledge on anatomy and physiology of the male and female reproductive systems, stressing primary sex characteristics, secondary sex characteristics, and hygiene.
- Imparting knowledge about pregnancy, including factors influencing maternal and infant health, proper pre-natal care, the birth process, pregnancy complications, and abortion.

- Information about diseases of the reproductive system, with special stress on the danger signs of reproductive cancer and frank discussion about STD's and AIDS and their consequences and prevention.
- Understanding the physiology of sex, with emphasis on normal adults' emotional development and management of impulses.
- Premarital counseling to help individuals be supportive partners and wise parents.
- Counseling to overcome sexually deviant behavior.
- The sex education program must appropriate to the individual's age and fill their needs and requirements.

Family Life Education in Schools

A modern health program will have to take responsibility for helping develop an appreciation of the family and the child's place in it. Children's and adolescent's relationships with parents and other family members and the development of self-understanding must be emphasized. School becomes the appropriate venue to take over sex education. The school can give more detailed and systematic teaching than the parents. Thus, family life education at school needs to include the details of human reproduction and sexuality.

From kindergarten up to the higher secondary level, the program could be worked out and implemented without even mentioning the word "sex" through subjects like nature study, life science, and civics. Suitable curricula should be drafted to cater to the needs of youth both at school and university levels. In the schools, colleges, and universities, attempts should be made to provide sex education through talks, lectures, audiovisual aids, and suitably illustrated text books, as well as individual guidance and counseling. In this relationship the effective use of seminars, workshops, and refresher courses would enable parents, teachers, doctors, nurses, priests, health officers, social workers, and educators working with children and adolescents to develop a better understanding and ability to provide appropriate and accurate information to students. At the same time, research work by teachers and health workers in the fields of sex education and family life education needs to be addressed. Finally, preparation of a brief question and answer booklet by the health care workers, research scholars, and the Family Planning Association of India would prove useful to parents and teachers by providing clear answers to the questions that trouble growing children.

Conclusion

Renewed interest in reproductive health in India has spurred the need for the development of a comprehensive program that addresses issues that affect all members of a family. The importance of such issues as pregnancy, abortion, family planning, prevention of reproductive cancer, and sex education for children and adolescents have been addressed in the context of a woman's right to make decisions about her own healthcare and how these issues impact the family unit and society. In order to lead a quality family life, it is essential that an individual must be aware of the various issues, problems, and challenges associated with reproductive health. Providing accurate and appropriate information through sex education will certainly pave the long way in achieving the goal of a ***healthy, wealthy, and happy family life.***

References

Berger, M. (1991). *Challenge of AIDS*. New Delhi: National Book Trust.

Brannol, L., & Fiest, J. (2000). *Health psychology*. Australia : Brooks Publishing Company.

Deshprabhu, R. (2001). *Child development and nutrition management*. Jaipur: Book Enclave.

Devadas, R. P., & Jaya, N. (1984). *A text book on child development*. Madras: Macmillan India Limited.

Fathalla, M. (1988). Research needs in human reproduction. In E. Dicyfalusy, P. D. Griffen, & J. Kharima (Eds.), *Research in human reproduction, biennial report*. Geneva: World Health Organization.

Grugani, A. (1988). *Sex education*. Bombay: Better Yourself Books.

Jackson, G., Garlick, J., & Kelly, T. C. (1987). *The bupa manual of fitness and well-being*. Great Britain: Macdonald & Co.

Jeyaraj, N. (2001). *Women and society.* Madurai: Lady Doak College.

Mangal, S. K. (1996). *Abnormal psychology.* New Delhi: Sterling Publishers.

Memoria, C. B. (1981). *Social problems and social disorganization in India.* Allahabad: Kitab Mahal.

Papalia, D. E., & Olds, S. W. (1996). *Human development*. New Delhi: Tata McGraw Hill Publishing Company.

Park, K. (1995). *Preventive and social medicine.* Jabalpur: Banarsidas Bhanot Publishers.

Pati, R. N. (2002). *Reproductive child health.* New Delhi: APH Publishing Corporation.

Rao, D. B., & Latha, D. P. (1999). *Women and family health.* New Delhi: Discovery Publishing House.

Ratan, V. (1994). *Human psychology.* New Delhi: Jaypee Brothers Medical Publishers.

Sigelman, C. K., & Shaffer, D. R. (1995). *Life span human development.* California: Brooks Publishing Company.

Stoppard, M. (1993). *Conception, pregnancy and birth.* London: Dorling Kindersley.

Suriakanthi, A. (1997). *Child development–an introduction.* Gandhigram: Kavitha Publications.

Wardlaw, G. M., & Insel, P. M. (1993). *Perspectives in nutrition.* Chicago: Mosby Publishers.

11

New Age Parenting: The Role of Fathering in Indian Families

Aparajita Chowdhury
and
Arundhati Rath

Abstract

The parent-child relationship has undergone a sea of change during the past few decades. What were once straightforward relationships where the parents had a complete control over their child's activities have now evolved into ones marked by power struggles, arguments, and destructive conflict. New age parenting techniques are needed where conservatism and liberalism go hand in hand, and where freedom and control are balanced so that there is feeling of harmony and trust within the family. Men's issues have been in the current public spotlight, as changes in gender relationships have led to a questioning of what it is to be a man and a father in contemporary India. Family and workforce composition have changed due to increasing rates of unemployment for men and women.

> *This change has triggered a debate over children's well-being. Moreover, rapid social change has led to an increase in the number of children who do not have a consistent male figure in their lives. A man's role as a father is a relatively new area of study in Indian society. The need to understand the influence of fathers becomes especially imperative at a time when high divorce rates and non-marital child bearing have lead to the prediction that the majority of children will at some point experience the lack of a father figure. The younger generation is being increasingly exposed to crime and violence, and good parenting (achieved by both fathers and mothers) can serve to protect children and help prepare them to cope successfully with negative societal influences.*

"Children are very delicate and impressionable. Just like a sapling, they require the right amount of sunshine and water in the form of love, understanding, and affection to ensure they grow up into well-balanced and confident individuals."

One of the most important challenges facing Indian society today is to ensure that its children and adolescents grow in to healthy, happy, and responsible adults capable of achieving and contributing to the common goals of the nation—*"India Rising"* and *"The Incredible India"*. Parents are chiefly responsible for meeting this challenge. Parenting is the most important job an adult will have in his or her lifetime (Monagle, 1998). It takes precedence over other professional tasks because of its unique commitment to the protection and well-being of the next generation. If the family community is acknowledged as the basic building block of society, then parents must be acknowledged as society's first teachers of children and youth. Parents prepare children physically, socially, emotionally, and intellectually for the world, which in turn determines the health and dynamics of society. However, evidence increasingly shows that by the time many children in India reach adolescence, they are vulnerable to manipulation by depersonalizing influences, including materialism, drugs and alcohol, and petty crime. They become ill-equipped to sustain stable relationships or go on to make good parents themselves. Thus, it appears that parents are failing to deliver what is necessary for the general well being of their children.

One of the major relationships to have undergone a sea of change in India during the past few decades is that of the parent and child. It has gone from being a straightforward relationship where the parents had complete control over their child's activities, to one marked by power struggles, arguments, and conflicts. Regardless of the amount of money or education a person possesses or one's prior experiences with handling children, when our own child comes into this world, we feel powerless, inadequate, and frustrated. What is more revealing that, the wisdom passed on from grandparents, elders, and friends also seems to sound irrelevant—it may seem as if nothing can help you get through the tough spots (Gupta, 2003).

There are universal trends today that pose more tangible challenges to parents. Increasing technological sophistication continues to impact the way human beings think and behave and interrelate. It is most important that parents, who are first and foremost responsible for humanizing their children, understand the positive and negative repercussions that result from human behavior in the world their children will inhabit. New age parenting techniques are needed where conservatism and liberalism go hand in hand, and where both freedom and control are exercised, creating a balance and feeling of trust within the family. With the traditional method of childrearing, the Indian joint family included grandparents, uncles, and aunts who shared the role of parenting, while biological parents played a minor role. Children were brought up amidst different age groups, which perhaps made prepared them to understand society better. Today's nuclear family system is radically different.

Drastic change occurred slowly in Indian society during the post-independence period. Industrialization compelled people to move to cities, resulting in a gradual disintegration of the joint family system. Now parenting became the sole responsibility of the mothers, as fathers were frequently absent from home due to work. Over time, women's education and the growing demands of life contributed to the need for a dual-income system, further complicating the parenting process. As result, childcare centers sprang into existence. The decline of the extended family system, influence of Western Culture through education and the media, and the manifold increases in day to day life challenges has relieved the father as sole decision-maker of the household. Today it is vital that both the parents are equally responsible for their children's overall well-being and development, and the father is expected to cooperate with the mother in choices such as child rearing, kitchen chores, day to day household work, dropping children off at school, helping them with their homework, listening to their problems, and offering them advice. The mother's education and awareness of the world around her enables her to participate in major household decisions. Hence, the roles of the father and mother overlap to a certain extent. In sum raising a child in today's milieu consists of greater challenges regarding external influences, changing family structure, and extensive peer pressure. These factors have imparted a totally new dimension to the concept of parenting. Thus, effective parenting in contemporary society requires the following

P – Patience and Perseverance
A – Affection and Positive Attitude
R – Resourcefulness and Reasonableness
E – Effective Communication.
N – Nurturance
T – Tactful and Truthful Behavior
I – Intelligence and Insight
N – Negotiability & natural.
G – Guidance and Generativity

Further, to become an effective parent, the dynamics of parenting need to be understood. Increasing social complexity and educational challenges make parents more vulnerable and in need of assistance at times. According to Monagle (1998), the basic parental attitudes required for becoming a successful parent are:

- Openness to learning about children and adolescents and their stages of development.
- Readiness to reflect on their own approach to handling their children and their children's education, and a willingness to share experiences with other parents and to learn from their own mistakes and the mistakes of others.
- Willingness to improve themselves, and to attempt to overcome their own limitations, and to become not only better parents but better persons as well.

Parenting and the Healthy Development of Children

A child is just like a tiny sapling, which needs water, minerals, and protection from the elements to grow into a healthy plant. Similarly, a child needs proper food, clothing, guidance, and protection from hardships and problems, so that they can grow up into mature, sensible, responsible person. Besides the physical aspects of growth, the child's mental and emotional development also needs to be nurtured. It is the duty of parents to provide stimulation and a proper environment for the overall development of the child.

Physical development – Parents must provide healthy and nutritious food for their child, proper clothing, and a safe and clean dwelling in which to live. The diet should be balanced, including carbohydrates, proteins, fats, fibers, vitamins, minerals, and sufficient hydration. Healthy food is required for proper growth and development, and parents need to have a sound knowledge and awareness regarding the nutritional requirernents for children in different stages of their lives.

Personal habits and hygiene - These are two important aspects of healthy physical and personality development. Parents can help shape a child's personal habits such as appearance, behavior and personality in a positive direction. The issue of personal hygiene requires a lot of patience, tact, and toughness. Parents need to try to inculcate good habits in children at an early age so that they become a part of the daily routine. Enforcing these guidelines will be much easier if the parents cite the reasons for doing so and the negative effects of not doing so, even at an early age. Some concern, a little justification, and a bit of encouragement will help in cultivate good habits that lead to a pleasant personality.

Physical activities - There is an old saying, "A healthy mind resides in a healthy body," which holds true even today. Nowadays, because of the pressures of studies and diversions such as videos, computer games, the internet, mobile phones, and television, few children can be seen playing on playgrounds, in gardens, or on the streets. As a result, children are becoming lethargic and many are prone to becoming overweight. Parents must ensure that physical activities are a part of the child's daily routine. Cycling, hockey, cricket, swimming, badminton, etc., are all acceptable activities. The child can also join a sports organization. Physical activity serves as a way for children to release their pent-up emotions. Negative emotions like anger and fear are neutralized through vigorous play. Strenuous play also aids the development of gross and fine motor skills.

Extracurricular activities - For complete development of the child's personality, it is essential that their emotional and spiritual development occur simultaneously. Participating in extracurricular activities helps provide an outlet for the child's emotions, thoughts, and frustrations. Parents need to determine their child's interests. It may be music, dance, painting, sculpture, participating in debates and speeches, theatre, and so on. Meditation, yoga, and self-improvement classes are offered at various places to promote spiritual development. Participation in these classes helps release the stress of modern life that affects children as well as adults. Extracurricular activities provide immense satisfaction to children, fostering creativity and spontaneity in the child and promoting all around development.

Social development – Children should be provided with ample opportunities outside the family to interact with others and build close relationships, for in doing this the child's social competence is enhanced. Children should also be encouraged to spend time with their grandparents since many elders prefer to spend most of their time with their grandchildren even more than their grownup children. Taking children to family functions and festive occasions will increase the sense of familial bonding and the child's tolerance towards others.

Inculcating etiquette and manners – Beginning in childhood, etiquette and manners need to be taught and modeled. The child should be instructed to speak clearly and politely with elders and warmly with younger family members at home. The use of abusive words should be discouraged. Moreover, the child must realize that it is the proper etiquette of a person that leaves a favorable impression on others.

Intellectual development - The term cognition refers to the process of knowing, thinking, remembering, and judging. It refers to the interpretation of sensory events, their registration and efficient recovery from memory, and the ability to manipulate images, symbols, and concepts in thinking, reasoning, and problem solving. Cognition also has to do with the acquisition of knowledge and beliefs about the environment, people, and society. Parents can create an atmosphere in which the child can acquire different intellectual abilities such as attention, concentration, observation, memory, retention, and recall. Approximately 80% of brain development is complete by the time a child is two years old. Parents need to make their child understand that for success in any field or activity in life, sound education is a priority. Only if the child studies hard and has a desire to learn can they reap the benefits in later life by securing a good job or conducting business successfully.

Emotional development - Emotions and feelings play a major role in child development, and an individual's emotional development has a profound influence on their effectiveness and happiness as an adult. Emotions can be both constructive and destructive. Excessive emotion can disrupt action, making a person restless and acutely uncomfortable. Proper emotional development prepares the individual to appreciate the joys of life and to cope with stress in a constructive manner. The well-developed personality should be expressive and emotionally responsive in a disciplined manner. Children experience both positive emotions like love, affection, and joy and negative emotions like anger, fear, sorrow, grief, envy, and jealousy. Parents should encourage children to engage in strenuous play, which will help release the pent-up, negative emotions. A conducive and relaxing atmosphere in the family will instill positive emotions among the children. Children can be trained to express their negative emotions in a socially acceptable manner. Strong bonds of love and affection between parents and the child provides emotional security to the child and reduces aggressive behavior.

Attitude building - Our attitude towards life is a crucial element that influences our actions. Factors such as moral values, past experiences, frame of mind (mostly influenced by parents), and present environment affect the child's attitude towards life. Parents must encourage children to have a positive attitude at all times so they can contribute towards the progress and welfare of society, since how they behave, interact, and live will have a bearing on the future of our society.

Learning to face life's challenges - Life is full of challenges. It is a parent's duty to help children face challenges bravely and without the fear of losing or making mistakes. Parents should support their children at all times and indicate that they are always behind them. This will give children the confidence-boosting morale they need. Only then will they be able to take up greater challenges in life and succeed. The philosophy of Bhagwat Gita (The Holy book of Hindus) is very helpful in making one understand the need for putting forth one's best efforts without worrying about the results.

Moral development – The development of a conscience is fairly well in place by the time a child is 3 to 4 years old. A conscience helps the child decide what is right and what is wrong and is strongly influenced by paternal values, informal teaching, school values, peers, and electronic media to some extent. Parental role models also play a vital role in developing moral values in children.

Aesthetic development - This is another aspect of development generally expected to begin in early childhood. This trait enables the child to appreciate different forms or phenomena in nature. Parents must inculcate aesthetic appreciation among children by taking them to parks, zoos, forests, seashores, and so on. Aesthetic appreciation promotes positive mental health and relaxation and boosts imagination and creativity. Drawing and coloring pictures, modeling shapes, singing songs, and dancing simple dances aid aesthetic development.

Language development – The preschool period is the most important for the development of language and it is essential to provide children with opportunities that enable the growth of expression. Telling stories, singing songs individually or in groups, visiting important places, nature study, dramatization, free conversation, and group play contribute to the language development of preschool children. Sometimes parents are annoyed with preschool children for their talkative nature and instruct them to keep quiet, which is detrimental to the children's development. In order to increase the size of their vocabulary and enable them to speak correctly and fluently the child needs to be provided with opportunities to speak freely. It is natural for very young children to ask questions out of curiosity. Parents should not stop the child from asking those questions, and should try to give a satisfactory answer to each question.

Development of understanding, thinking, and reasoning- For survival, every living being has to adjust to its environment, and this adjustment is made possible when the given situation is understood. Likewise, children have to understand their environment and the people in it. The parents' role in instilling the development of understanding, thinking, and reasoning in children is extremely important. Understanding paves the way for thinking and reasoning. Reasoning involves the understanding of cause and effect relationships, and even though this is a complex process, many psychologists believe that even young infants begin to acquire it. Exposure to nature and study of the environment helps children have a greater understanding, better reasoning capacity. , and expanded knowledge.

Development of self-concept - Self-concept is instilled in children's minds during their preschool years and continues throughout childhood and adolescence. A positive and healthy self-concept is central to all other areas of development, as well as one's mental and emotional health. Developing a positive or negative self-concept profoundly influenced by the degree of parental acceptance or rejection of the child from birth.

Fathering and Children's Development in Contemporary India

There is an old saying to the effect of, "Home is the place where Mother is." Much truth lies hidden in these simple words, for the mother is usually the first person to be remembered when thinking of home. But the father also has a definite place there as well, especially with so much chaos among older children in families today. Respect for authority is a necessary part of proper training in childhood and adolescence, and the example of a wise and sensible father is the best way to instill this. Both parents are needed for the emotional health and wellbeing of their children, as neither parent can ever take the place of the other. This is particularly important during adolescence, when life presents many challenges.

The father's role in Indian society has slowly but gradually changed during the last few decades. There has been a shift from a strict authoritarian and distant figure to a more involved, caring person who plays a major role in fulfilling developmental needs and shaping children's futures. Increasing awareness of women's rights issues and education has enabled more women to enter the workforce, so women are taking full-time employment outside the home. Fathers are now ready to perform their role flexibly, unlike earlier days. Further, increased unemployment rates in men and increased employment rates for women have placed more focus on the father's role in child development. Regardless of their personal interaction style, most fathers are rather interested in having a satisfying relationship with their children. Although Indian fathers might not verbally express themselves like fathers in other cultures, most do know they are important to their children at every stage of development. Regardless of socioeconomic status or any other social condition, it has been shown that the main variable for successful negotiation of childhood, adolescence, and young adulthood is having two parents at home (Boxi, 2005). A growing number of more fortunate children and adolescents also have a nurturing father.

Generally, fathers in Indian society have always taken up the slack when mothers were unavailable to care for children and adolescents. However, they have not been expected to be competent in the role of caregiver, enforcer of household activities, or nurturer until recently. The last few decades have changed the Indian scenario of parenting and child rearing to the extent that children and adolescents need involved and active parents (both father and mother) in order to develop into independent citizens. Training is now provided to interested males who want to become a good parent. Disinterested males also have opportunities to shrink their responsibilities as parents. It is for the man to decide whether or not to be a successful parent for his children.

The presence of a father figure at home is of great significance for young people, as the absence is associated with many behavioral and emotional problems. According to Erickson (2000), father absence is strongly associated with high rates of school failure and drop-out, early sexual activity and teen pregnancy, youth suicide, juvenile delinquency, and adult criminality. Regardless of family circumstances, a father's involvement in the care and protection of his adolescent child is a significant part of that child's development. Sons need the care of a warm and nurturing father for cognitive development, sexual development, good peer relationships, and self-esteem. Fathers impact their children's psychosocial development from infancy through adulthood. A study on parenting skills with adolescents noted that adolescents need firm guidance followed by explanations and reasons for the guidance given (Patnaik, 2005).

A father's most important role in parenthood is the influence of the example he sets. He does not have to preach sermons or arrange counseling sessions with his children in order to affect their lives for better or for worse. His personal conduct goes further in setting the family's ideals and standards than any rule he can lay down or any words he can speak. A father may advise his children not to smoke or may punish the use of foul language, but if the same father smokes or uses foul himself in a moment of stress, all his preaching and threatening looks like hypocrisy. Children can often see a father's ulterior motives and size up his character rather easily. A child's standards for integrity and of kindness come from their father and mother alike, so if a father's behavior is not ethically sound, a child's standards will be lowered accordingly. A father's faith and religious convictions also have a strong influence on his children. If a father make light of religious matters, the child's confidence in religion is likely to be shattered. But when a father expresses faith in God and shows confidence in divine justice, the child's soul benefits accordingly.

A father's concept of clean and noble living is passed on by example to his children. When a father treats his wife and daughters with love and kindness, both the boys and girls in the family learn valuable lessons in morality and purity. The sons adopt their father's standard as their guideline in conducting themselves outside of the home, and the daughters measure the personality of others using the father's as a yardstick.

It is easy to become a father, but the responsibility the role bears is not. What Indian society expects from fathers has changed over the course of history. New expectations continue to emerge, and fathers have to decide how they will carry out their roles. Men may look to their own fathers as role models or they may look to other men in their lives for examples of positive parenting. These influences can leave fathers wondering, "What are the expectations of me as a father," and "How can I meet these expectations?" In these circumstances, men may need to reconsider the demands placed on them and what their personal interests and goals are. They need to ask themselves how their children fit into their life and then make a conscious effort to balance their life to meet the needs of their children. Recognizing and developing their own personal and parenting strengths will enable them to better meet their children's needs.

Fathers can easily get involved in their children's lives. Meeting children's needs quickly and frequently establishes trusting and secure relationships. As children are growing, fathers can show their teens that they care about them by talking with them about their interests and attending their school and community activities. Fathers can also be supportive by providing comfort to their children when they are disappointed by their failure, encouraging children to try again, supporting them in their efforts, and listening and responding to their ideas and feelings. A father can be involved in a child's life above and beyond meeting their basic need for nutrition, shelter, clothing, and safety. Developing special activities for the family around holidays, birthdays, and certain days of the week is another way to stay involved in children's lives.

Fathers' Involvement in Child Development:

Many Indian fathers today support the cultural ideal of the nurturing father, at least in principle, but their participation in everyday childcare is often very limited. The basic factors underlying the father's role in childcare and development include:

- Motivation to spend more time with their son or daughter and participate more actively in youth development within the family.
- Skills and self-confidence to deal with the adolescents. Parental incompetence, especially the father's skill in dealing with boys during this period, can negatively shape future development.
- Social support from the spouse, family, and friends in dealing with young children goes a long way towards helping the father manage the children at home. The attitude of family members, particularly the wife at times, may restrict the involvement of the father in parenting tasks.

Types of Fathers and Their Roles in Child Care:

Fathers in India have been willing to take up certain responsibilities towards their children, but cultural, familial, and sociological factors, along with a lack of skills and effort and a negative attitude, have kept fathers from having the chance to do their jobs. However, contemporary fathers have moderately increased their involvement with their children. Fathers can manage their adolescent's unruly behavior by using certain parental strategies, such as caring for oneself, better understanding their children, nurturing, providing guidance and motivation, and being an advocate for their children (Taylor, 2000). There are various types of fathers who can have a tremendous positive influence on their children's growth and development. They are discussed as follows:

Fathers who care for themselves – These are father who care for themselves, manage their own stress, and reach out and accept help from others when it is needed. They know and develop their own personal and parenting strengths, so that they can manage their children efficiently. These men manage family resources and plan and set parenting goals. Fathers must take care of themselves physically and mentally to bear the stress of both family and professional life. Understanding ones' own strength and weakness and accepting them is an essential for the father to lead a natural, stress-free life.

Fathers who understand their children – Fathers are also required to know and understand the growth and development of their children and identify specific needs, problems, or challenges faced by them in their environment. This can only be done through play, talk, and everyday activities with children, so that the physical closeness can enable them to be honest with their father. The behavior of father is translated to the children to a certain extent.

Nurturing fathers – Nurturing fathers build positive relationships with their children and give frequent and consistent messages of love and support. They usually pay attention to and meet the needs of their children. Further, they are the fathers who celebrate life and make connections with family history and cultural heritage. Both sons and daughters benefit from a nurturing relationship with their fathers. Young boys with positive qualities and behaviors report that their fathers were nurturing and emotionally available to them, especially in times of need. Similarly, girls with high intellectual and job accomplishments are more likely to have had positive relationships with fathers who expected them to be capable and determined.

Fathers who provide guidance – The role of fathers in Indian society is best described as a guide to their children. They serve as positive role models, monitor activities, and establish and maintain reasonable limits based on the age and maturity level of the children. They also assist their children in developing self-control, fulfilling responsibilities, and encouraging positive involvement with peers and other adults within and outside of the family. Throughout different stages of life, parents' guidance is sought and provided. Children will always be children to their parents, no matter their age.

Fathers who advocate for children– There are fathers in our society who try to locate and use community resources to help their adolescents develop competence. They make efforts to develop connections with family, the neighborhood, and the community to which the children belong. The father's positive involvement in the child's life results in lifelong positive outcomes for his children. Mothers can teach both abstract values and personal skills, while fathers can teach personal issues and help girls and boys learn how to function in the world.

Father as disciplinarian - A father's responsibility to the maintenance of order and discipline in the home is often overemphasized. Children try to pitch one parent against the other when they want to get around regulations or try to escape punishment for their misdeeds. Parents must therefore present a united front when disciplining their children. This can be achieved by jointly discussing the operating principles of the home beforehand and reaching agreement on them. One of the first principles of child training requires parents to respect the individuality of the child. Even a small child has the right to their own preferences.

Another requirement for successful discipline is consistency. Children are more likely to cooperate when they know what to expect of their parents. If a parent stands firm on one occasion and easily caves on another, the child will modify their behavior with the expectation that this time the parent will be indulgent. If the child guesses wrong they interpret it as unexpected rigidity. When dealing with children and their behavior problems, it is best to keep them busy with wholesome enterprises. Here the father can form a particularly strong connection with his sons. However, many family activities that keep children busy require planning by both the father and the mother.

Keeping children busy consists of more than just assigning chores around the home. Activities should also include recreational and creative activities, physical exercise, hobbies, and social events. Some activities will be completed individually by the child, while others will include the whole family. Children are more cooperative if their parents can participate with them part of the time. Even though parents have difficulty finding the time to play with their children, spending time together provides the most natural setting for the kind of bonding that carries a lasting influence.

Ideal Fathering: Fathers should occasionally provide each of their children with exclusive attention. During their time together, fathers need to enjoy their children's company without allowing outside distractions to interfere. There are many options for how this might be accomplished. A father and child might play and talk, learn a skill, or read together. What is important is that they notice each other and acknowledge a common interest. This type of undivided attention fosters a sense of bonding with one another and allows the child to feel noticed and special. Fathers can also give their children a glimpse of the work they do outside of the home. Children admire their father's strength, determination, and self-confidence and also respect their power at the same time. Walking the middle ground between dominance and permissiveness can be difficult for a father. Instead of always telling children what to do, fathers need to listen and be responsive to their children's suggestions. Tenderness can be difficult for some fathers to express because of its association with weakness of femininity. Every father should try to develop his own style of showing affection to others in his family.

Difficulties in Fathering: Today's parents' primary concern lies with the material welfare of their children, while moral and spiritual wellbeing has become less of a focus. When a child is born, the goal in contemporary Indian society is that he should be educated, sent abroad, and encouraged to make as much money as possible by whatever means necessary. However, it is not wealth that is of primary importance, but character. Nowadays, parents do not teach their children to cultivate positive qualities or control their children when they go astray. In fact, many parents often inadvertently encourage them in their bad habits.

It is the parents' duty to set children on the right path in their early years. They should not hesitate to correct or punish their children when they make poor decisions. The best way parents can show love for their children is to do everything necessary to make them follow the right path in life. Firmness is necessary when dealing with children to ensure that they develop the right way. Men want to become good fathers, but they experience barriers that can cause difficulty for them. Gadsden, Pitt and Tift (2001) identified some of the difficulties faced by fathers as:

✓ Poor education – Lack of education limits employment options for fathers and makes it harder for them to provide for their families. Men can overcome these difficulties by going to a vocational school, community college or university to become more marketable.

✓ Isolation, poverty, and hopelessness – Fathers earning a low income who live in poverty-stricken areas tend to experience a sense of isolation and hopelessness about their future. They may not know how to plan for the future or have much information about how to be a good father. These difficulties can be overcome by doing everything in their power to find work and gain an education in a more economically stable community. It is not easy, but it can be done with persistence and determination.

✓ Lack of preparation for fatherhood and family life - Young men need to be educated about parenting and its responsibilities. They need to be prepared for the hard work and sacrifice that occurs in day-to-day family life. These men must learn adult roles and the responsibilities of marriage, finances, and child rearing.

✓ Beliefs about the roles of men and women - Sometimes ideas about masculinity and femininity devalue the personal qualities needed to become an involved, caring father. The common idea that men should control and suppress their emotions interferes with creating a healthy family life and nurturing environment for children. Society's messages that say men need to be in control while women need to take care of the home keep men from playing an active role in family life. Men can resist these beliefs by rejecting the idea that participating in traditionally feminine activities means they are any less masculine. Learning about childcare and child development, sharing feelings with their children spouse, preparing meals, doing laundry, and cleaning the house does not detract from masculinity.

✓Understanding how much work it takes to be a good father - Good fathering, like good mothering, does not come automatically. It is a skill that develops with time and effort. When a father arrives home from his job, his work isn't over. It is then time for him to assume his role as a father in the home, which can be both hard work and fun.

Fathers try to avoid these difficulties by becoming more involved with their children. They express love, concern, appreciation, and forgiveness often and provide verbal praise for their children as well. They show genuine interest in their children's daily experiences, attend parent-teacher conferences, spend time listening and talking to their children about heir day, plan activities, attend music recitals and school events, tell stories, and plan vacations with their children. If difficulties in fathering occur, it is important that they be overcome.

Paternal Involvement and Children's Personality Development:

A higher level of paternal involvement with children in daily activities contributes to a higher level of sociability and school performance in children and adolescents. The father's involvement has been found to be a more reliable predictor in academic achievement than the mother's involvement. The father's love, attention, and guidance are very important. Not all fathers are able to live with their children. In cases where fathers live separately, positive outcomes in the overall wellbeing, cognitive development, academic achievement, and behavior of children have been found when an adequate amount of support has been provided to the child.

Research on father-child involvement demonstrates that fathers can be as sensitive to their child's needs as mothers, and that they engage in play differently than mothers do (Patnaik, 2005). Fathers' involvement with children is a basic need and helps a sense of personal power be constructed that promotes feelings of self-worth and respect in the child. A father's ability to make decisions and set limits increases his influence on the family, particularly his sons.

If children are frequently punished and dominated by their fathers, their personality will suffer, and they may face difficulty in school. Fathers who provide firm and gentle guidance for their children and are warm and accepting tend to have children with high self-esteem. When fathers are perceived as rewarding, gratifying, and understanding, sons usually score high on a masculinity scale questionnaire. Fathers should find a balance between tough and tender when necessary. Nothing gives a father more pleasure than to see his children gradually growing into adulthood.

As fathers have become more involved with their children, researchers have been investigating the advantages of father-child interaction. Studies have found that children whose fathers are involved in their lives benefit in many ways. When a father cares for a child at home without the mother present, a stronger father-child bond is facilitated and the father's confidence increases (Russell, 1983). Fathers' involvement is generally conceptualized in the social science literature as including three dimensions: *accessibility, engagement, and responsibility*

(Lamb, Pleck, Charnov & Levine, 1987). King (1994) found that children whose fathers provide financial support do better in reading, mathematics, and other areas in school. Fathers whose children report frequent interaction with them are more likely to view themselves as understanding and emotionally close parents (Ishii-Kuntz, 1994). Ishii-Kuntz also found that if fathers become involved in their growing children's lives, a positive self image continues to develop. Palm (1985) claimed that "Children put pressure on fathers to be as good as they want their children to be." It was also found that children whose fathers are more involved with them and have fewer problems overall (Amato & Rivera, 1999). Involved fathers learn quickly that their children look to them. When a father is involved, he learns new ways of caring, nurturing, listening and expressing affection. A Buddhist saying states, "A child without a father is like a house without a roof." Every child needs an involved father to positively build their personality. Without proper paternal involvement, daughters are more likely to become depressed and sons are more likely to engage in criminal activities. Interpersonal relationships between the father and the child are a necessity. Therefore, paternal and maternal roles each have their own significance in children's lives.

Fathers can help their children begin to develop self-control by encouraging them to make responsible decisions. They should also provide opportunities for their children to take care of themselves in order to learn responsibility based on their level of development. Kindness and responsibility for others is also encouraged. It is important to give children praise for their good behavior and accomplishments. Good fathers develop their own ways of showing emotion and responsiveness. A nurturing father can involve his children in meal preparation, cleaning, fixing objects, yard work, and gardening. Showing children how to save money for the future helps encourage financial responsibility in children. Ways of instilling responsibility include: saving money in a piggy bank for a future purchase, taking older children to the bank to set up a savings account, teaching children to comparison shop, giving children opportunities to earn money doing special tasks, helping teens look for a summer job, teaching teens how to balance a check book and responsibly use a credit card, teaching teens how to file a tax return, assisting in writing a resume, and practicing interviewing skills.

Good fathers also motivate their children, creating conditions that improve their learning. They teach their children about themselves, the world, other people, encourage them to be curious, to use their imaginations, and help them seek out knowledge and organize information. Children's early experiences help determine the way their brains develop and function. Fathers can encourage healthy brain development in infants and preschoolers by singing, reading, and talking to them and providing safe places for them to explore and play. It will impact the child's way of thinking and acting throughout their lifetime. Children should be taken on outings that encourage them to use their imagination and curious nature in the pursuit of knowledge. Places such as a library, museum, zoo, science center, or drama performance. Children learn about other people, themselves, their neighborhood, community, state, country, and other places in the world from their fathers. Fathers also help children obtain and use information by providing access to books, newspapers, educational TV, radio, and computers. Reading books to children on topics they are interested and discussing the information in them is an excellent way to become more involved.

Researchers suggest that children perform better in school when their fathers are involved in their lives and provide them with encouragement. Children's motivation and success can decrease when their father frequently intrudes and places too many restrictions on them. Good fathers also locate, use, and in some cases develop community resources to meet the needs of their children. They develop connections with family, neighborhood, and community groups, and help initiate social changes that support children and families.

Children who have special needs benefit from having both their fathers and mothers involved in supportive relationships with them. Fathers make social change happen by creating environments that support children and families. Fathering is a big responsibility and a learning process. All fathers make mistakes, but using positive parenting practices can help meet their children's needs. A positive father who is involved in his child's life will yield positive lifelong outcomes for his children.

Parental Paranoia in India Today and Pressure on Their Children to Achieve:

There is an obsessive condition of panic striking parents in urban India today—***parentitis.*** The parents' desires to have their children excel in every activity—academics, sports, or extracurricular activities—have put tremendous pressure and stress upon their children. It peaks every March-April during final examinations with the severity differing between each parent and child. Panic parenting actually begins while the child is still in the womb. Added family pressure to know the sex of the child, anxious mothers-to-be scanning the internet for information, books and magazines about what to expect, struggling to find a meaningful name, pushing the child into kindergarten at a very early age, and the stress and tension of getting the child admitted into a reputable school are just a small part of the whole process. When the child has barely started learning to talk or walk they are put into a playschool to prepare for admission into a proper school.

There is no respite after admission: homework, weekly exams, tuition, extra classes, extracurricular activities, sports, and so on are always occurring. As children grow up, new issues arise, like flirting, alcohol, drug abuse, and the lure of sex and crime. Parents have to be on the alert constantly, praying that their child are well-prepared enough not to succumb to these temptations. In the age of cutthroat competition, parents push their children to perform harder and better, thus putting a lot of pressure on them. The situation is not easy on the parents either though, and they can become emotionally and financially drained. They restrict their social outings and other luxuries in order to pay for high school fees, tuitions, and study materials. Parents may even sacrifice their own basic needs and comforts to provide coaching classes, new clothes, vehicles, mobile phones, and brand name consumer goods to their children.

The excessive pressure from parents, peers, elders, teachers, and society puts tremendous pressure on the child, doing more harm than good at times. The overwhelming expectations may lead to frustration when the child is unable to perform up to the required expectations. Thus, the child can end up with stress-related disorders like palpitations, nervousness, high blood pressure, insomnia, loss of appetite, and other ailments. Parents and children alike are grappling with cultural dualities, and parents are adapting to new age parenting concepts and trying to find an appropriate blend between freedom and control. Parents first need to realize that not every child is born a genius—they cannot all be Bill Gates, Sabeer Bhatia, Sachin Tendulkar, Abdul Kalam, or Donald Trump. Parents need to support and respect their children and guide them appropriately. They must refrain from exerting undue pressure on their children or pushing them to achieve too far beyond their abilities. Some pressure is inevitable and is required for the child to work harder and perform better, but too much goading and pushing might have the opposite effect. Today's children are quite clearheaded and focused about their objectives. Thus, the parents' role should be more of a friend, guide, and philosopher, rather than being critical, demanding and pushy. That is perhaps the best way to achieve parental success in present day Indian society.

CONCLUSION

There are many ways fathers can become more physically and emotionally involved in their children's lives. Some ways of doing this include: exercising with the child, getting involved with the child's sports team, taking the child shopping, monitoring the child's TV and computer viewing habits, sharing a common hobby with the child, involving the child in daily chores (i.e., planning meals, budgeting, shopping,), engaging the children socially and intellectually, knowing the child's friends, giving affection to the child, learning to talk and listen to the child, taking an active role in children's learning, and helping children with their home work. Being a successful parent is hard work. Raising well-behaved and well-balanced human beings requires courage, patience, skill, and a good attitude. Thus parents need training, especially in the present day context to develop the understanding and confidence necessary to bring up the future citizens of India. Ten keys to new age parenting can be suggested for both fathers and mothers to raise their children in this complex and competitive world:

- Use genuine encounter moments
- Use actions, not words
- Give children appropriate ways to feel powerful
- Use natural consequences
- Use logical consequences
- Avoid conflict
- Separate the deeds from the doer
- Be kind but firm
- Parent with the end in mind
- Be consistent and follow through

Parents need to set goals for their children that are consistent with the child's interests, personality, and capabilities. Setting expectations that are too high or too low can lead the child to have feelings of inadequacy or having ambitions that exceed their capabilities. Placing too many expectations on the child that are beyond his capabilities will result in depression, frustration, or other negative feelings on the part of the parents and the child. Parents need to have sound convictions about their parental skills and healthy ambitions regarding their children. Parents need to be realistic and accept their children for who they are. Parents can be like the tree that provides protection to the young sapling below by blocking excess sunshine, rains, winds, and storms, while allowing it to grow and seek its own space. With the proper perspective, the overindulgence and overprotection provided by Indian parents today that is hampering children's growth and development will be understood and changed, allowing for the betterment of children's lives.

References

Amato, P. R., & Rivera, F. (1999). Paternal involvement and children's behavior problems. *Journal of Marriage and Family, 61*, 375-384.

Boxi, S. (2005). *Fathering: A study on families of different socioeconomic background.* Unpublished master's thesis, Berhampur University, Orissa, India.

Erickson, M. F. (2000). Research confirms what dads and kids tell us. *Seeds of Promise, 3.* Children, Youth and Family Consortium, University of Minnesota. Retrieved from http://www.cyfc.umn.edu/Parenting/Seeds/volume3.html

Gadsden, V. L., Pitt, E. W., & Tift, N. (2001). Research can practice on fathers in high-risk families: Exploring the need and potential areas for collaboration. In J. Fagan & A. Hawkins (Eds.), *Clinical and educational interventions with fathers* (pp.257-283). New York: The Haworth Clinical Practice Press.

Gupta, S. (2003). *The joy of parenting.* New Delhi: Unicorn Books Pvt, Ltd.

Ishii-Kuntz, M. (1994). Paternal involvement and perception towards fathers' role: a comparison between Japan and the United States. *Journal of Family Issues, 15*(1), 30-47.

King, V. (1994). Non-resident father involvement and child wellbeing: Can dads make a difference. *Journal of Family Issues, 15*(1), 78-96.

Lamb, M. E., Pleck, J. H., Charnov, E. L., & Levine, J. A. (1987). A biosocial perspective on paternal behavior and involvement. In J.B. Lancaster & J. Altmann (Eds.), *Parenting across the life span: Biosocial dimensions* (pp. 111-142). Hawthorne, NY: Aldine.

Monagle, V. (1998, November 25-27). *Parents – A challenge for the future*. Paper presented at the 6th Australian Institute of Family Studies Conference, Melbourne, Australia.

Palm, G. F. (1985). Involved fatherhood: A second chance. *Journal of Men's Studies, 2*(2), 139-155.

Patnaik, S. (2005). *Critical analysis on the paternal role in children's personality development*. Unpublished master's thesis, Berhampur University, Orissa, India.

Russell, G. (1983). The changing role of fathers? St. Lucia, Australia: University of Queensland Press.

Taylor, D. E. (2000). *Fathering to meet the needs of children*. University of Missouri Extension Publication. Retrieved from http://muextension.missourri.edu/explorepdf/hesguide/humanrel/GH6500.pdf T

12

Family Counselling As a Form of Crisis Intervention

Tapati Das

As the human family is changing, problems are becoming more complex and emerging at an ever-increasing rate. It therefore becomes necessary to view the family from a fresh perspective. Political, social, economic, religious and cultural demands in India placed on the families today are creating considerable stress for family members. Family counseling is one form of crisis intervention that may help maintain the integrity and dignity of the family. This chapter discusses family counseling from different perspectives and summarizes various types of counseling when working with members of the family system. Specific examples of real-life situations are provided.

The family has been the social institution that has stood at the very center of India society for centuries. The family is the most important group to which most people belong. It provides intimate and enduring interactions, serves as a mediator between family members and the larger society from birth until death, and transmits the traditional ways of a culture to each new generation. However, during last few decades, Indian families have been greatly affected by the uncertainties of social, political, and economic upheaval, thus putting families at risk for a host of difficulties. Major problems Indian families are facing vary greatly. However, millions are subject to poverty and its concomitants. More recent crises in Indian families rich and poor include marital strains and dissolution, parent-child conflicts, various forms of family violence, substance abuse, juvenile delinquency, and low school attainment, to name a few. Some specific areas of concern today include the pressure of both parents working outside the home, the unique stresses experienced by single parent families (most women headed), unemployment, a lack of family values and ethos, and an increased life expectancy that leads to many problems related to caring for the elderly. Given these conditions and difficulties, the future well-being of the Indian family is uncertain. Family centered intervention is one solution to defining the tension and stress within today's families.

The family is deeply ingrained in Indian culture and philosophy. An individual is a part of the family unit, and his or her identity is defined in and through the family. The image and status of the family, and its goals and achievements, are more important than anyone's individual needs and aspirations. Family counseling encompasses any and all professional techniques and activities that are undertaken to resolve family problems. It involves the participation of the principal family members, both immediate and extended. It is often difficult to successfully help a family member who is experiencing psychological problems that has its roots in the family. If a family member is treated without the family, temporary change in the individual may occur as a result of treatment. However, for long-term results, it is essential to involve the other family members in the counseling process. Family counseling is also the treatment of choice for marital and family problems.

Understanding Today's Families: A Systemic Approach

To be maximally effective in working with couples and families, the counselor needs to conceptualize the family as the client and be capable of treating the family system as the client. The family is the basic, cohesive and integrative unit of the larger social system. Its members are bound by interpersonal relationships in a wider social and cultural milieu. Culture defines one's roles, responsibilities and expectations that help to maintain family solidarity. However, urbanization and modernization have created a stressful situation for the family, threatening its very existence, solidarity and continuity. Technological advancements and mass communications have completely changed the landscape in which families live and work, and the changes have not all been positive. Some social scientists believe that there has been a gradual deterioration in the quality of human inter-personal relationships and breakdown in religious, moral and social values, with the consequences being an increase in conflicts, emotional disturbances, human maladjustment and emotional instability.

To understand family systems and to practice counseling from a systematic approach, it is important for therapists to understand that systems exist at many levels. Each individual human being is a subsystem of a "larger living system" called the "family". The family is part of a living system called the "extended family", which is part of a larger system known as the "community". The community is a part of larger system, known as the "State", which is also part of a larger system, and so on. Because of these interrelationships between systems and their subsystems, if a problem occurs in one of the subsystems of a social organization, that problem sometimes affects other subsystems and has ripple effects throughout the family system (e.g., an economic recession at the national level affecting employment openings and possibilities for real workers). The systems framework also comes to life when counselors treat a family in which the problem seems to reside in only one of the members. Counselors recognize that, although the "presenting problem" is centered on the individual, it may be maintained by behaviors of other family members. Furthermore, the counselor recognizes that the "problem" affects the feelings and behaviors of other members of the family system. Other key concepts central to a family systems paradigm are discussed as follows. In sum, basic to the concept of the family as a system is the notion that "the whole is greater than the sum of the parts." One implication of this conceptually is that each and every family as a unit takes on its own unique personality that is resistant to change and also makes it difficult for individual members to vary much from the "normal" and expected ways of thinking, feeling, and behaving. Some families, of course, are much more flexible and growth-promoting over time, whereas others are more rigid or chaotic and thus hinder the healthy development of it members.

Family subsystems: Salvador Minuchin (1974) states that the family system is composed of smaller units called "subsystems". Several family subsystems exist, including the "spouse subsystem", the "children's subsystem", the "female system", the "male subsystems" and the "individual subsystem". In addition to these, the potential of other subsystems configurations exist, such as mother-son, father-son, mother-daughter father-daughter, grandparent-grandchild, and so on. Each family system has a set of rules that govern the behavior of family members, and each member has certain roles to play in the larger whole.

Family Homeostasis: Homeostasis is the tendency of living systems to desire to be at rest or in balance. When all members abide by the family rules and act in ways consistent with their roles, family homeostasis or balance is achieved (Minuchin, 1974). However, when a family members deviates from the established family rules or roles, homeostasis is violated and members of the family system begin to engage in certain behaviors in an attempt to return the system to its former state of balance. Hence, families have self-righting tendencies. For example, a family rule right be that teenage children will be home at six o'clock evening. The parents allow for some fluctuations in the arrival time of the teenager, but when he or she regularly returns home over an hour late, the parents become upset and begin enforcing measures to bring the system back into balance. These expectations may or may not be adhered to by the teenager. Disequalibrium is often needed in families to bring about change. Families that are not able to do so may seek counseling or therapy for their child's acting out behavior. Even though the son or daughter becomes the "presenting problem," it is really the family unit that is in need of help and change.

Family Boundaries: As mentioned, families are composed of several subsystems. The flow of information from one subsystem to another is controlled and regulated by the boundaries between the subsystems. Boundaries are created primarily by rules the family creates for defining and regulating appropriate behavior. Boundaries in families range from rigid to diffuse. For example, a husband and wife may have a rigid boundary that makes inclusion of "outsiders" difficult. Sibling boundaries within the family, on the other hand, may be too diffuse and in need of clarification and monitoring, if, for example, a teenager is having a negative influence on a younger child. The character of the boundaries of the family determines the flow of information within the family and the inclusion or exclusion of participants within the family.

Family Adaptability: Adaptability refers to the family's ability to modify its rules, roles and structure in response to the pressures and conflicts of family life. Chaotic families have little structure for dealing with the problems of family life; rules are unclear and frequently not enforced. Flexible families are quite receptive to change and have the ability to resolve problems through appropriate changes in rules and roles. Structured families are less able than flexible families to modify rules and roles. However, these families are able to adapt and change when necessary. Less adaptable families are reluctant to change rules and roles and tend to maintain the status quo at all costs.

Family Cohesion: Cohesion refers to the degree of togetherness in the family and the amount of individual autonomy granted to family members. Disengaged families have low cohesion. Members are afforded maximum autonomy and may not identify significantly with their family. Separated families value individual autonomy; however, they have a sense of family unity and identity. Connected families value closeness. However, connected families also recognize and support the development of autonomy in their members. Enmeshed families value family closeness above all else, but not to a healthy degree. Family members are not allowed to develop and become their own person are exceedingly limited, and their individual identities are fused with others in the family (e.g., mother and daughter) or the family as a whole. To sacrifice togetherness for independence is considered a major violation of family rules in enmeshed families.

Family Communication: Communication is critical to healthy family functioning. This is because members need to be able to express their thoughts, feelings and needs to others. When family members are unable to truly be who they are, emotional or psychological problems may develop in one or more family members. Alexander and Parsons (1982) maintain that an effective negotiation style is an important general goal for all families. This is because negotiation is the key to conflict resolution.

Family Life Cycle:: Carter and McGoldrick (1980) have suggested that families move through stages of development in the process of marriage, child rearing, and preparing for life as a couple with grown-up children. Typically, three generations of the family are directly involved in the life cycle process. In counseling, knowledge of these stages prepares counselors to help their clients deal with these significant issues in acceptable ways. Further, it allows counselors to reassure family members that many events which are stressful to the family are normal aspects of family development.

Family counseling may includes several different types of treatment for needy members, including parent counseling, marital counseling, child or adolescent therapy, or working with the entire family conjointly. Counseling in part aims at helping individual reach a state of self-autonomy through self-understanding, self-direction, and self-motivation. Such individuals tend to experience minimal inhibitions, conflicts and anxieties (Rao, 1992). However, the ultimate goal of family counseling is to help the family as a unit experience a higher level of acceptance, coping and conflict-resolution. Different manifestations of counseling from a family perspective are discussed as follows.

Marital Counseling

"Marriage is that relation between man and woman in which the independence is equal, the dependence mutual and the obligation reciprocal." - Louis Kaufman Anspacher.

Marriage involves the joining of two families and two ways of life. Each partner brings from their families of origin not only issues in relating that were not resolved from childhood, but also ways of believing, thinking and acting. The relationship issues and tasks involved in mate selection are not merely those springing from one's parents, but also those that come from the entire family (Nicholas, 1996). Moreover, individuals are different when witnessed in relation to and interaction with their spouse than when they are seen alone. A seemingly sensible, reasonable and mature man or woman who is otherwise a social or vocational success may become irrational, unreasonable and immature in attitudes and behaviors when involved in interaction with his or her spouse.

Successful resolution of relationship issues with one's family of origin is essential to the formation of a marital relationship that has adequate opportunity for growth and resolution of its own tasks and problems (Framo, 1970). Optimally, the joint marital and individual task appears to be that of securing and maintaining an appropriate distance from the family of origin that involves some contact and closeness, but not so much that it interferes with individual and marital development. All families and couples have problems, although most people can usually work through them. But sometimes problems become so persistent or severe that families must turn to outside professionals or agencies for help. In the past families with problems were likely to turn to kin members or elders or a religious priest or guru for assistance. Many couples still use these resources today, at least as a first step, but more and more people need professionally trained personnel to deal with family and marital difficulties.

Until recently it was a common practice in India that, before marriage, friends, elders, parents, relations, or a priest gave advice and counsel to the young boys and girls regarding family life. However, today this occurs with much less frequency. Hence, there is a tremendous need for trained professionals who are able to work therapeutically with couples and families in all geographical areas and segments of Indian society (Natrajan, Rastogi, & Thomas, V., In Press). Marriage and family counseling can be defined as the process through which a professionally trained counselor assists two or more persons in developing abilities which help them manage stress and resolve difficulties in their relationship (Mudd, 1955). A part of marriage and family counseling involves education, both before couples get married and during the course of child-bearing and child-rearing. The "client" is the family or married couple and not the individual. Adjustments in marriage are usually needed in matters of sex, child bearing, in-law relationships, economic matters, religion, work and personality conflicts (Stokes, 1959).

Types of Marriage Counseling

There are three major types of marriage counseling, each following various stages of the couple's relationship.

Premarital Counseling. This starts from the time of dating. In modern day "love" relationships (i.e., not traditionally arranges marriages), young boys and girls meet at various times and get to know each other before entering into matrimony. Pre-marital counseling typically occurs once couples have made a definite decision to marry. In many societies around the world today young people entering into marriage are advised by elders, friends, parents or relatives about the golden rules of marriage from their own experience. This is still largely the case in India, where most marriages are arranged by the parents. The social structure in India (except in some isolated urban areas) does not permit or at least encourage a period of courtship. Again, the exception occurs in free-choice relationships where the partners are not strangers to each other before marriage. When pre-marital counseling starts before mate selection, whether in arranged or choice marriages, the marriageable aged boys and girls are taught what marriage is, and what they can and should expect from marriage. The main purposes of premarital counseling can be summarized as follows:

- To know and realize the goals and purpose of marriage. It may mean different things to different persons, including a means of recreation, procreation, and/or partnership and having a happy conjugal life.
- To overcome the apprehension of meeting and living with a total strangers in cases of arranged marriage.
- To receive instruction about the planning of family, and the sexual needs of men and women. In India sex is a taboo subject and therefore many young boys and girls face many adjustment problems after marriage.
- To remove ignorance, suspicion, fear and tension of marriage relating to the wedding day and potential conflict between families that are being untied.
- To prepare mentally and physically for marriage, and become aware of unhealthy attitudes, negative feelings, egos, and jealously and possessiveness dynamics.
- To educate couples about mutual love and respect towards each other and each other's family. Also, to make them aware of the interpersonal relationship, sensitivities, and adjustment needed in relation to in-laws.

- To understand the importance of sharing responsibilities in the home and with children. Many young couples are simply not prepared for their domestic responsibilities and working together as a team.
- To learn to cope with potential family problems that can involve dowry, marriage rituals, the honeymoon, settling down, and managing finances.

Counseling for Newly Married Couples. Marital counseling for newlywed couples can be very helpful to them as they begin to face the challenges of married life. The new couple has to learn each other's habits, attitudes, emotions, and likes/dislikes. They also have to learn to adjust to a whole new family and the blending of two often large family systems. Moreover, disagreements may arise due to small matters such as eating patterns, spending habits, work styles and schedules, or a lack of constant concern of one of the partners towards the other. Problems may also arise because of interferences from in-laws. In addition, there may disagreements that arise from conflicting role expectations and role performance. A conflict or crisis in the marriage relationship may develop because of the dowry system in Indian society. Differing sexual needs and expectations in marriage is also a frequent source of stress.

Counseling to Help Troubled Marriages. Conflicts may develop at any point in time after the honeymoon phase of marriage is gone. Sometimes familiarity breeds contempt, and significant numbers of couples today are growing apart from each other for a multitude of complex reasons from both partners working outside the home to unfilled emotional needs to conflicts between extended family members. Still, the sacramental nature of marriage pressures couples to remain together in spite of their differences, even though there is an ever-increasing philosophy among educated Indians that that marriage is not necessarily life-long, and if one of parties wants to get out of the marriage he or she should have the freedom to do so. The enactment of marriage law has stipulated certain conditions for divorce, and although the divorce rate in India is still low compared to many countries of the world, the current state of marriage is not always a positive one.

Every community interested in supporting married couples and preventing separation and divorce should look for creative ways to integrate and maximize the resources and expertise of teachers, physicians, psychologists and counselors, lawyers, religious leaders, academicians, social workers, and other professionals. Counseling can be provided for couples and families at colleges and universities, schools, religious institutions, and NGO's; e.g., through setting up Marriage Counseling Bureaus. Each medical college in India has a psychiatry department where marital counseling can be offered. The family court system, as well as the Women's Commission, can also include marriage and family counseling units. These types of services are provided in some locations in India at Family Welfare Clinics and places like Parivar Seva Sanstha. The Social Welfare Department in each state of India can also start family life education programs in an effort to support couples and families and better prepare couples for married and family life. Police departments can also provide or refer couples for counseling in cases involving spouses and/or family members. In sum, marriage and family counseling can take place on many fronts and in a variety of unique ways.

Counseling Children and Adolescents

Raising happy, healthy, and well-adjusted children is the greatest challenge parents face today. Most of us are still searching for ways to improve our relationship with our children irrespective of whether they are tiny tots or teenagers. Children with behavioral or emotional problems are in need of a stable and supportive family and school environment that enforces healthy rules and limits (Sharma, 1999; Thompson and Rudolph, 1988). Before successful intervention can take place, counselors and others who work with children and their families need to understand that root causes of a child's difficulties. These are influenced by both heredity and environment, as indicated in Figure 1 below.

Figure 1

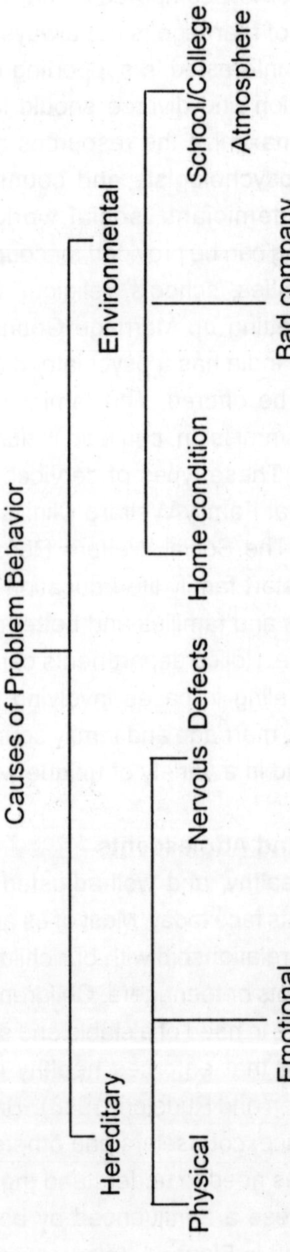
Causes of Problem Behavior
Hereditary
Environmental
Physical
Emotional
Nervous Defects
Home condition
Bad company
School/College Atmosphere

Children who are acting out (externalizing) problem behavior are of great concern to parents and teachers, particularly in the area of discipline (Vernon, 1999). These children have poor relationships with their teachers, parents and peers. However, children can also have internalizing types of problems or disorders such as depression or a host of anxiety-related disabilities (Thompson & Rudolph, 1992). These internalizing and externalizing behavior problems can range from mild to moderate to severe. Environmental contributors to children's difficulties and psychopathology include the home atmosphere (e.g., permissive or authoritarian parenting), peer network (e.g., bad company), school (e.g., poor or uninvolved teachers, and community milieu (e.g., poverty or crime-ridden).

Children exhibit abnormalities in their character in addition to defects and complications that pose a threat to their physical and mental being. Character building is an important process in the child's development. Character formation is largely dependent on parents, family, teachers, friends, and environmental factors. Timely instruction and intervention can divert many common problem behaviors such as stealing, lying, cheating, bullying and teasing other children, poor study habits in school or low school attendance, and other related behavioral problems. Character development requires a multimodal approach with children and youth, with parents and school personnel cooperating and playing the major role. Often children with behavioral difficulties are slow learners in school; hence, they need proper educational remediation as much as individual and family therapeutic intervention. Some of the common causes of both learning disabilities and concomitant behavioral problems are summarized as follows.

- Physical Illness or Disabilities
- Mental Defects
- Educational Immaturity
- Chaotic, Abusive, and/or Resource-Limited Home Environment

- Lack of Interest
- Unhealthy School Atmosphere/Low Quality Learning Environment/Poor Teachers
- Non-Adapted Educational Curriculum Based on the Child's Special Needs
- Intellectual Giftedness That is Not Identified and Nurtured at Home or School

Counseling Delinquent Adolescents

Adolescence is a period through which a person passes from childhood to maturity. A series of physiological, mental and emotional changes take place. It is a time when the roots of identity are established and a sense of true independence from parents, although limited, is sought. This period brings with it significant changes in the parent-child relationship. If parents and professionals have a better understanding about what to expect during this stage of development, they will have a more realistic perspective from which to assess and help with problem areas (Vernon, 1999).

Adolescents can be easily overwhelmed by their feelings. Anger, depression, and changes in mood are common. There are some problems of adolescence which have to be dealt with great care, sensitivity, and understanding on the part of parents and teachers. Some of the more common characteristics of adolescence that can be a breeding ground for conflicts between them and their parents and other authority figures include: excessive sentimentality and emotional instability; social awkwardness and the need to impress others; daydreaming and fantasy proneness that can result in insufficient study habits and learning difficulties; inability to understand and sometimes control their aggressive and sexual impulses and desires; struggles with their body image, poor self-concept, and/or low self-esteem; stress experienced from pressures to achieve academically; and for older adolescents, anxiety over their educational and vocational future (Berger & Thompson, 1991; Sharma, 1999).

Delinquency is the most common problem among post puberty and early adolescent children. According to Reckless (1986) the term 'juvenile delinquency' applies to violations of criminal code and pursuit of certain patterns of behavior disapproved of by society. Earlier, Hirsh (1937) classified delinquents into six groups:

1. Incorrigible (keeping late hours and disobedience).
2. Truancy (staying away from school)
3. Larceny (Petty theft to armed robbery)
4. Destruction of property (both private and public)
5. Violence (against individual or community)
6. Sex offences (sexual misconduct to rape)

Delinquency in India today is also sometimes accompanied by alcohol use/abuse and drug addiction. A study by Ahuja (1997) showed that a high number of drug user's families were dysfunctional (i.e., lacking in affection and healthy interactions). Parents play a crucial role in controlling the drug and alcohol usage of their children. The history drug addicts indicates marital disharmony in the home, as well as parental neglect, hostility, permissiveness, or rejection. Addiction does not evolve overnight. Symptoms of addiction may include loosing interest in one's studies, irritability, spending too much money, erratic behavior towards family members, withdrawal and dazed expression, locking oneself up in a room for a long time, or spending more time outside away from the home. These early symptoms should not be ignored by parents, and action should be taken immediately. If parents are vigilant and spend quality time with their children, usually drug use can be detected and eliminated before it gets out of hand.

Parents and teachers can prevent drug usage in children and adolescents by putting into practice the following steps suggested by Ahuja (1997).

(1) Communicate with children openly and listen to their problems.

(2) Set an ideal example by not using alcohol or drugs.

(3) Take interest in children's activities and their friends.
(4) Keep track of prescription drugs at home.
(5) Learn and educate children about drugs.
(6) Ask teachers to discuss the dangers of drugs with students openly.
(7) Take interest in children's hobbies and leisure time activities.
(8) Talk freely with adolescents about their problems and solutions.
(9) Help children talk about their life goals and career planning.
(10) Discuss common crises of growing up and how to cope with problems.

Case Study #1: Rama, a girl of 18 years, came from a broken home where her parents lived separately. She lived with her father and one brother and sister. Her father was an alcoholic. All of her relatives had sympathy for the girls, especially Rama as she managed all of the household responsibilities along with her studies. Rama had the tendency to steal things wherever she went. For example, when she visited her paternal relations she lifted money or gold jewelry. It became a regular feature and she was caught several times, but she did not abandon the habit. She was also caught cheating while taking her graduation examination and was given a warning. Her good qualities were overshadowed by her antisocial behaviors. After graduation she worked in a school. There she stole money from a colleague's purse and also the jewelry of the woman with whom she stayed. She always wanted to be rich and live in luxury. Rama's biggest problem was that she did not have parents who were concerned about her. At last one of her aunt's started counseling her. The aunt tried to help Rama with her self-esteem issues and made her realize how she is loosing love and affection of others to the extent that nobody welcomed her in their homes. Her aunt also helped Rama understand how her bad choices contributed to her worry and anxiety. Eventually Rama moved to a new location and began a new job as a teacher. Her old habits disappeared, all because of her aunt's counseling and concern. Now she is married and leading a normal and happy life. The jest of this story is that one life was turned around because a family member, even though untrained in the area of professional counseling, took the time and effort needed to help another person in the family. This story points to the extreme power and influence that one member of the family can have on another within the Indian family system.

Case Study #2. Anuj is a young man of 20 years working on his MBA in Bangalore. He comes from a family where there was severe marital disharmony. He is the oldest child in the family. A few months after he entered his graduate studies he stopped communicating with his family either through letters or phone calls. His parents thought he was busy in his studies, and that this was the reason he did not communicate. Anuj did not appear for his first semester examination. This was reported to the parents by the local guardian. When his parents reached Bangalore they were shocked to find out that Anuj had become a drug addict. He has spent all the money his father has kept in his account for study. Anuj's health had deteriorated. His father took a long leave and stayed with his son and helped him somehow complete his studies. However, Anuj went on to become addicted to other drugs. After his final examination he was left in a drug dead diction center where he went received the benefits of both individual and family counseling, meditation, and yoga. Anuj became drug free. He got a job and started earning a salary. Although he had one relapse, Anuj was eventually able to stay drug free and get his life in order, again through the assistance of some professional counselors. The family component of his counseling was what was needed in order to enlist the help and support of his family as he surmounted one of the most difficult barriers of life.

Conclusion

This chapter provided information about the family as a living system and outlined the need for and advantage of a family-based approach to counseling. Basic concepts and terminology necessary to understand family health and dysfunction were presented, and some of the different kinds of family-related counseling were briefly described. Since education and therapy are intimately intertwined, there is little doubt that family life education and family counseling are two sides of the same coin. Family counseling has many uses in a wide range of settings in India and remains a *tour de force* in both crisis intervention and longer term treatment of a host of individual and relational disorders.

References

Ahuja, R. (1997). *Social problems in India*. New Delhi: Rawat Publications.

Alexander, J.F, & Parsons, BV. (1982). *Functional family therapy*. Montercy CA : Brooks/Cole.

Berger, K., & Thomson, R. (1991). *The developing person through childhood and adolescence*. New York:Worth Pub.

Blochere, D.H. (1996). *Developmental counseling*. New York: The Ronald Press.

Boy, A.V., & Pine, G.J. (1963). *Client centered counseling in the secondary school*. Boston : Houghton Muffin Co.

Carson, D.K., & Chowdhury, A. (2000). Family therapy in India: A new profession in an ancient land? *Contemporary Family Therapy, 22*(4), 387-406.

Colanzelo, C., & Zaffrann, R.T. (1979). Special issues in counselling the gifted. *Counseling and Human Development, 11*, 1-12.

Fenell, D.L., & Weinhold, B.K. (1989). *Counselling families : An introduction to marriage and family therapy*. Denver: Love Publishing Company.

Glasser, W. (1986). *Control theory in the classroom*. New York: Harper & Row.

Gustad, J.W. (1953). The definition of counseling. In R.F. Berdie (Ed.), *Roles and relationship in counseling.* Minneapolis: University of Minnesota Press.

Hallahan, D.P., & Kaufman, J.M. (1986). *Exceptional children: Introduction to special education* (3rd edition) Eaglewood Cliffs, NJ: Prentice Hall.

Jullian, J. (1977). *Social problems.* Englewood Cliffs, NJ : Prentice Hall.

Mamoria, C.B. (1961). *Social problems and social disorganisation in India.* Allahabad: Kitab Mahal.

Mc Cully, C.H. (1965). *The Counselor-Instrument of Change.* Teachers College Records.

Mudd, E.H. (1955). Psychiatry and marital problems: Mental health implications. *Eugenics Quarterly*, June, p. 3.

Nicholas, W.S. (1996). *Treating people in families: An integrated framework.* New York. Guilford Press.

Patterson, C. (1959). *Counseling and psychotherapy : Theory and practice.* New York: Harper and Brothers.

Pepinsky, H.B., & Pepinsky, P. (1954). *Counseling theory and practice.* New York: The Ronal Press.

Perez, J.F. (1965). *Counseling theory and practice.* Reading MA: Addision Wesley.

Rao, S.N. (1992). *Counseling and guidance.* New Delhi: Tata McGraw Hill Publishing.

Reckless, W. (1956). *Handbook of practical suggestions for the treatment of adults and juvenile offenders.* Govt. of India Publication.

Sharma, R.N. (1999). *Guidance and counselling.* Delhi: Surjeet Publications.

Steinberg L.D., & Lewins, A. (1987). *You and your adolescent.* New York: Harper Perennial.

Stroup, A. (1996). *Marriage and family: A developmental approach.* New York: Appleton Century Crofts.

Stroup, A.L., & Glasser, P. (1959). The orientation and focus of marriage counseling. *Marriage and Family Living, 21*, pp. 25-26.

Thomson, C.L., & Rudolph, L.B. (1992). *Counseling children*: Pacific Oaks, CA:: Brooks Cole Publishing Company.

Tyler, L.E. (1969). *The work of the counselor.* New York: Appleton Century Crofts.

Vernon, A., & Mubuk, R. (1995). *What growing up is all about: A parent's guide to child and adolescent development.* Champaign, IL: Research Press.

Vernon, A. (1999). *Counseling children and adolescents.* Denver Love Publishing Company.

Youngs, B. (1985). *Stress in children.* New York : Arbor House.

13

Creating a Safe Haven for the Elderly in Indian Families

Visala Patnam

and

Fauzia Khan

Abstract

In India, where a value-based extended family system has historically prevailed, family support has not until recently been a concern for elderly people. Respect and support for elders has been ingrained in Indian culture for centuries. However, due to rapid development and globalization, families in India today are much less likely to provide care for their aging members. The present chapter discusses needs and requirements of elderly people and provides suggestions as to how the home can become a safe haven for elders during the last phase of their journey through life.

"Our society must make it possible for the elderly not to fear the young or be deserted by them, for the test of a civilization is the way that it cares for its helpless members."

Societies, cultures, and nations have often been evaluated on the basis of how they treat their elderly, young, disabled, and disadvantaged individuals in the course of their development. This is even more relevant for developing countries as they face radical demographic transitions where the number of people in each of the aforementioned population segments is likely to be quite large (Ramamurti & Yamuna, 2002, 2004). India has the second largest population of elderly persons subsequent to China. In 1991 there were about 57 million older adults (6.7 percent of the population). The Technical Group on Population Projections, Government of India, has projected the number of elderly persons to be around 113 million by 2016, accounting for nearly 9% of the total population (Prakash, 2005).

Population growth, modernization, globalization, the trend towards a nuclear family system, increased life expectancy, and a deterioration of cultural values and norms are some factors that function as stumbling blocks in the changing environment of the elderly in India (Bhatia, 1983). Indian society has come a long way from its idealistic state. Until recently Indian society was known for collective, normative, and group-oriented behavior. Now an individualistic style of living is becoming more prevalent. Under these circumstances, aged people are finding it increasingly difficult to meet their needs. Resources available to elderly persons and their families need to be augmented so that the quality of their lives can improve.

The traditional norms and values of Indian society focused on respecting and providing care for the elderly. Consequently, elderly family members were normally taken care of within the family unit itself. The joint family and social networks provided an appropriate environment in which aging family members could spend their lives. However, the advent of globalization and growth of an individualistic philosophy have eroded the traditional values that vested authority with family elders. Social scientists report a general lowering of social status of elderly people in India. Increasingly, aged people are being perceived as burdens due to their disability and dependence on others for care. Rapid changes in the family system, both in urban and rural areas, are reducing the family's capacity to provide quality care for elderly people (Shandilya, 2005). One bi-product of these changes is a defiance toward and decline in respect among members of the younger generation towards elders. This has occurred to such an extent that aging family members are being moved away from their own homes into *Ashramas*, or old age homes. Thus, the negative effects of aging seem to be compounded because Indian elderly have been socialized to expect family support in old age, especially from their sons, who by default inherit all paternal property.

The continuous commitment of every family member in fulfilling the constantly changing and growing needs of the family is essential to creating a safe haven for elderly people in Indian society. The elderly provide the backbone of the family, while the young provide the hope for the future. Balanced, nurturing care is important for aging family members. Family is a living institution, which becomes crippled without inclusion of the elderly in it. Old age is an inevitable phase of life, with declining capacities and changing physical and psychological needs. The presence and involvement of the elderly in the family keeps bonds intact and connects generations. Values, traditions, culture, and wisdom are imparted on younger generations, and checks and balances maintain structure in the family. Elders also help provide a congenial environment for children's sound upbringing. Parents, grandchildren, and other young family members must therefore be sensitive to the changing needs of aging family members. Allowing the elderly to remain productive family members would enable them to better cope with the challenges of aging.

Understanding the Needs of Elderly People

The needs of the elderly are similar to the needs of any other human being. They include physical needs (i.e., food, clothing, and shelter), security needs, emotional and social needs, and the need for self-actualization. Maslow's (1954) hierarchy of needs is as relevant for the elderly as it is for people of other ages. The ideal for every elderly person is good health; emotional, psychological, and social well-being; and optimization of his or her capabilities—all of which contribute to personal, familial, and societal health and stability.

In the context of the Indian lifestyle, responsibility for care of the elderly is primarily borne by family members. There is a legal provision that allows the aging person to claim maintenance from their children if the elderly person has no resources of their own (Section 125 of the Code of Criminal Procedure, 1973). However, few parents go to court to claim maintenance from their children (Veedon, 1994). The Constitution of India recognizes the duty of the State towards the elderly (Prakash, 2004, 2005). According to Article 41, "The State shall, within the limits of economic capacity and development, make effective provision for securing the right to work, to education, and to public assistance in case of unemployment, old age, sickness and disablement, and in other cases of underserved want."

Therefore, efforts need to be taken to revive cultural values and reinforce the traditional practice of interdependence among generations. Families need assistance in caring for their elderly family members. Such help may be in the form of emotional support to help deal with the stresses of providing long-term care, or in the form of practical support related to care-giving issues. It is neither desirable nor affordable to open a large number of retirement homes in India. Thus, reinforcing the existing sense of duty to family may be the only feasible option (Mohanty, 2000). Families need to be strong enough and adequately prepared to take care of and provide necessary supports to the elders within their families. The status of the elderly in Indian society will not only be increased, but their wisdom and experience in family living can make a positive impact on their families and society as a whole.

Taking Care of the Elderly

Aging is an inevitable part of the life cycle. The elderly undergo many physiological and psychological changes, which in turn may cause them stress and lead to changes in behavior. Empathy, concern, and understanding are required of family members at this point in their loved one's life.

Health Care : Deterioration in the functioning of the various bodily systems occurs during old age, resulting in general health problems. Ghosal (1982) reported that multiple health issues are more predominant than single ones. Some of the somatic diseases of elderly people in India include: high blood pressure, heart disease, stress, cancer, diabetes, and diseases of joints and bones (Rao, 1975). Furthermore, 43% of the elderly had some form of morbidity, predominantly respiratory illnesses, skin infections, bowel disorders, and dysenteries (Mehortra, Pandey, & Dabral, 1979).

These health issues demand attention and care, especially from family members. Timely monitoring of appropriate diet, exercise, health checkups, use of medicine, rest, and personal assistance are a priority. Planning and distribution of workload among various family members can make meeting these demands easier and more effective. Even in busy daily routines, these health demands must be addressed in order to prevent magnified health complications.

Engagement in Life : Retirement is an important event in the life of elderly people, and studies have shown its impact on the individual's adjustment, attitude, and life style. According to Mani (1980), retirement can make one dependent, dull, and lonely despite comparatively good health. Further, retirement appears to have a negative effect on personal adjustment in so far as there is economic deprivation and difficulty in keeping oneself pre-occupied.

Retirement from work-related responsibilities can make the day feel long, monotonous, unproductive, and tiresome. Staying mentally and productively occupied and engaged is a challenge to the individual and the family, which can be met by intelligent planning. Keeping the elderly individual's capacities and interests in mind, some familial responsibilities should be allocated in a way that boosts their sense of worthiness to the family. Recognition of and expression of gratitude for their contributions will make the elderly family members feel appreciated and may help improve physical and mental health.

Feeling Valued : It is necessary to help make the elderly feel important, appreciated, and respected. Crucial family issues should be discussed with them, and they should be involved in decision making. The family as a whole would benefit from spending a period of time each day talking with their older family members. Keeping elderly family members informed about what is happening each day and special occasions coming up is a way of showing respect. Contributions to the household and community should be acknowledged. Celebrating their birthdays, wedding anniversaries, and holidays, such as Grandparents Day (3rd Sunday of November) and International Day for the Elderly (October 1st), are ways to make the elderly feel special. Occasional small gifts, specially prepared food items, and paying attention to their complaints can help them feel important and enhance their self-esteem. This ultimately contributes to happiness and optimism and prevents undue stress and strained relationships in the family.

Aids and Accessories : Items such as eyeglasses, magnifying lenses, walking sticks, hearing aids, arm chairs, and nonskid footwear become necessities for the elderly as health issues accumulate. Family members should be sensitive and considerate in providing, repairing, and replacing these aids that are an important aspect of daily life. Without these items, the individual could experience handicap and irritation. Being sensitive and responsive to elderly family member's requirements and needs is essential for younger family members.

Clothing and Personal Belongings : It is difficult for older people to adapt to climatic fluctuations with advancing age. Therefore, special clothing, bedding, fans, or toiletries may be needed. Special attention needs to be paid to the elderly family member's attire during hot and cold seasons. Similarly, personal belongings such as radios, headphones, tape recorders, and religious books can provide a source of entertainment. Family members need to be concerned about the acquisition and maintenance of these items.

Autonomy : Freedom and autonomy are basic needs of all individuals. Financial freedom goes hand-in-hand with autonomy. Each elderly person must have some amount of money to spend according to their wishes since it provides a sense of independence. Decisions regarding property, travel, donations, and purchases are also fundamental to freedom and autonomy. Those choices must not be taken away. Every sphere of their life should have a certain amount of autonomy. The elderly should always be respected and protected by their family members.

Privacy : Every human being is entitled to some degree of privacy. At times the elderly prefer solitude, and they must be provided some time and place for privacy. In Indian culture, the concept of "personal space" is virtually nonexistent, as Indian families hardly place any value on this aspect of life. Elderly people must be given some privacy for themselves, and it is essential that family members facilitate this.

Recreation : The elderly must be encouraged to develop hobbies and to utilize their leisure time for activities that interest them. Family members must make sure that aging family members maintain old friendships and relationships with relatives, and that they develop new friendships when possible. Occasional social gatherings should be arranged. Visits to parks, clubs, places of worship, cinemas, theatres, music programs, and picnics can be arranged to make their social lives more interesting. Reading materials, television, and recorded movies are other sources of entertainment. Younger family members can play an important role in providing these opportunities for the older family members.

Religion and Spirituality : The closer a person comes to the end of the life cycle, the more inclined they may be to spend more time devoted to their religion and/or spirituality. The sentiments and desires of the elderly regarding these issues should be respected. In India, the elderly spend more time with people engaged in various religious activities, and this positively affects their level of personal satisfaction. Therefore, necessary personal space, transportation, and religious material should be provided for them. It is the responsibility of the family members to respect the sentiments of the elderly towards their religious and spiritual journey.

Reciprocal Role of the Elderly : All relationships in life are based on give-and-take and can disintegrate if proper balance is not maintained. As people age it is possible that they may become unrealistic, exaggerating, demanding, hypersensitive, insecure, stubborn, resistant to change, or negative in attitude. These possibilities could create an unhealthy environment in the family and could lead to the elderly family member being ignored and ostracized. The attitudes of older people in the family in turn affect younger members. The younger generation needs to be considerate and understanding towards the elderly, but the elderly individuals, with their experiences, wisdom, and patience, need to show warmth and empathy for the younger generation as well. It is through guidance and counseling that the young family members will find the direction to move forward. The following responses from elderly persons would prove to be beneficial for the entire family:

Broad Outlook and Emotional Stability : Oversensitivity can be very injurious to interpersonal relationships. The younger generation has many responsibilities in life, and they are deeply involved in their routines. The elderly have more time at their disposal and may feel ignored and forgotten. Elderly persons must make a conscious effort to maintain a broad outlook, and attempt to avoid feeling hurt by unintentional events. Emotionally stable, reasonable, and mature elders are an asset to the family.

Positive Attitude : Attitude is a major factor contributing familial happiness. Ones own perspective is central to the feeling of contentment. Accommodative attitudes, and small sacrifices on the part of the elderly, are more likely to strengthen relationships among family members. Furthermore, a nurturing, positive attitude can help the person overcome a sense of insecurity or of being ignored. Excessively complaining about ailments and discomforts to the other family members can strain relationships as well.

Consideration : One must realize that every family member has their own demanding routine, with duties to fulfill, personal areas of interests, and likes and dislikes. Some elders may forget this in their eagerness to talk about their own achievements and past experiences. Elderly family members need to have consideration for the hectic schedules of their loved ones. If they do not, younger members of their family may ignore them or will avoid talking with them, which would lead to emotional upset on the part of the elderly family member.

Interference : Our elderly members possess a tremendous wealth of wisdom and experience. They are anxious to prevent the new generation from making mistakes in life. These fears could be either genuine or perceived, but the new generation has the right to have their own experiences and make their own decisions. Advice and guidance from the elderly is extremely important, but care must be taken that it does not border on interference and intrusion. In Indian families, elderly members try to involve themselves in the daily affairs of the younger family members with good intention, but this is not always met with a positive response. Therefore, elderly family members need to understand to what extent they can be involved in their children's affairs so that conflict can be avoided.

Favoritism : Older family members need to balance their attention between their children and grandchildren and try not to show favoritism. This is of significant importance in the family. Pressuring the more responsible, hardworking children into shouldering the burden of their lazy, irresponsible siblings can create an unhappy environment and strain familial relationships. Sensible and mature behavior on the part of the elders aids in promoting healthy relationships within the family.

Responsibility : Weakened physical capabilities may not allow the elderly to shoulder much responsibility within the family. However, this does not justify their taking no responsibility at all. The elderly must try to explore areas in which they are capable of extending support to their family members, especially in raising grandchildren, supervising household work, and in helping with household duties when unexpected situations arise. This can boost the aging family member's sense of personal satisfaction because they are productively contributing to the family's needs and taking responsibility for the betterment of the family.

Adaptability and Flexibility : Age can increase rigidity of personal beliefs, and advancing age creates a cultural gap between generations in the family. Adaptability to changing values and situations is vital for mental health. The elderly need to make a voluntary effort at being more adaptable to the inevitable transitions in the life cycle. Flexibility in molding daily routines according to new demands is essential for the elderly. These small gestures can have a great impact on the family's well-being.

Forgiveness : Mistakes are a given aspect of life. Impulsivity and the naivety of youth go hand in hand. The elderly must not forget that forgiveness is an important part of life. Therefore, it is equally necessary that the elderly play a role in creating a safe haven in the family. Ideal conditions cannot be realized without sensible and balanced input from every family member, whatever their age or status within the family.

Contributions of the Community : A family is the smallest unit of a larger community. The overall value system, structure, decency, dignity, peace, discipline, traditions, culture, and social commitment of the community as a whole directly affect the family. At the same time, it is the combined family units that form a community. The two are reciprocally affected by their own values and structure.

India, being a nation with an enormous population, cannot rely solely on the government to fulfill the needs of its elderly. Community participation is crucial. The community can pool its resources and plan and establish need-based institutions and facilities that will function effectively for the welfare of the elderly. Such facilities would provide supplementary or complementary care, which in turn would directly or indirectly help families and the elderly by catering to their needs. The heart of the community is reflected in the families it has constructively served and strengthened. Consideration for the elderly is shown by providing items such as wheel chairs, lifts, and reserved seats at places like hospitals, reservation counters, banks, ration stores, milk booths, bus and railway stations, and airports. The community must also play an active role in protecting the elderly from injustice, exploitation, and abuse. Community members must also be vigilant in supervising the policies and programs meant for the elderly by making sure they are implemented properly by government agencies and NGOs.

Conclusion

Elderly people will be able to enjoy a high quality life if they have a sufficient income, maintain good health and strong relationships with family members and friends, and are able to optimize the use of their own capabilities. These traits may not be attainable by every elderly person, but they can form guidelines for policies being formulated explicitly for the elderly, or for other areas that may impact the elderly such as health, housing, and the environment (Veedon, 1994).

The central and state governments in India must formulate new need-based policies and programs for the elderly, instead of simply modifying and updating existing ones that are long outdated. Government policies and programs should also encourage improved care for the elderly by declaring tax deductions for families, free medical facilities, and other incentives. The integrated efforts for care of the elderly provided by families, the community, and the government can have a profound impact on the quality of life for older adults in India today. Elderly persons have been agents of change in their world, and they deserve to reap the benefits of those changes.

References

Bhatia, H. (1983). *Aging and society: A sociological study of retired public servants*. Udaipur, India: Arya's Book Center.

Ghosal, B. C. (1982). Care of the aged. *Yojana, 20(10),* 10.

Mani, M. P. (1980). Probing the mind of the aged. *Social Welfare, 27(4),* 4-5.

Maslow, A. (1954). *Motivation and personality*. New York: Harper.

Mehrotra, S. K., Pandey, D. N., & Dabral, S. B. (1979). Urban aged population: A social study. *Indian Journal of Public Health, 23(2),* 71-75.

Mohanty, A. (2000). Population aging in India and the effectiveness of social assistance program in Orissa – A human right perspective. Bhubaneswar, Orissa, India: People's Cultural Center.

Prakash, I. J. (2005). Aging in India: Retrospect and prospect. Bangalore, India: Bangalore University.

Prakash, I. J. (2004). Improving intergenerational relationships through monitoring programs. *Indian Journal of Gerontology. 18 (3/4),* 501-508.

Rao, B. S. (1975). Old age can be made happy. *Social Welfare,* 9-10.

Ramamurti, P. V. & Yamuna, D. (2002). Aging in developing countries: The Asian perspective. In S. D. Gokhale & N. Pandit (Eds.), *Aging in search of its identity*. Pune, India: Ameya Prakasan.

Ramamurti, P. V. & Yamuna, D. (2004). *Handbook of Indian gerontology*. New Delhi, India: Serials Publications.

Shandilya, B. (2005). *A critical study of multigenerational attitudes towards aged and adjustment towards aging*. Unpublished Ph.D thesis, Jai Narayan Vyas University, Jodhpur, Rajasthan, India.

Veedon, R. (1994). Need for a policy for the aging. In, *Enhancing the role of the family as an agency for social and economic development*. Bombay, India: Tata Institute of Social Sciences.

14

Nurturing Youth Potentials Within Indian Families

Rita Choudhury
and
Aparajita Chowdhury

Abstract

The future prospects of young individuals ultimately depend upon the families, communities, and nations into which they are born. Today's youth are living in an exciting time of unprecedented changes. The family remains the training ground which prepares the young person to navigate the journey to adulthood. However, the changes in family structure and functions during the last half of the 20th Century in India has altered the capacity of families to provide resources to its youth. Due to the exceptional nature and variability of the conditions faced by young people today, there are many challenges for them and society as a whole. The present chapter discusses family diversity, the changing family situations for youth in India, and various associated stresses related to their growth and development. Suggestions for families to foster creative potential and resilience while preparing youth for adult life in the emerging global high-tech world are also provided. When the pathways of youth are well marked, stable, and supported by the family, society can be confident that new generations will join the ranks of adulthood well-prepared.

"The young are any country's greatest resource and hope for the future."

The future of all societies in the world rests, in part, on how well they succeed in preparing youth to be productive adults who contribute to their respective communities. In the 21st Century, there are innumerable reasons to worry that this vital life stage may be in peril. New demands of adulthood, frenetic lifestyles, entrenched poverty, alienation of youth, and a geopolitical climate marked by conflict and terrorism jeopardize the transition to successful adulthood for many youth today (Larson, Brown, & Mortimer, 2002). The role of young people and their ability to shape the societies in which they live cannot be ignored. Disproportionate attention has been given to the problems of young people in the literature, particularly the ways in which they are victims or perpetrators of negative behaviour. The constructive roles played by young people, however, are frequently overlooked.

Youth is a distinct stage of preparation for adulthood. This is a period in which young people experience changes in their roles and shifts in social expectations of them. It marks a time that abounds with potentials as well as problems. The young are recognized as an important resource for the future of any country. However, this period of life is often the most neglected and overlooked. Youth represent a tremendous source of positive creative energy and they have enormous potential to contribute to the betterment of societies.

Contemporary Youth in India

There are currently about 200 million adolescents in India between the ages of 10-19 years (22% of the total population) and 300 million between the ages of 10-24 years (30% of the total population). Thus, the major portion of India's population lies in the youth category. Indian youths not only create the major resources for the community but their potentials have remained intapped even today. The Draft National Youth Policy (DNYP; Government of India, 1997) recognizes youth as an important asset for developing human resources. Further, it recommends better opportunities and support systems to empower young people.

The present Century speaks of the emergence of a 'global youth culture' (Schlegel, 2000) in which middle class young people wear the same styles of clothing, listen to some of the same music, and adopt similar slang expressions in many cultures worldwide. This not only signifies the onset of a new culture, but is also a common voice for care and development within and outside of families. Young people develop and grow through interactions and situations they are exposed to in this environment and shape themselves in preparation for their future lives, especially within their families.

The family remains the training ground which prepares the young person to navigate the journey to adulthood. The home, with its network of intimate relationships, is the first place young people learn pro-social behaviours such as sharing, helping, and cooperating. The home environment provides the foundation for building a strong sense of self, laying the groundwork for building inner psychological resources and coping skills in later life (Stinnett, 1981; Swick, 1987). However, in recent times the family has been experiencing transformations in structure and functions. New types of household arrangements have emerged which have included major changes in family roles and expectations.

The primary domain in which young people gain, or fail to gain, valuable resources from their families are in areas that affect their later lives. Families provide not only a reservoir of experiences to draw from, but offer models, guidance, teaching, social control, and material resources that prepare youth for adulthood. However, there is increasing evidence that by the time many children reach adolescence they are vulnerable to manipulation by depersonalizing influences, such as materialism, drugs, and alcohol. They are also ill-equipped to sustain stable relationships. The inevitable conclusion is that many adults are failing to deliver what is necessary for the proper social development of young people during this stage of their life. One of the main contributing factors is a widespread sense of helplessness among parents due to aggressive values and messages from the media and peer groups that challenge their own competencies in bringing up young people within the context of a healthy family.

Families in India have undergone tremendous changes, with far-reaching consequences in social, cultural, economic, and political spheres. Increases in social mobility, women's education, migration to cities, urbanization, industrialization, ad liberalization have profoundly affected the family system in India. This has led to changes in interrelationships among family members and in family dynamics.

Types of family units today are varied and are in a process of transition. Across nations, the expansion of varying family forms has been well-documented in recent years. Apart from the traditional joint families in India, many other family forms have evolved, including nuclear, women-headed, single parent, divorced, remarried, adopted, and gay and lesbian families. The nature of the family system across the world has also undergone a sea of change. Larson et al. (2002) inficate that these major changes in trends are due to family mobility, family members working in distant cities and countries, smaller family size, and an increase in women's employment. These changes alter the capacity and types of resources families are able to provide to their younger members. When parents and extended relatives live apart, it deprives the young family member of the warmth and security of a cohesive family environment and support, as well as daily access to role models, sources of advice, and different types of support in crisis situations.

A positive aspect of the contemporary Indian family is that the mother's employment allows her to receive support outside her family. The mother's employment brings additional resources to the family in the form of money and new social capital, and provides a role model for female offspring. However, it also brings various problems for which the family is not prepared. In India, more and more women with their own families are working, without the proper skills to manage the personal, social, and professional aspects at once. Thus, a kind of confusion and discontentment is evident which greatly affects the young family members. At this stage various risk factors need to be examined and understood. Unless families are strengthened, individual members cannot be empowered to face the future effectively.

The fast pace and discordant sequence of changes has contributed to individual stress, which has in turn affected youth development. The ambiguity of values young people observe in the adult world, the absence of powerful role models, and the increasing gap between aspirations and possible achievements, has, not surprisingly, lead to alienation and identity diffusion (Singh & Singh, 1996). The key concern now is the stress created by the changing composition and dynamics of the family, with different expectations, values, competencies, and copying styles between parents and children.

Parents themselves appear ill-prepared to cope with this rapid social change, having grown up in hierarchically structured and interlinked social groups and collectives that have included the extended family, kinship network, and caste groups which provided stability and solidarity (Singhal & Mishra, 1994). The conflict between a parent's desire to help their children cope with the competitive demands of the market economy, and society's achievement orientation and its rootedness in the safety of tradition, expresses itself in the "cold feet syndrome" when things go wrong (Saraswathi & Pai, 1997). Parents who seem modern in their child rearing practices get anxious when their adolescent child breaches established social codes. Intergenerational conflicts related to marriage, career choice, education, or separate living arrangements result in the tendency to fall back on tradition, which in turn can be a breeding ground for intergenerational conflict.

Clinical practitioners have expressed concern regarding the implications for youth mental health, especially the tensions experienced by the weakening of social supports from kinship groups and the community. Thus, youth development is a major agenda of policy not only in India, but across the world. It has been universally recognized that the future of societies depends on the success in providing pathways by which children and young people can develop and prepare themselves to be contributing members of their communities as adults, while still maintaining healthy family ties.

Developing Youth Potentials within Families

Families are found worldwide and are considered the most significant social context for youth development. They not only foster development in children and adolescents, but also shape the quality of their lives by serving as a source of nurturance, emotional bonding, and socialization. The family unit has the potential to provide stability, support, and act as a safety net in the face of crises in the environment. The basis for an individual's competence in coping with and shaping their environment is primarily a function of the family system.

Parents and communities invest in children and youth by providing for their health, education, and physical, vocational, and cultural preparation for a productive adulthood (Fussell & Greene, 2002). Therefore, it is the role of the family—the basic social unit—to enhance the potential of its young members and create an environment that provides the opportunities to do so, despite fast paced social change. Ways to nurture the potentials of young family members include:

1. ***Developing self-esteem, self-efficacy and personal responsibilities :*** Realistic confidence is a hallmark characteristic among competent children. Hence, parents and teachers especially need to assist with infusing confidence in children to enhance their self-esteem. They can do this by providing unconditional love and emotional support, while at the same time lovingly enforcing healthy rules and boundaries. As a result, the child internalizes a strong sense of confidence each day as they do things that confirm their ability to create the results they want in their lives. Further, adequate use of rewards and praise produces higher self-esteem, competence, responsibility, self-reliance, and independence in children and adolescents. On the other hand, the use of force and punishment by parents tends to create poor self image in children.

2. ***Developing positive personality traits :*** Training may be imparted within families through socialization process to enhance a young person's personality, for instance, in developing a positive outlook of life, enhancing adaptive skills, encouraging self-regulation, and discouraging negative social behavior. Disadvantaged children and adolescents in particular may be trained to make the use of the available family resources and to develop coping skills to adapt to stressful situations successfully.

3. ***Family support, coping, and competence development*** : Research has identified the family unit as the most significant contributing agent in developing competencies among children and adolescents (Blechman, 1991; Blechman, Tinsley, Carella, & McEnroe, 1986; Choudhury, 2003). Effective

communication within the family contributes to children's and youth's adaptive ability through development of coping skills and relevant competencies. Families try to shield children and youth from experiencing developmentally appropriate challenges and avert the occurrence of negative life events. However, participation in effective family communication teaches children strategies for coping with developmentally appropriate social and achievement challenges.

4. *Effective parenting* : High-quality parenting and the empowerment of parents through developing family resilience have been identified as the focus areas for optimizing youth potentials. A good parent-child relationship serves as a scaffold for building adaptive skills in a child. Sensitive and consistent care-giving and warm but firm authoritative parenting is necessary for the development of self-regulation in children and adolescents to prevent aggressive and disruptive behavior problems. The new role of the father in parenting within Indian families has been emphasized in some recent studies (Choudhury, 2003), and co-parenting relationships are necessary for effective stress-free parenting, especially among working and low socioeconomic status families.

Supportive parenting behavior in which fathers provide affection, nurturance, interest, and companionship enhances children's self-esteem, life satisfaction, and social and cognitive competence (Biller, 1993). This supportive dimension of parental involvement has been shown to influence certain behavioral outcomes of adolescents such as delinquency, drinking, and other behavioral problems (Simons, Johnson, & Conger, 1996). According to Monagle (1998), parents contribute to the development of their children and adolescents in a unique way. They foster development of the child's personhood, provide emotional stability, socialize the child and educate them in social tolerance and citizenship, provide a link to culture and traditions, and provide unconditional acceptance for the child's sense of self-worth.

5. *Adequate learning in the home environment* : The home environment is vital for human development because it provides the necessary ingredients for learning. Thus, adequate resources should be provided to adolescents in areas such as literacy, wellness promotion, rituals for nurturing healthy relationships, building a positive attitude towards learning, social connections for pursuing higher education, and strategies for sustaining a positive, well-balanced family system (Thomson & Hupp, 1992).

6. *Positive family relationships* : Family relationships are considered an important resource for psychological well-being and competence development among children and adolescents. Researchers have linked the emergence of resilience in children to key protective influences in the family and social contexts. Within the family system, a warm, nurturing, supportive parent-child relationship is considered the key factor in developing competence in children. A close parent-child relationship enables an individual to enter adolescence with better self-regulation skill and better ability to establish supportive relationships with persons outside the family (Wills & Clearly, 1996). During adolescence parental warmth continues to be positively related to optimal psychological adjustment and parental control. When warmth is combined with high parental support, it is particularly associated with high self-esteem.

Parents remain an emotional touchstone in adolescents' lives. Even if adolescents spend little time with their parents, they remain emotionally attached and rely on them for comfort and support. Conflict between parents and adolescents is higher mainly because of the ambiguity of parental authority and parental helplessness in dealing with difficult and complex issues today. Therefore, parental competency in managing their young children is required. This can only be achieved through a deeper understanding of the needs, requirements, and problems faced by the adolescent during this transitional stage between childhood and adulthood. Relationships with parents are not the only family interactions that will have an impact on the adolescent's development. Uncles, aunts, and grandparents are of significant importance as well. Grandparents play an especially important role in Indian families as their involvement, interaction, and assistance has a variety of positive effects on the lives of Indian youths.

7. Family functioning style : The family functioning style is basically determined by the style of parenting used within the family system. There are two dimensions of parenting behavior: parental responsiveness and parental demandingness. Parents vary on both of these dimensions, and these dimensions are more or less independent of each other. This makes it possible to look at various combinations of the parenting characteristics. The scheme developed by Maccoby and Martin (1983), and illustrated below in Figure 1, shows that parents can vary both in demandingness and in responsiveness, resulting in four types of parenting behavior. Parents can be classified as indulgent, indifferent, authoritative, or authoritarian. *Indulgent parents* behave in a benign, accepting, essentially passive manner. They are unlikely to set standards or to have high expectations for their children and do not see punishment as important. *Indifferent parents* are often also called neglectful. This group knows little of what their children are doing and tries to minimize the time they spend on child care activities. *Authoritative parents* are warm but firm. They set standards and hold to boundaries and are more likely to give explanations and to reason with the young person than to be punitive. Finally, *authoritarian parents* place a high value on obedience and conformity. They are more likely to punish misbehavior and tend not to encourage autonomy.

Adolescents brought up in indulgent households are often less mature, more irresponsible, and more likely to conform to peer pressure. Those who grow up in neglectful or indifferent

Fig. 1: A scheme for classifying parenting types

Responsiveness	Demandingness	
High	High	Low
	Authoriativ	Indulgent
Low	Authoritarian	Indifferent

Source: Maccaby and Martin (1983)

families are those most at risk, as might be expected. They are more likely to be impulsive and to get involved in high-risk behavior at an early age (Kurdek & Fine, 1994). In most cases children and adolescents reared in families with authoritative parents do better on a range of measures, including self-esteem, perspective-taking, and the likelihood of avoiding risky behavior (i.e., drug abuse, excessive sexual activity, etc.). Authoritative parents love and nurture their children and provide structure so that the young person has expectations and rules for their behaviour. Further, the parents accept and encourage autonomy. Equally important is monitoring and supervision provided by the parents. Poor monitoring is linked to a variety of risky behaviors, including offending the law, drug use, poor school performance, and unsafe sex. Knowledge regarding what, when, where, and with whom the young people are spending time is of particular importance. Authoritarian parents can damage a child's self-esteem or cause rebellion against strictly enforced rules.

8. *Disciplining the young at home* : The goal of all discipline is to mould behavior so that the child or adolescent's behavior will conform to the roles prescribed by the cultural group to which the individual belongs. Today it is recognized that children need discipline if they are to be happy, competent, and well-adjusted individuals. It is through discipline that they learn to behave in accordance with the members of the social group. In order to inculcate this value, parents need to be disciplined themselves in their daily activities, behaviors, and thinking, so that their children have a role model to follow.

Parental deeds and actions have tremendous impact on youths' psyche. Certain childhood needs can be fulfilled by disciplining them at home. They are:

- Discipline gives children and adolescents a feeling of security because it gives them behavioral guidelines to follow.
- Discipline helps young individuals to avoid the feeling of guilt and shame of misbehavior—feelings that inevitably lead to unhappiness and poor adjustment.
- Developmentally appropriate discipline serves as an ego bolstering motivation which encourages one to accomplish what is required of them.

9. *Encouraging positive peer relations* : In some ways peers play an even more critical role than parents in shaping social skills and sharpening identities. Furthermore, a multiage peer setting can foster intergenerational transfer of cultural knowledge and skills. Experience with peers also has major effects on later development, including orientation towards friendships and sexuality issues that are central to quality of life. It is essential to view peer influence in both its positive and negative aspects. Parents need to guide their children in selecting a peer group and may counsel them in terms of positive and negative influences of peer relationships. Positive peer relations may be encouraged through inviting the child's friends to the home, observing functions, keeping in touch with other children's parents, and bringing the families together so that each set of parents is kept involved.

10. *Care for physical and nutritional well-being* : Young individuals in Indian society may suffer from various physical and nutritional deficiencies which can lead to stunting of growth, under-nutrition, malnutrition, etc. All growth parameters can be profoundly affected, along with their reproductive health (especially of females). The health scenario of more than 40% of adolescents in India is plagued by under-nutrition. Improper eating habits, such as overeating or engaging in the fast food culture, also affect Indian youth to a large extent. Older family members need to provide accurate information regarding food choices and their impact on health. Good eating habits can be encouraged by focusing on home made food, requiring less dependence on fast food. The family's attitude towards food is very important because it has a tremendous impact on the food habits of the younger generations.

11. *Sexuality and reproductive health care* : Gopalan (1993) rightly terms the high incidence of teenage pregnancies in India as "child labour at its worst." He stated, "we witness the said spectacle of millions of children (girls 14-18 years) compelled to engage in child-bearing and child-rearing even before they have had a chance to complete their own physical growth and development and attain adulthood...It is labour which carries greater risks than some other forms of child labour over which there is public outcry." Despite the acquired immunodeficiency syndrome (AIDS) scare, sexual activity is on the rise, and the age of initiation into sexual activity has been steadily lowering into the early teens. Data indicates that more than 50% of young adults are married by the end of their teenage years and are therefore engaged in socially acceptable sexual relations. Double standards do exist, whereby unmarried adolescent boys are far more likely than unmarried adolescent girls to be sexually active (Verma & Saraswathi, 2002).

All of these given facts indicate that information, knowledge, and awareness among the youth are of vast importance for a healthy future life. Young individuals can and should receive the right kind of information from within their families. Otherwise they may receive incorrect, inappropriate knowledge that may lead to unhealthy sexual activities.

12. *Mental health care* : Prevalence of psychiatric disorders in school children in India ranges from 8-36% (Malhotra, Kohli, & Arun, 1999). The most common types of mental health disorders have been identified as: enuresis, sleep disorders, mental retardation, epilepsy, emotional disturbances, and conduct disorders. Scholastic underachievement in India is found to be inversely related to mental health, highlighting the importance accorded to school success by both teachers and parents. Thus, providing quality mental health care to children and teenagers is a primary concern of today. Understanding the cultural, social, and economic contexts of problems associated with mental health of adolescents is important, especially parents and for other family members. The family focus needs to be placed on enriching the quality of life for Indian youths and improving mental health by providing a quality home environment and an encouraging family atmosphere.

Family "Resourcing" to Enhance Youth Resiliency

Family resourcing encourages the identification of family strengths and focuses on collaboration, highlighting the interdependence of family members (Karpel, 1986). It promotes coping and survival, limits destructive family patterns, and enriches daily family life. One of the most important factors that affects adolescents' resiliency is a strong parent-child relationship. Parental commitment gives the family particular a sense of cohesion and stability. Out of this family experience, resilient youth learn to feel that life makes sense and they can exercise control over their lives. This sense of meaning is extremely motivating. Family support is another important factor that can promote resiliency in young people, as it improves family adjustment to life cycle changes and stresses.

There are different ways families can enhance youth resiliency through family resourcing. One way is the ability to access coping and survival techniques used by the family members to face day-to-day family difficulties and life challenges. Younger family members need to be made aware of these challenges and day-to-day struggles, so that they will get used to the various types of family issues that require attention. Further, destructive actions and patterns of behavior displayed by young family members can be limited to prevent stressors from piling up within the family. Focusing on the rewarding aspects of life allows children and adolescents to connect with the family in an enriching and enjoyable way. Concentrating on caring, sharing, satisfaction, and pleasure allows youth to learn from positive and rewarding elements of family life, which enhances their ability to enjoy simple aspects of family life and reap the maximum benefits. Other ways a quality family life can be fostered include:

- The family's inner language identifies it as a family to all members—young, old, adults, children, males, females, boys and girls—and the language serves as a resiliency-building strategy.
- Individual and family commitments serve as loyalties, or a sense of connection, on the part of the each and every family member.
- The capacity of the family to interact with the outside world preserves and enhances the integrity of the family.
- The sibling subsystem is also a valuable source of support in Indian family context that can be utilized for enhancing youth potentials.
- Extended family support (especially grandparents) is another potential strength of the Indian family system that can be used for engaging, encouraging, and energizing youth power.

Conclusion

Economic globalization is functioning in parallel with cultural globalization to alter young people's tastes, lifestyles, and values. Most significantly, their relationships, attitudes, beliefs, and perceptions regarding their own families, parents, and community as a whole are severely challenged. Not surprisingly, evidence suggests increasing materialism in adolescents' values and aspirations across class, caste, and socioeconomic levels. Globalization has eroded the traditional upbringing of children in which the extended family shared the responsibility of socializing youth. Distractions and lack of proper role models are significantly contributing to the systematic disadvantages of the youth in Indian society. The role family is able to play in providing the necessary support, assistance, and guidance is disheartening and distorted as well, and the future growth and development of many of today's young people are affected. There seems to be separate youth culture that fails to be understood by the family members, so these families feel helpless.

Despite greater pressures due to globalization, most youth are rising to the challenges and developing higher level of skill and maturity than were common in the prior generations. What the youth of the 21st Century require now is a safe haven in the family to develop their potentials, capabilities, and competencies to face the challenges of future. The youth of today need to be equipped with more effective skills that will promote psychological well-being and resilience and help them to keep pace with changes in the society. Building youth resilience is a complex issue that has multiple dimensions in relation to the characteristics of the young person, the family, and the environment, (the community) in which the youth develops, within the broader social milieu. Therefore, we need to examine and understand what builds resilience in young people within the family context in this increasingly diverse and rapidly changing world. Strong, healthy families are more likely to launch well-adjusted young people that actively participate in their own development while successfully contributing to the larger community as a whole.

References

Biller, H. B. (1993). *Fathers and families: Paternal factors in child development*. Westport, CT: Auburn House.

Blechman, E. (1991). Effective communication enabling multi problem families to change. In P. A. Cowan & M. E. Hetherington (Eds.), *Family transitions - Advances in family research,* 2, 219-245. NJ: Lawrence Erlbaum Associates.

Blechman, E. A., Tinsley, B., Carella, E. T., & McEnroe, M. J. (1986). Childhood competence and depression. *Journal of Abnormal Psychology, 95*, 223-227.

Choudhury, R. (2003). *Family support system of invulnerable children in India*. Unpublished D.Litt Thesis, Berhampur University, Orissa, India.

Fussell, E., & Greene, M. (2002). Demographic trends affecting youth around the world. In. B. Brown, R. Larsen and T.S. Saraswathi (Eds.), *The world's youth: Adolescence in eight regions of the globe*. New York, Cambridge University Press.

Gopalan, C. (1993). Child care in India – Emerging challenges. *Bulletin of the Nutrition Foundation of India, 14*(3), 1-3.

Government of India. (1997). *Draft national youth policy*. Ministry of Human Resources Development, Department of Youth Affairs and Sports.

Karpel, M. (Ed.). (1986). *Family resources: The hidden partner in family therapy*. New York: Guilford.

Kurdek, I., & Fine, M. (1994). Family acceptance and family control as predictors of adjustment in young adolescents: Linear, curvilinear, or interactive effects? *Child Development, 65*, 1137-1146.

Larson, R., Brown, B. B., & Mortimer, J. T. (2002). Edited book on. 'Adolescent's preparation for the Future: Perils and Promise. A report of the Study group on Adolescence in the 21st Century, Miami: The Society for Research on Adolescence.

Maccoby, E. & Martin, J. (1983). Socialization in the context of the family: Parent-child interaction. In E. Hetherington (Ed.), *Handbook of child psychology*. New York: Wiley.

Malhotra, S., Kohli, A., & Arun, P. (1999). Prevalence of psychiatric disorders in school children in India. Unpublished manuscript, Chandigarh, India: PGIMER.

Monagle, V. (1998, November 25-27). *Parents – A challenge for the future*. Paper presented at the 6th Australian Institute of Family Studies Conference, Melbourne, Australia.

Saraswathi, T. S., & Pai, S. (1997). Socialization in the Indian context. In H. Rao & D. Sinha (Eds.), *Asian perspectives in psychology* (pp. 74-92). New Delhi: Sage Methodology Series.

Simons, R. L., Johnson, C., & Conger, R. D. (1996). Parents and peer groups as medicators of the effect of community structure on adolescent problem behavior. *American Journal of Community Psychology, 24*, 145-171.

Schlegel, A. (2000). The global spread of adolescent culture. In L. J. Crockett & R. K. Silbereisen (Eds.), *Negotiating adolescence in time of social change* (pp. 71-88). London: Cambridge University Press.

Singh, L. B. & Singh, A. K. (1996). Alienation: A symptomatic reaction of educated employed youth in India. *International Journal of Psychology, 31*(2), 101-110.

Singhal, R. & Mishra, G. (1994). Achievement goals: A situational-contextual analysis. *International Journal of Intercultural Relations, 18*(2), 239-258.

Stinnett, N. (1981). *Family strengths: Roots of well-being*. Lincoln, NB: University of Nebraska Press.

Swick, K. (1987). *Perspectives on understanding and working with families*. Champaign, IL: Slipes.

Thomson, T. & Hupp, C. (1992). *Saving children at risk: Poverty and disabilities*. Newbury Park, CA: Sage.

Verma, S., & Saraswathi, T.S. (2002). Adolescence in India: Stress urchins or Silicon Valley millionaires? In B. Brown, R. W. Larson, & T. S. Saraswathi (Eds.), *The world's youth: Adolescence in eight regions of the globe*. New York: Cambridge University Press.

Wills, T. A. & Clearly, S. D. (1996). Stress-coping model for alcohol/ tobacco interactions in adolescence. In J. Ferting & J. Allen (Eds.), *Alcohol and tobacco: From basic science to policy*. NIAAA Research Monograph.

15

Preparing Families for the 21st Century: The Need for Family Life Education in India

David K. Carson, Cecyle K. Carson, Aparajita Chowdhury

Indian families in the 21st century are truly at a crossroads. This chapter discusses the need for Family Life Education (FLE) in India and presents a case for FLE as an essential component of professional practice for those who work with married couples, families, and youth. Included is a discussion of the numerous factors placing Indian families at risk today, and the common and more extreme difficulties experienced by couples and families. The potential benefits of Family Life Education to strengthening families and marital relationships are discussed. Targets of and settings for Family Life Education and its training are highlighted, and a brief outline of a training-the-trainer approach is provided.

India is the world's largest democracy and the second largest nation on earth. Although it is a rapidly developing country, India is a land steeped in tradition. It is also unparalleled in terms of ethnic, cultural, economic, political, linguistic, and religious diversity. Despite the fast-paced socio-cultural and economic changes that are challenging marriage and family life, the family unit remains at the core of society. Indeed, contemporary Indians continue to hold marriage and family life in the highest possible regard and reverence (Mullatti, 1995). Children and adolescents have a special place in the family and community (Mandan, 1990), and interdependency, support, and nurturing across the generations are commonplace in the Indian family system (Simhadri, 1989). Parents and extended family members maintain their roles as the primary socializers of children, and parents and adult children strive to retain close relationships even when they are separated by long distances (Baral & Bishoyee, 1999; Misra, 1995).

On the reverse side, Indian families today are experiencing a complex array of problems and challenges. Some of these difficulties are ancient and deeply embedded in Indian society, and some of them have seemingly never before been encountered in this country's history (Baral & Bishoyee, 1999; Baral & Chowdhury, 1999; Desai & Bharat, 1989). The majority of the roughly 80% of Indians who live in villages and rural areas remain poor and are generally lacking in social resource and supports. They continue to be isolated from mainstream society. Urbanites are also facing a multitude of problems that are challenging traditional family structures and relationships, and putting marriages and families at risk. An over-abundance of urban and rural dwellers continue to experience a plethora of difficulties, including: poverty and disease; overcrowding; water and air pollution; migration of individuals and families from rural to urban areas due to a lack of viable employment and vocational opportunities; a gradual weakening of age-old traditions including transformations in religion, caste, and other social institutions; natural disasters that make transportation, communication, and modernization difficult; ethnic conflicts and ongoing political instability; increased crime, social violence, and terrorism; inadequate housing and sanitation; poor nutrition and health care; illiteracy and low quality (and sometimes non-existent) education for children; minimal enforcement of child labor laws; and especially in rural areas the continual promotion of early marriages and large families which facilitates more than impedes the cycle of poverty. In addition, families in contemporary India are experiencing newer kinds of problems similar to those which have permeated most Western societies the past 40 years or more. These include: marital strain and dissolution, parent-child conflicts, various forms of family violence, substance abuse, juvenile delinquency, school dropout or low school attainment among the lower class, and excessive pressures in many middle and upper class families for adolescents and young adults to achieve academically (Agarwal, 1989; Chowdhury, 1999; Das, 1999; Madan, 1990; Nanda & Dash, 1996; Parikh & Krishna, 1992; Patnaik, 1999; Sarkar, 1988). The result of all of these changes and difficulties has been a gradual segmenting of Indian society into the very rich, a flattening of the middle class, and a rise in the percentage of people living in deplorable conditions with little hope of ever improving their lives. In short, the future and well-being of the Indian family is highly precarious. Families are in tremendous need of assistance, resources, and support.

As part of a comprehensive mental health promotion effort in India, Family Life Education (FLE) is an essential component in helping professionals and concerned citizens work with the populace in maintaining and restoring family strengths and traditions. However, FLE is a relatively new concept in India, and one that, with few exceptions, has not been implemented in current mental health, social welfare, or educational programs. Yet, the need for educating families about various aspects of parenting, child and adolescent development, and other facets of family life, has been emphasized by key Indian social scientists. For instance, the prominent Psychologist Durganand Sinha (1988) noted that there was a general consensus in the mental health community in India that (echoing the words of Channabasavanna and Bhatti, 1982, p. 149), "a patient is only a symptom of a troubled family." More recently, Oommen (2000), Professor of Sociology at Jawaharlal Nehru University in Delhi, indicated that today's Indian family is ripe for and in great need of family-based education and intervention.

This chapter examines the range of marital and family difficulties in light of the undercurrent of social and economic changes in India today, and how a Family Life Education (FLE) "movement" might take root in the current mental health, social service, and educational system. We also discuss the potential benefits of FLE training and services in meeting the tremendous needs of married couples and families in India today. This discussion will include an integration of the authors' practical experiences and observations in India that are based on the research we have conducted on Indian couples and families, educational programming we have engaged in with couples and families, and the counseling we have done with those experiencing a wide range of difficulties. Before we begin our discussion, however, it is important that we share three key assumptions that in many ways set the stage for FLE in this vast and diverse society.

First, Family Life Education (as with the notion of counseling or therapy) is generally an unknown, misunderstood, and sometimes devalued enterprise in India (Carson & Chowdhury, 2000). Any activity or movement promoted by professionals which implies that couples and families need education or training, especially with regard to sacred areas such as marriage or child-rearing, can easily be viewed in negative terms. This is partly because such practices connote a "deficit" in marriage and family life or functioning that needs to be fixed or remedied. Second, it is likely that FLE in India will entail a much greater involvement of extended family members, as well as interdisciplinary integration of prevention practices, than in many western countries, which emphasize both education about and treatment for existing problems and disorders. Finally, the training and practice of family life specialists in India, and the growth of FLE as a profession, is likely to follow a radically different pathway than it has in other countries around the globe, including the United States; for example, a widespread lay training component that involves a high level of volunteerism. Each of these issues will be discussed in greater depth as this chapter unfolds.

The Changing Indian Family and the Need for Family Life Education

In rural areas, villages, and even in large cities today, family life in India continues to be deeply rooted in the community. In fact, for centuries, friends, neighbors, relatives, and community members have shared responsibility for children's lives and well-being. The family system remains a source of stability and support when problems arise and maintains the physical and psychological integrity of individual family members over time. Traditional Indian society has been based on the joint family system, which, while in transition, is still the norm. This is particularly the case in rural areas where mobility of family members is much more restricted. The family as a social system consists of well-defined rules, roles, and sentiments that bind people together. Members share feelings of solidarity (familism) and strive to uphold family dignity and status in the society. A high premium is placed on family unity and cohesiveness, which are necessary for family stability and survival. Any behavior that threatens this cooperative spirit and unity is discouraged both from within and without. Sharing and mutual dependence are common at all stages of the family life cycle, which contributes to a sense of safety and security in the family. Elaborate family practices and rituals foster feelings of belongingness and convey the message that family bonds are immutable, dependable, and life long (Bharat, 1997; Mullatti, 1995). Yet, the family structure has not gone unchallenged in recent years.

There are numerous and fast-paced changes occurring in India, which are having far-reaching implications in family, social, cultural, economic, and political life. These include the widespread growth of education (especially women's education), the impact of the mass media and modern communications, westernization (i.e., gradual adaptation of values and life-styles of western nations), industrialization and modernization, and economic liberalization. In an age of the electronic media, including televisions and computers in even remote areas, the Indian family is being exposed to ideas, ideals, and values that are sweeping across the entire nation (Baral & Bishoyee, 1999). Some Indian social scientists and family scholars have proposed that, once the conditions of equality are negotiated and obtained at all levels, mental and relational well being will be an inevitable outcome for a large portion of the society, including the family (e.g., see Bharat, 1991; Belle, 1990; Sinha, 1984). However, in the modern age these changes continue to be slow and are often met with resistance (Baral & Bishoyee, 1999; Misra, 1995; Sinha, 1988).

Other everyday problems encountered by contemporary Indian families include the stresses and strains of rearing children, conflicts with in-laws, difficulties associated with various chronic illnesses, and developmental delays and disabilities of children or other family members. Sinha (1984,1988) argues that the majority of urban and rural dwellers today prefer to live in small nuclear family units. At the same time, however, they want to maintain close relationships with their extended family and have them available during times of crisis. The gradual trend toward nucleation has created greater role strain, ambiguity, and conflict between family members (such as authority over children between mothers and their mother-in-laws), as well as confusing expectations for children. Moreover, unlike the scenario in the traditional joint family system, elderly persons today have few roles to play in child-rearing and socialization. They are also less likely, especially in educated families, to live with their adult children and grandchildren. The result in many families is an absence of clear and consistent role models for children beyond their own parents. In addition, parents are becoming more restrictive of their children (partly due to safety reasons) in having free time to interact with peers either at school or in the neighborhood. This situation not only limits children's social network but also tends to instill more feelings of fear and distrust in them. The mass media (especially the electronic media) also aggravates the situation by creating unrealistic aspirations in children and parents, including a "you can and should have it all" materialistic kind of mind set.

Additional influences on the family include increased exposure to "western thinking" (e.g., European and American), which has brought about changes in attitudes towards conventional methods of disciplining, toilet training, feeding, and other child-rearing practices (Mullatti, 1995; Sinha, 1984, 1988). However, because traditional attitudes have not been completely abandoned, many parents alternate between permissive and strict (authoritarian) child-rearing, thus creating anxiety and confusion in children. This ambivalence and ambiguity makes them more vulnerable to acquiring a variety of behavioral and emotional disorders (Bharat, 1997). Moreover, difficulties in marriage relationships, coupled with inadequate or conflictual co-parenting practices, are becoming more prevalent, in part because women are breaking out of traditional roles, becoming educated in greater numbers, and advocating for equal rights both at home and in the work place (Baral, Das, & Dash, 1999; Mohanty, 1999). Given that so many women are employed outside the home today, some Indian researchers contend that children's needs are not being met nor their development facilitated (Desai & Bharat, 1989; Mullatti, 1995). Research on female-headed households has shown that these women face numerous problems, including low income, a lack of social support, and discipline problems with their children (Pati & Patnaik, 1999). Some social scientists are convinced that the increase in single-parent families has contributed to a greater number of children and adolescents experiencing serious difficulties (Bharat, 1991; R. C. Das, 1999). Hence, increased role strain, marital difficulties, parent-child conflicts, feelings of guilt, and status confusion, are commonly observed among working women (Chowdhury, 1995; Muni, 1995), despite the fact that there may be some economic and self-esteem related advantages in some of these families (Mohanty, 1999). Since more women in India are joining the labor force without proper support and assistance (often in the face of extended family and community opposition), the increase in family-related problems is perhaps not surprising (Das, 1999; Kapur, 1995).

Other Factors Placing Children and Families at Risk:

• ***Inadequate teacher training and changes in school functioning and curriculum:*** Also contributing to child and adolescent difficulties (with repercussions to the family) is a school curricula and environment that often does not meet children's needs, whether they are academic or personal. It is not uncommon for teachers to use strict and sometimes physical punishment to maintain order, practices which today's Indian youth are not always in agreement. Perhaps most notable in educated families are the extreme pressures for children to achieve academically so they can gain entrance into the better colleges and universities (often with little free time with peers or family play time). This pressure tends to increase the vulnerability of older children and adolescents to various personal and relational difficulties (Nanda & Dash, 1996). Further, Carson, Chowdhury, Perry, and Pati (1999), as well as Padhi and Dash (1994), have found strong evidence of a connection between positive parental attitudes and adolescent social and academic competence. Among lower income families in India, studies have indicated that children who are the most at-risk for school difficulties and failure are from multiply disadvantaged groups, including those commonly referred to as Scheduled Castes (SC) and Scheduled Tribes (ST) (Chowdhury & Chowdhury, 1996; Gupta, 1987; Misra & Mohanty, 1995; Padhi & Dash, 1994; Sahoo & Sia, 1988). Those SC and ST children who are rejected by their higher class and caste peers are particularly at risk for developing behavior problems, dropping out of school, and experiencing disorders such as anxiety and depression (Chowdhury & Chowdhury, 1996; Ota, 1995; Sarkar, 1988). However, Chowdhury and Chowdhury suggest that, if such children received the necessary resources and support to successfully navigate this transition, patterns of long term poor achievement and school failure might be averted.

- ***Families with disabilities and multiple crises:*** Indian families with a disabled or chronically ill member experience all of the burdens associated with life-long care (Kapur, 1995). These families need social support and require special coping skills to manage. Further, families facing situations caused by demoralizing events, such as suicide, rape, family violence, unwed motherhood, "bride burning"(caused by the dowery system), and loss of home or property due to exploitation, job loss, or natural disasters, run the risk of breakdown or disintegration (Davar, 1999; Desai & Bharat, 1989). Serious marital maladjustment in families is more likely to result in abuse, conjugal separation, juvenile delinquency, mental health problems, extended family disputes, and an unhealthy environment for children (Baral, Das, & Dash, 1999; Das, 1999).

- **Mental illness as other handicapping conditions:** Mental health problems in India are often associated with inter relational or intra family conflicts. These are typically everyday difficulties that in many cases could be prevented or resolved, but frequently tend to accumulate. Due to decreasing assistance or support systems within communities, more serious problems such as suicide, homicide, rape and sexual harassment are increasing (Devar, 1998,1999; Kapur, 1995; Sharma & Chadd, 1990). In the last 50 years, philosophically at least, and to some limited extent pragmatically, medical and mental health efforts have gradually moved from the institutionalized care of the mentally ill to the promotion of mental health. Yet, relatively little is available to individuals and families in immediate distress. Furthermore, public attitudes toward couples and families in crisis, or person's with mental or emotional disorders, are often judgmental and compartmentalizing. For example, research not too many years ago conducted in Delhi indicated that educated laypersons generally viewed the mentally ill as aggressive, violent and dangerous (Prabhu, Raghuram, Verma, & Maridass, 1984). Optimism about the outcome of psychiatric treatment for these individuals was not high, and there was a lack of awareness about available facilities to treat the mentally ill. Another study (Boral, Bagchi, & Nandi, 1980) revealed that relatives of the mentally ill preferred magic healers, ayurveds, and homeopaths to psychiatrists and psychotherapists. Moreover, a majority of participants believed that marriage would cure mental illness, even though (paradoxically) a majority did not want to forge marital alliances with a mentally ill person. Hence, treatment of personal and family difficulties is still at a rudimentary stage of development in India.

A survey of prevalence studies of child mental health problems (Sitholey & Chakraborthi, 1992) highlighted a number of issues relevant to intervention, education and prevention. These investigators found that there were considerable differences in psychiatric disorders in the small number of general population studies that had included children. Disorders varied greatly across age, gender, social and demographic status. When the extremely high or low reported prevalence rates were excluded (about 1% of children under 18), the acceptable range of mental and emotional disorders ranged from 50 to 150 per 1000 children and adolescents (approximately 5 to 15 percent). Often these individuals had accompanying developmental delays and/or scholastic difficulties.

Considering the pervasiveness of psychiatric disturbances among youth, inpatient and outpatient mental health care facilities are extremely sparse. Presently there are only about 100 child guidance clinics in the entire country, and most of these clinics are located in large cities such as Mumbai, Poone, Bangalore, Hyderabad, and Delhi. These clinics do provide services to children with mental retardation and emotional problems. Indeed, much of the emphasis on mental health treatment in India is geared toward children in accordance with the National Mental Health Program for India. However, while this Program covers adults and children alike, whole family mental health coverage receives little attention and is downplayed in its importance, despite the abundance of research showing a string connection between conjoint marital and family functioning, and the social/academic competence and psychosocial well-being of youth.

In sum, mental health professionals in India are presented with numerous challenges in working with couples and families. Individual psychopathology is often is associated with family problems and dynamics. When individuals are treated apart from the family (as is customary), therapy sometimes yields positive results (Sharma & Chadd, 1990). However, when someone who has had counseling or has undergone psychiatric treatment returns to the family, it is believed that this person more often than not regresses to earlier patterns of behavior and functioning. This is because even though the individual may have changed, the family system has not (Devar, 1998, 1999; Sethi & Manchanda, 1978). Until family units are transformed through education and sometimes therapy (Carson & Chowdhury, 2000), individual family members have little chance of maintaining any gains made.

Strong Families and Child/Adolescent Resiliency and Competence

As we have observed, there are seemingly countless millions of young people in modern India who are failing to acquire the competence and skills needed for success in adult life. The adolescent segment of India's population has been rapidly expanding since the early 1950's, and individuals between 10 and 21 years of age make up more than half (57%) of India's population (Shukla, 1994). The number of rural adolescents is rising at unprecedented rates and now constitutes approximately 73% of the total youth population. Indian society has generally been unsuccessful in providing the necessary assistance and guidance to today's children and youth, most notably (but not exclusively) among lower caste rural dwellers. Even in villages and small communities today youth are exhibiting a host of difficulties that include disobedience and even violence toward parents, school dropout, smoking, alcoholism and other drug use, petty crime, and various other manifestations of juvenile delinquency (Chowdhury & Choudhury, 1993; Shukla, 1994; Simhadri, 1989).

Despite these increasing problems and risks, however, many children and youth are thriving in their development, and it is from these children and their families that we have much to learn. Elsewhere these individuals have been referred to as resilient (Garmezy, 1983; Rutter, 1987) or invulnerable (Anthony, 1987), and in an Indian context they are like "lotus in the mud" (Chowdhury & Choudhury, 1993). Even though these youth are growing up in resource-limited and often stressful environments (familial, social, cultural, economic), they generally find ways to cope well with stress and are socially and academically competent. Understanding the processes that contribute to their adaptation, particularly family dynamics and relationships and key community factors, will provide crucial clues for improving education, prevention, and intervention efforts.

Resilient children and adolescents are those who turn their disadvantages into advantages and emerge as successful and competent individuals in society. While constitutionally based individual characteristics and abilities certainly play a role in resiliency or invulnerability (e.g., health-related, temperamental), familial and extra-familial support systems, especially in an Indian context, are believed to be the most powerful influences (Acharaya, 1992; Choudhury, 1991; Chowdhury, Muni, Rath, & Pati, 1996). Results from several empirical studies have suggested that highly competent Indian adolescents, regardless of whether they are socio-economically advantaged or disadvantaged, share a common set of characteristics, including an emotionally healthy family climate (Carson et al., 1999, 2002; Choudhury, 1991, 1999; Hariharan, 1991; Padhi and Dash, 1994; Sahoo and Sia, 1988). Parents of adolescents in these families tend to have a positive attitude toward themselves, each other, and their adolescent, as well as high expectations of their adolescent with regard to behavior, education, and achievement. They are highly nurturing and consistently involved in their child's school and extra-curricular activities. Despite differences in living conditions, more competent youth generally have strong family, peer, and community supports (Chowdhury et al., 1996; Chowdhury & Choudhury, 1997). Findings from other investigations (e.g., Sharma, Saraswathi, & Gir, 1981) indicated that firm and consistent discipline, both at home and in school, promoted mature behavior patterns and cognitive and social competence in older school-aged children (see also Gore, 1983; Hariharan, Dash, & Acharaya, 1987; Nanda and Dash, 1996; Sahoo & Sia, 1988).

In summary, a substantial body of research has shown that the family plays a major role in augmenting successful coping in children and adolescents, and in facilitating their learning and school performance (Carson et al., 1999; Chowdhury, 1990; Chowdhury & Choudhury, 1993; Gupta, 1987; Hariharan, 1991; Nanda & Dash, 1996; Padhi & Dash. 1994; Sahoo & Sia, 1988; Sethi & Manchanda, 1978; Simhadri, 1989; Tiwari, 1990). Parents in particular, along with siblings, grandparents, and other relatives, thus serve as protective factors against stress and risk in the lives of youth. This is still normative in Indian families today, despite the growing tendency of youth toward independence, self-definition, and departure from some beliefs and practices of the past (Chowdhury & Muni, 1995). However, protective factors do not automatically result in positive outcomes. As Rutter (1987) indicates, protection does not lie in the availability of potentially supportive resources, but in the use made of them. It is in this context that Family Life Education (FLE) can perhaps make a unique and long-lasting contribution in Indian society.

Targets of and Settings for Family Life Education Training

Recipients of family life education training. There is a currently a severe shortage of professionals who have received training and supervised experience in family life education theory and methods. Information about Family Life Education is almost non-existent in traditional academic disciplines, such as in psychiatry, psychology, sociology, social work, and education. The field of Home Science education however, is one such exception, which is an applied academic field, built upon the discipline of science, arts, commerce and management for the purpose of achieving the welfare of whole family in an ever-changing society. Its curriculum provide an opportunity to integrate the knowledge from very many fields many from sociology, psychology, social work, anthropology, education and biochemistry etc., giving the subject a much needed practical applications with wholesome approach to family living in India. Thus, the academic program of Home Science education around the country can serve as pivotal place for training and dissemination of Family Life Education information and materials. Home Science as foundation education for FLE is already in existence throughout the country and with little inclusion of focused curriculum on FLE, can able to achieve effective result. Moreover, unlike Home Science program, FLE program can be started for both boys and girls or male/female for achieving its sole purpose of healthy and happy family life.

Rather than developing stand-alone FLE programs, it is our contention that, at this point in time, FLE training could most effectively be integrated into traditional academic programs mentioned previously. Indeed, these departments and programs already include some of the course work background essential to working with couples and families (e.g., human development, family studies, women and child welfare issues and practice). These programs are lacking presently certain basic theoretical issues, and at a minimum what an essential FLE curriculum should contain, may includes: (a) essential courses in family theory (including systems oriented theories) and human development as taught from various Indian perspectives; (b) identification and assessment of couples and families in need of education and prevention efforts, (c) current FLE theories, models, and methodologies that are relevant and applicable to Indian families; (d) professional ethics and practice in working with couples and families, and (e) supervised practical experiences which provide trained professionals and students at the graduate level opportunities to enhance their skills in working with couples and families. Whether some kind of credential is tied to such training is a matter of debate. However, it would be well within the realm of possibility to offer a 3- or 4-month post-graduate certification as a "Family Life Educator" to individuals who could take part in such a training experience.

A combined effort by psychiatrists (and other interested medical personnel), psychologists, sociologists, social workers, educators, and home scientists could involve the creation of different strategic centers around the country for FLE training. Involvement of those working in child and family welfare programs and services would also be vital to the success of this training effort. This is because government and non-governmental organizations (NGO's) run most of the Child and Family Welfare Programs in India. Although presently the training and competency of child welfare workers is exceedingly limited, provision of FLE training for these individuals is well within reach. Hence, these working professionals, as well as physicians, nurses, and other health specialists, academicians, and graduate students, are prime targets for FLE training. Promoting FLE as a legitimate and much-needed enterprise in India may also have secondary benefits, in that it may provide additional employment opportunities for trainees.

Settings for family Life education training. One ideal setting for FLE training is in *college and university academic departments,* and *colleges of medicine*, where this type of training and course work can be integrated into existing programs and curricula. Those with previous training and experience in FLE, including faculty members and students associated with various home science programs around the country, could serve as trainers and facilitators. Further, while many students who complete a degree in medicine or a graduate program in the social sciences (e.g., psychology or sociology), social work, or education, will seek employment in larger towns and cities, some inevitably go back to area in which they grew up (i.e., their town or village) to live and work. Undergraduate and graduate students in training who need to meet practicum or internship requirements, could also spend time in or visit centers, hospitals, or agencies which regularly to provide psychiatric, medical, or family counseling services. Part of what they offer could be FLE oriented.

Schools are also an excellent location for FLE training and services, and according to Kapur (1997), are the best places in India to develop mental health programs for children and adolescents. This is because community life in India often centers around the school and children's inter- and extra-curricular activities associated with school. Getting teachers, school administrators, and students to "buy in" to an FLE program by observing an effective program in action is often a turning point (Powell & Cassidy, 2001). Having timely and agreed-upon goals that are carried out in a cooperative manner are also essential. Since Indian parents (and other family members) are typically very concerned about the child well-being and educational success, they can become involved in (and recipients of) FLE efforts in a way that helps them feel empowered as well as, when necessary, save face in their community. Students too can benefit from a wide range learning experiences that include such topics as conflict resolution in families, relationship development and marriage preparation (e.g., so-called love marriages versus arranged marriages and everything on a continuum), effective parenting, and sexuality education.

As has been discussed, the large sector of professionals working with *child and family welfare agencies* that identify and work with families at-risk in both urban and rural areas would be prime recipients of FLE training. As in other countries of the world, which have discovered that "an ounce of prevention is worth a pound of cure," India's child welfare and social service contingent is in an ideal place to engage in. For example, early parent training and conduct marriage readiness and marital enrichment seminars and workshops on a large-scale basis can be started. In addition, training professionals associated with *mental health treatment centers and training institutes* in various aspects of family life is generally lacking in India. Some exceptions may include the 100 or so child guidance clinics positioned around the country. Other strategic centers for FLE training might include the National Institute of Mental Health and Neurosurgery (NIMHANS) in Bangalore, the Tata Institute of Social Sciences (TISS) in Mumbai, and a handful of other social science institutes (e.g., in Ranchi and Patna) and graduate training programs in counseling or clinical psychology (e.g., Chennai, Allahabad, Bhubaneswar). A mental health program in Amritsar (Vidyasagar) was one of the first in India to encourage families to stay with the patient during the entire treatment program. Bangalore and Vellore are two other cities which have programs where family members are actively involved in the active treatment of family members, as well as follow-up (Verghese, 1988). However, these few institutes and training programs cannot even begin to provide the educational preparation, research, and services to meet the needs of India's vast population (Devar, 1998; Shanker & Menon, 1991).

The *employment settings of parents* can also be an opportune place in which to involve parents or parents-to-be in various aspects of parenting education, marriage preparation, and marital enrichment. Admittedly, since approximately 80% of Indians live in rural areas, with many being self or sporadically employed, conducting FLE in work environments is a challenging task. These efforts may be better suited to those living and working in an urban milieu. Nevertheless, limited research from other countries of the world, including the United States, has shown that employee participation in regular FLE activities increases job satisfaction, commitment, productivity, social support, and longevity (Powell & Cassidy, 2001). Hence, there is much room for creativity when it comes to planning and implementing FLE programming for parents and others in work settings in an Indian context.

One can hardly travel anywhere in India, no matter how remote, without being reminded of the significance of *religious philosophies and practice*. Indeed, India is a country of intense religious activity and fervor. Religion permeates the lives of the vast majority of Indians, rich and poor, urban and rural, on a daily basis. Moreover, the concept of "family" is central to virtually all of the major religions of India (Hinduism, Islam, Sikhism, Buddhism, and Christianity, as well as a variety of sects, casts and tribal religions, etc.), as is the idea of service to others. Thus, working in the context of these religious traditions to provide training and outreach in FLE could (at least in many cases) be a natural and readily accepted activity, but only if conducted in a way that was in harmony with the essential tenets and practices each particular group. For example, in cities as well as rural areas, FLE services could be provided through Primary Health Centers (PHC), schools and *Anganwadi centers* where caring for women and children is a common undertaking. All the blocks of the country are covered by the Government sponsored program like ICDS (Integrated Child Development Services). Besides, under local self-government system (Panchayat Raj) in rural areas, this type of training can be given in "Panchayat level" for the benefits of the grassroots' level people.

Finally, South Asia in general, and India in particular, has a large number of *international development organizations and NGO's* (non-governmental organizations) operating within its boundaries. Our observations have been that, aside from various aspects of family planning and community health (e.g., prenatal care, disease prevention, nutrition education), there are a wide range of opportunities in these agencies and organizations for FLE that are yet to be tapped. Specialists working in various programs are prime candidates for basic training in FLE. Activities and information that can be realistically integrated with their regular duties and responsibilities may receive the greatest reception, as opposed to expecting or requesting that these professionals conduct additional programs and training with those whom they are involved. However, or impression is that these agencies are ripe for FLE training and implementation, whatever form and approach is taken. Trained FLE's in India can decide whether, and in what situations, they wish to adopt the role of expert, consultant, or facilitator, and with which group of professionals associated with particular NGO's and international development organizations. In sum, the success of any community mental health education and prevention program in India may depend on each community's sensitivity to mentally distressed children, adolescents, and adults, as well as married couples and families, in conflict (Sethi & Manchanda, 1978; Sinha, 1988). Thus, in order to meet the needs of a rapidly expanding society, mental health and social service agencies may need to be provided in large part by motivated para-professionals and citizens in cities, small towns, and rural areas (i.e., volunteerism). One untapped resource, for example, includes older adults and aging family members. Given the large percentage of retirees from government related services in India and the fact that the mandatory retirement age is now 55, these individuals would be ideal candidates for counselor training.

In our view, members of this age group not only have the time but also often have the need for a greater sense of purpose and involvement with others. As known and respected members (and often "elders") of their community, their impact as designated lay counselors could be significant. In this regard, families would be both a contributor to and receiver of services provided by a strong and encompassing force of lay family counselors.

Overview of a Training-the-Trainer Approach to Family Life Education

We are convinced that a "training the trainer" model, which has proved successful in the United States and other countries could be adapted for use in India. Training the trainer approach to education and preparation of family counselors/therapists in India has recently been proposed by Carson and Chowdhury (2000). This approach could be used for FLE training and implementation as well. Exchanges between family life specialists in India and other countries, where psycho-education and family therapy are common and respected forms of mental health treatment, can serve as the impetus to program development and identification of family life education trainees, supervisors, and training sites. As mentioned in the Carson and Chowdhury (2000) article, sources of funding for these exchanges might come primarily from NGO's, including various external grant-funding organizations, agencies and programs (e.g., WHO, UNICEF, Fulbright Commission, World Bank). A general outline of such a training approach to FLE is outlined below.

Phase One: (1) Identification of a "metavisor" in India for the entire training program; (2) Identification of FLE training sites in key areas (e.g., initially, three or four in one or more "test states" or geographical areas; and (3) Identification and training of an FLE supervisors or key trainers at each of these sites (i.e., "training the trainers") over a two or three month period through grant-sponsored international exchanges, where participating agencies and institutions would send designated supervisors abroad for FLE training, and/or host visiting family life educators as initial trainers in India. Supervisors-in-training might include experienced mental health professionals, social workers and child welfare specialists, physicians/psychiatrists, and university faculty in fields such as home science, psychology, social work, sociology, and education who have had some prior training in, or at least familiarity with, some of the core content and process components of FLE.

Phase Two: (1) Identification of interested and committed FLE trainees representing various disciplines, including, e.g., (a) post-graduate professionals in medicine, child/family welfare, social work, psychology, education, home science, etc.; (b) graduate students in appropriate academic disciplines (as indicated above); and (c) interested academic faculty in colleges and universities in the aforementioned (or related) disciplines.

Phase Three (The 3 Month Training Program). (1) Three months of academic (content-based) training (including in-class experiential learning and role-playing), which incorporates a minimum of 1 month of supervised internship experiences in FLE practice (at approved locations and sites, both urban and rural) with couples and families. Part of this practicum experience could include lay training of motivated community citizens (i.e., those who are concerned about families in their area/social milieu) in basic FLE knowledge, skills, and delivery. A community-based approach that includes some "home visiting" activities would be used extensively in both the practicum/internship and lay-training activities.

Training Processes and Procedures. FLE academic work in the classroom, as well as practicum/internship experiences, could be integrated with current academic programs in graduate schools of psychology, social work, home science, and even medicine. Training sessions for full-time working professionals could occur weekly (3-4 hours) in both professional (e.g., child/social welfare) and academic environments, as well as key locations in surrounding communities where trainees live and work. Trained supervisors would be responsible for coordinating and overseeing trainees' internship and lay training activities, both at designated learning (educational) sites and out in the community. Supervisors and trainees in particular geographical regions would meet once every month (total of three times) for one day of consultation. Each trainee's supervisor would provide on-going feedback to that person with regard to strengths and needed areas of improvement. The supervisor, in conjunction with the metavisor, would provide the final evaluation of the trainee that would determine successful completion of the training program.

The training approach described above, of course, could be modified and even reconstructed based on the needs and desires of the trainers, the trainees, and those couples and families who would be participating in such home and community-based education and services. Given India's mushrooming population, designers of programs and training will also need to have creative and empowering ways of involving lay persons of all ages and at all stages of life.

Concluding Remarks

Our observation has been that, while educated parents in India as a general rule may be more involved in their child's education than in countries such as the U.S., participation with their adolescents in both family and school-related activities that might enhance competence and self-esteem is still lacking in scores of families. Work, health and transportation problems, and limited family income may contribute to this lack of parental involvement. Many parents in India are also reluctant to violate school/home boundaries, and teachers and school administrators sometimes discourage parental involvement in the adolescent's process of learning while in school, and at times school-related functions. Hence, competency promotion needs to be part of a nation-wide thrust in family life education. School and community leaders, agencies and organizations are in an ideal position to assist parents not only in becoming more effective in their parenting roles, but also in augmenting marital and family strengths and providing education and opportunities for family recreation and activities. As Chowdhury *et al.* (1996, p.46) conclude, ".....positive interpersonal/social support within families such as positive help, mutual support and cohesion, provides opportunities for the development of mastery and competence....." Hence, parental counseling and education need to be ".....introduced to the parents regarding the child-rearing styles and positive support rendered to their children." Joint experiences for parents and adolescents might include the enhancement of communication and decision-making skills, problem-solving and conflict resolution abilities, anger management, self-esteem, and goal-setting/career exploration. Augmenting family strengths will tend to enhance adolescent competence, perhaps even more so in countries like India where immediate and extended family members play a unique and powerful role in the lives of the next generation. Family life education can positively and significantly influence the lives of couples and families who are struggling to balance traditional family structures and practices with the changing values, attitudes and life-styles that permeate contemporary Indian society.

References

Acharaya, S. (1992). *Personality, Motivational, and Cognitive Competencies of Invulnerable Children.* Unpublished Ph.D. Thesis, Utkal University, Orissa, India.

Agarwal, U.C. (1989). *Creativity and adjustment of adolescents.* New Delhi: DK Publishing.

Anthony, E. J. (1987). Risk, vulnerability, and resilience: An overview. In E. J. Anthony & B. J. Cohler (Eds), *The Invulnerable Child* (pp. 3-48), New York: Guilford Press.

Baral, J. K., & Bishoyee, A.P. (1999). Family in transition: Some theoretical and methodological questions. In J.K. Baral & A. Chowdhury (Eds.), *Family in transition: Power and development* (pp. 1-15). New Delhi: Northern Book Center.

Baral, J.K., Das, U., & Dash, S. (1999). Power equation in family. In J.K. Baral & A. Chowdhury (Eds.), *Family in transition: Power and development* (pp. 57-82). New Delhi: Northern Book Center.

Belle, D. (1990). Poverty and women's mental health. *American Psychologist, 45*(3) 385 389.

Bharat, S. (1991). Research on families with problems in India: Utility, limitations and future directions. In: *Research on families with problems in India* (Unit of Family Studies, Editors). Bombay: Tata Institute of Social Sciences.

Bharat, S. (1997). Family socialization of the Indian child. *Trends in Social Science Research, 4,* 201 216.

Boral, G. C., Bagchi, R., & Nandi, D. N. (1980). An opinion survey about the causes and treatment of mental illness and the social acceptance of the mentally ill patients. *Indian Journal of Psychiatry,* 22(3), 317 321.

Carson, D.K., Chowdhury, A., Perry, C.K., & Pati, C. (1999). Family characteristics and adolescent competence in India: Investigation of youth in southern Orissa. *Journal of Youth and Adolescence, 28*(2), 211-233.

Carson, D.K., & Chowdhury, A. (2000). Family therapy in India: A new profession in an ancient land?" *Contemporary Family Therapy, 22,* 387-406.

Carson, D. K., Chowdhury, A., Choudhury, R., & Carson, C.K. (2002). Competence and family support of vulnerable and invulnerable adolescents representing Scheduled Tribes and Scheduled Castes in India. *Journal of Comparative Family Studies, 33*(2), 249-270.

Channabasavanna, S.M., & Bhatti, R.S. (1982). A study of interact ional patterns and family typologies in families of mental patients. In A Kiev & A. Venkoba Rao (Eds.), *Readings in transcultural psychiatry* (pp. 149-161). Madras: Higginbotham.

Chowdhury, A. (1990). Development of social competence in children." *International Journal of Behavioral Sciences, 10,* 55-69.

Chowdhury, A. (1995). Employed mothers and their families in India. *Early Child Development and Care, 113,* 65 75.

Chowdhury, A. (1999). The Status and Perceptions of aged in Orissan families. In J.K. Baral & A. Chowdhury (Eds.), *Family in transition: Power and development* (pp. 47-56). New Delhi: Northern Book Center.

Chowdhury, A., & Baral, S. (1999). A study on Vulnerable Families. In J.K. Baral & A. Chowdhury (Eds.), *Family in transition: Power and development* (pp. 131-138). New Delhi: Northern Book Center.

Chowdhury, A., & Choudhury, R. (1993). Exploring research strategies for identifying invulnerable children: An Indian context. *Early Child Development and Care, 93,* 87-100.

Chowdhury, A., & Choudhury, R. (1996). Peer socialization: A new direction towards socio-personal growth. *Trends in Social Science Research, 3,* 105-112.

Chowdhury, A., & Choudhury, R. (1997). Peer social support: A protective factor for children in poverty. *Experiments in Education, 25,* 163-171.

Chowdhury, A., & Muni, A. (1995). Role of parental support in children's need satisfaction and academic achievements.*Journal of Community Guidance and Research 12,* 135-144.

Chowdhury, A., Muni, A., Rath, A., & Pati, C. (1996). Assessing social support network among socio-culturally disadvantaged children in India. *Early Child Development and Care, 121,* pp.37 47.

Choudhury, R. (1991). *Invulnerable Children: An Exploratory Attempt to Identify and Study Them.* Unpublished Ph.D Thesis, Utkal University, Orissa, India.

Choudhury, R. (1999). The changing family scenario in Orissa: Its impact on mental health. In J.K. Baral & A. Chowdhury (Eds.), *Family in transition: Power and development* (pp. 21-30). New Delhi: Northern Book Center.

Das, R.C. (1999). Marriage in transition: A biosocial approach. In J.K. Baral & A. Chowdhury (Eds.), *Family in transition: Power and development* (pp. 16-20). New Delhi: Northern Book Center.

Das, T. (1999). Employed women and problems of childcare. In J.K. Baral & A. Chowdhury (Eds.), *Family in transition: Power and development* (pp. 139-147). New Delhi: Northern Book Center.

Desai, M., & Bharat, S. (1989). Research on families with problems in India: A seminar report. *The Indian Journal of Social Work, 50*(4), 531-536.

Davar, B. V. (1999). *Mental health of Indian women: A feminist agenda.* New Delhi: Sage Pub.

Davar, B. V. (1998). Writing phenomenologies of mental illness. Extending the universe of ordinary discourse. Paper presented at the Annual Culture Studies Workshop, Centre for Studies in Social Sciences, Bhopal, India, January 15-20.

Garmezy, N. (1983). Stressors in childhood. In N. Garmezy and M. Rutter (eds.), *Stress, coping, and development in children* (pp. 44-83). New York: McGraw-Hill.

Gore, M. (1989). *Socialization of Rural Adolescent Girls from an Ecological Perspective.* Unpublished master's thesis, M.S. University Faculty of Home Science, University of Baroda, India.

Gupta, A.K. (1987). _*Parental influences on adolescents.* New Delhi: Ariana Pub. House.

Hariharan, M. (1991). *Invulnerable Children: Some Studies on Disadvantaged Children's Competence and Coping Styles.* Unpublished Doctoral (Ph.D.) Dissertation, Utkal University, India.

Hariharan, M., Dash, A.S., & Acharya, S. (1987). School, grade, sex, and academic achievement differences in peer rating. *Journal of Educational Psychology, 45,* 32-36.

Kapur, M. (1995). *Mental health of Indian children.* New Delhi: Sage Pub.

Kapur, M. (1997). *Mental health in Indian schools.* New Delhi: Sage Pub.

Madan, G.R. (1990). *Social welfare and security.* New Delhi: Vivek Prakashan.

Misra, G. (1995). Reflection on continuity and change in the Indian family system. *Trends in Social Science Research, 2,* 27 30.

Mishra, P.K., & Mohanty, R.P. (1995). Some demographic characteristics of the Scheduled Caste population of Orissa. In R.N. Senapati, P.K.Nayak, & P.K.Das (Eds.), *Population profile of Orissa* (pp. 129-144). Bhubaneswar, Orissa: Association for Population and Development (OAPD).

Mohanty, B. (1999). Dual-earner family: A journey to freedom and equality. In J.K. Baral & A. Chowdhury (Eds.), *Family in transition: Power and development* (pp. 120-130). New Delhi: Northern Book Center.

Mullatti, L. (1995). Families in India: Beliefs and realities. *Journal of Comparative Family Studies, 26* (1), 11-25.

Muni, A. (1995). *Development of Competency Among Advantaged and Disadvantaged Adolescents.* Unpublished Ph.D. Thesis, Berhampur University, Orissa, India.

Nanda, G.K., & Dash, A.S. (1996). *Disadvantage, schooling, competence, and invulnerability.* Bhubaneswar: Panchajanya, c/o URPL House.

Oommen, T.K. (2000). Family therapy: Challenging the system. *Hindu,* 26th March .

Ota, A.B. (1995). Changing demographic scenario of the Scheduled Tribes in Orissa. In R.N. Senapati, P.K. Nayak, & P.K. Das (Eds.). *Population profile of Orissa* (pp. 113-128). Bhubaneswar, Orissa: Association for Population and Development (OAPD).

Padhi, J., & Dash, A.S. (1994). The relation of parental attitudes to adolescent competence. *Psycho-Lingua, 24,* 33-42.

Parikh, J.C., & Krishna, K.S. (1992). *Drug addiction: A psychosocial study of youth.* New Delhi: Friends Pub.

Pati, C., & Patnaik, S. (1999). Status and problems of single women. In J.K. Baral & A. Chowdhury (Eds.), *Family in transition: Power and development* (pp. 166-172). New Delhi: Northern Book Center.

Patnaik, M.M. (1999). Family violence in traditional Oriya society. In J.K. Baral & A. Chowdhury (Eds.), *Family in transition: Power and development* (pp. 148-156). New Delhi: Northern Book Center.

Powell, L. H., & Cassidy, D. (2001). Family life education: An introduction. Mountain View, CA: Mayfield Pub. Co.

Prabhu, G.G., Raghuram, A., Verma, N,. & Maridass, A. C. (1984). Public attitudes toward mental illness: A review. *National Institute of Mental Health and Neurosurgery Journal, 2(*1), 1 14.

Rutter, M. (1987). Psychosocial resilience and protective mechanisms. American *Journal of Orthopsychiatry 57,* 316-331.

Sahoo, F., & Sia, N. (1988). The socio-cultural antecedents of helplessness among rural adolescents. *Indian Joumal of Comunity Guidance Services, 5*, 34-47.

Sarkar, C. (1988). *Juvenile delinquency in India.* Delhi: Daya Pub. House.

Sethi, B. B. & Manchanda, R. (1978). Family structure and psychiatric disorders. *Indian Journal of Psychiatry, 20*(3), 283 288.

Shanker, R., & Menon, M.S. (1991). Family intervention programme in schizophrenia: The SCARF experience. In: *Research on Families with Problems in India,* (Unit of Family Studies, Editors). Bombay: Tata Institute of Social Sciences.

Sharma, S., & Chadd, R.K. (1990). *Mental hospitals in India: Current status and role in mental health care.* Delhi: Institute of Human Behaviour and Allied Sciences.

Sharma, P., Saraswathi, T.S., & Gir, S. (1981). Role of parents and teachers in promoting social competence in children. *Child Psychiatry Quarterly, 14,* 134-137.

Shukla, M. (1994). India. In K. Hurrelmann (Ed.), *International handbook of adolescence* (pp. 191-206). Westport, CT: Greenwood Press.

Simhadri, Y.C. (1989). *Youth in the contemporary world.* Delhi: Mittal Pub.

Sinha, D. (1984). Some recent changes in the Indian family and their implications for socialisation. *The Indian Journal of Social Work, 45,* 271 286.

Sinha, D. (1988). The family scenario of a developing country and its implications for mental health: The case of India. In P.R. Dasen, J.W.Berry, & N.Sartorius (Eds,), *Health and cross cultural psychology: Towards applications* (pp. 48-70). Newbury Park, CA: Sage Pub.

Sitholey, N., & Chakraborthi, A. (1992). Child psychiatric research in India: Epidemiology, assessment and treatment. In S. Malhotra, A. Malhotra, & V.K. Varma (Eds.), *Child mental health in India.* Delhi: Macmillan.

Tiwari, R. (1990). *Adolescents' personality and frustration.* New Delhi: DK Publishing.

Verghese, A. (1988). Family participation in mental health care: The Vellore experiment. *The Indian Journal of Psychiatry, 30*(2), 117 121.

Index

T